AF606878

DISPOSABLE WIVES

MURDER AND MENACE IN GREEN BAY'S RURAL BELGIAN SETTLEMENT

LYNDA DREWS

Little Creek Press
5341 Sunny Ridge Road
Mineral Point, WI 53565

To contact Lynda directly:
lyndadrews@gmail.com or www.lyndadrews.com

Printed in the United States of America

Cataloging-in-Publication Data
Names: Drews, Lynda, author
Title: Disposable Wives
Description: Mineral Point, WI Little Creek Press, 2026
Identifiers: ISBN: 978-1-969183-10-2
Classification: TRUE CRIME / Murder / General
BIOGRAPHY & AUTOBIOGRAPHY / Women
HISTORY / United States / State & Local / Midwest
(IA, IL, IN, KS, MI, MN, MO, ND, NE, OH, SD, WI)

Book cover original art by Debra Riggs: www.debrariggs.com/works
Book design by Little Creek Press

To my adventurous siblings, Gail and Chris,
and each of our loving spouses,
Randy, Cathy, and Jim,
who have each vowed to stay connected
and to keep the memories of our incredible parents alive.

Door Peninsula in Wisconsin

Homes of Major Characters & Bay Settlement Area (Courtesy of Dennis Jacobs)

FAMILY TREES IN 1873

Villiesse		Coppersmith		Minsart		Soquet		
Henry	Pauline Coppersmith	Alexis	Desiree Meuron	Jacques	Anne Connart	Marie Gillard (1st wife)	Jean Philippe	Esperance Hannon (2nd wife)
Flora		Desire		Virginia Francart		Mary	Jennie	
Celinda		Marcel		Ignace			Fred	
Anton		Isadore		August (Elvira)			Elisabeth	
		Pauline Villiesse (Henry)		Alexandre			Josephine	
		Elvira Minsart (August)					Jule	
		Fannie Vandenbusch (Peter)					Rose	
		Fred						
		Flora Lancelle (William)						

NOTE TO READERS

Belgian-American Farm on Door Peninsula (Petiniot Farm, Photo 270, Belgian-American Research Collection, University of Wisconsin-Green Bay Archives Department)

NESTLED BETWEEN THE WATERS of Lake Michigan and Green Bay extends the Door Peninsula, a panoramic patchwork of Wisconsin farmland. The southern section, spanning from the cities of Green Bay to Sturgeon Bay, is where the largest rural settlement of people of Belgian origin in America is located. Five generations of farming families have toiled and celebrated in this region since the land was cleared of primeval forests in the 1850s.

In the decades following the Civil War, Jean Philippe Soquet, the patriarch of one of these families, had earned many titles: the Bay Settlement Bruiser, the Belgian Archfiend, and the Bloody Bender of Wisconsin. Within this tranquil Belgian community, gossip and legend surrounded J.P. Soquet, including a series of purported murders, three of those his wives, which spanned four decades.

What follows is the true story of the remarkable means by which Appolonia Villiesse, the sister of Soquet's third wife, and the Belgian translator Xavier Martin sought justice for the wives of Jean Philippe Soquet, who he had treated as disposable.

Note: All quotations are provided from archival records, letters, or other written documents. The thoughts and scenes of Pauline Villiesse and Xavier Martin are extrapolated from the same sources, as imagined by the author.

PART I

THE FIRST INCIDENTS

(1873-1878)

SHAMEFUL GOSSIP

PAULINE

APPOLONIA VILLIESSE maneuvered a horse-drawn wagon off the rutted Green Bay to Sturgeon Bay State Road in late May of 1873, the powerful scent of manure in the air. Unlike city women, twenty-eight-year-old Appolonia, better known as Pauline, had the liberty to drive a wagon without a man, choose her own destination, and use the reins tightly clasped in her calloused hands. That morning, she was doing just that. Pauline was on a mission. Her shameful younger sister, Elvira, would soon get a piece of Pauline's mind.

Pauline had left the farm she and her husband Henry owned near Dyckesville, Wisconsin, on the Door Peninsula, to travel twelve miles south to her sister's Humboldt township farm, about eight miles east of Green Bay. Pauline's three children, all under six, sat on the flat wooden buckboard cushioned with blankets, their little legs tucked beneath them, their small frames strapped together so they would not fall out of the wagon.

Along the roadside, white-throated sparrows chirped in search of seeds. Between the rains and warm weather, farmers had nearly finished sowing the small grains. Pauline scanned the expansive farmland, which was bordered with split-rail or stacked-rock fencing and was owned primarily by Belgian immigrants who had risked everything to forge a new life in Wisconsin. Pauline knew their stories because it was her story—a story of hard-won survival.

Pauline smiled down at her children, grateful for the freedom she and her family benefited from. Here was a place where hard work paid off, where everyone worshipped as they pleased, where Henry's vote counted. Pauline dreamed about the unlimited opportunities her children would have for their own success. Such a rewarding American life she and her seven siblings had inherited due to their parents' sacrifice.

Pauline would remind her disgraceful and thankless sister of all she was forsaking, and by doing so, all the shame she was bringing to their family.

Ahead was Bay Settlement. The Belgian family of Gregoire Denis owned the general store attached to a saloon. Pauline pulled up beside the two-story clapboard Denis General Store, which also served as the post office. Here, they stocked everything from dry goods to fabric, liquor to harmonicas, and farm equipment to drugs.

Gregoire Denis Store and Bay Settlement Saloon (Courtesy Dennis Jacobs)

Pauline's eyes widened when she saw one of her sister's neighbors, Martin Simonar. The nimble man, with his black beard hanging low, was scampering across the saloon's front porch on all-fours, drawing laughter and applause from the men milling around.

Simonar noticed Pauline's arrival and clambered to his feet, a self-righteous look in his eyes.

Pauline's gaze pierced his. She knew he loved gossip, the more scandalous the better. Today his antics had gone too far. They were personal. She was quite certain he had been imitating her sister's married lover, Jean Philippe Soquet, also called J.P. Word had it that the farmer had worn a path from his home to Elvira's, crawling behind fences to avoid discovery.

Now, more than ever, Pauline needed to give her married sister a good talking to. Adultery was a sin against God and a crime against society. What Elvira was doing carried the risk of significant social stigma and condemnation within their close-knit Belgian community, not only for Elvira, but for everyone in her extended Coppersmith family. If Elvira's shameful conduct continued, Pauline was worried her sister could even be arrested and thrown in jail.

Pauline climbed out of the wagon and tied the horse to a post near the communal water trough. Head held high, she unstrapped her children. Five-year-old Flora jumped down and stretched while Pauline lifted the two little ones to the ground. Pauline held onto Anton's hand, and Flora took Celinda's as the small band entered the store filled with scents of pickles, ripe cheese, and kerosene. Glass containers of enticing penny candy stood by the cash register. Those jars were the reason for Pauline's stop. She had promised each child a piece of taffy, a caramel, or a sugar-coated fruit chew as a reward for their good behavior.

Her children radiated delight while carefully selecting their candy.

Pauline smiled. Their joy made it worth suffering the scrutiny of those outside the store.

Pauline returned to the wagon and her horse lifted its head in greeting. She gave the animal's velvety muzzle a rub before securing the children and taking her own seat. All the while, Simonar and his appreciative audience eyed Pauline. She ignored them with her chin raised, slapped the reins, and the horse plodded off.

Pauline brushed away that irksome encounter as another wagon passed, its buckboard straining from the weight of stacked caskets, one of the high demand items sold in the Denis Store.

Death was always near due to infectious diseases like cholera, scarlet fever, diphtheria, and malaria, as well as farming accidents and childbirth complications. So far, Pauline, Henry and their children had escaped those maladies more by chance than anything else. But the year Pauline was born, her five-year-old sister, Victorine, had died from an infectious disease, so Pauline was the family's oldest sister to make the journey to America.

Across the road, Pauline gazed at the modest steeple and bell tower of the white-painted Holy Cross Church, the Roman Catholic immigrant community's spiritual haven for more than two decades. The rectory to the north housed the cheerful and energetic Father Daems, a Crosier Belgium priest, who also doctored to the community. After he had arrived in 1852, four years before Pauline's family, Father Daems had erected the church and built a parish school where three sisters from the Racine Dominicans taught and helped him minister to the sick.

Holy Cross Church and G. Denis Store (Courtesy Dennis Jacobs)

Pauline's wagon drove past the Holy Cross Cemetery followed by thickets of tall pines like those which had covered her family's new Wisconsin land. From those woods her father, Alexis Coppersmith, and Pauline's three older brothers had chopped down trees and dug out stones to build their new homestead. To clear the land for farming, they had continued that arduous process of felling trees and dragging them into piles to be burned or split into shingles. All the while, ten-year-old Pauline had helped their mother plant a kitchen garden. Eight-year-old Elvira had tended to their two younger sisters and little brother. Elvira had always loved children.

Pauline entered her sister's neighborhood where the townships of Preble, Humboldt, and Scott bordered each other. The home of her sister's lover, J.P. Soquet, was about a mile down the road and situated on 160 acres, twice the size of Pauline and Henry's farm. To Pauline's dismay, the approaching wagon held J.P.'s wife, Esperance Soquet. Beside her sat J.P.'s adult daughter from his first marriage.

Pauline knew Esperance was more than a decade older than Pauline's sister and the mother to six children, with another due, by the looks of her, within the month. But in addition to J.P.'s affair with her sister, Pauline knew people still whispered suspicions about the circumstances of his first wife's death.

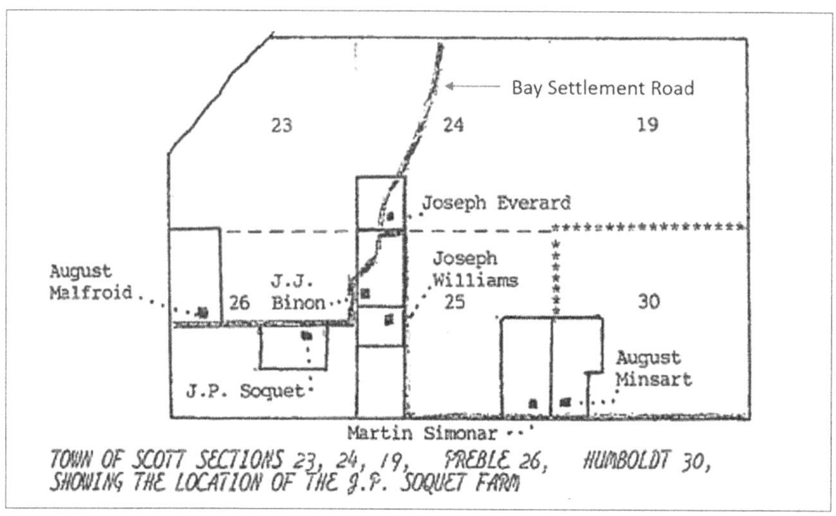

Soquet and Minsart Neighborhood (Courtesy John Mertens)

Pauline felt deeply unsettled when Esperance's eyes met hers. Pauline quickly looked away, a flush of heat on her neck. The idea that Elvira was running around with that very pregnant woman's husband was mortifying—so clearly wrong. Pauline could still sense Esperance's eyes on her as Pauline used the reins to turn the wagon off Bay Settlement Road toward her sister's home. Pauline urged the horse on, thankfully creating a distance from the Soquet wagon.

Pauline passed the farms of Joseph Everard and Joseph Williams before she turned east to reach Martin Simonar's house and barn. Next came her sister's farm. Pauline assumed Elvira's husband, August Minsart, would be working in the fields, and she hoped to find her sister there alone.

Pauline knew her sister's marriage had been unhappy for years. Elvira constantly complained about her husband, a Civil War veteran, twelve years Elvira's senior, who treated her more like a servant than a wife.

Pauline drove the horse over dirt tracks onto the Minsart farm where honeysuckle clung to the split-rail fence. The farm contained a good dwelling house and barn. Her sister and August kept horses, cows, and poultry, along with farming tools for planting and harvesting grain, hay, and straw. Elvira's life was not perfect, but she had achieved the prosperity their parents had worked so hard for.

Elvira's two-story house was similar to Pauline's, built of carved and fitted logs, the gaps sealed with limestone chinking. But Pauline's narrow windows would have had small faces peeking out awaiting a visitor's arrival. During Elvira's eight years of marriage to August Minsart, they had not been blessed with any children, and this was truly a heartache for Elvira.

Behind the Minsart house, Pauline caught sight of her sister, squatting over the four-quadrant kitchen garden planted with the same vegetables Pauline grew such as onions, carrots, and potatoes. The last time Pauline had visited her sister, J.P. Soquet had been inside the Minsart farmhouse drinking coffee with Elvira. Pauline had remonstrated her sister for entertaining J.P. when her husband was absent. Elvira had rebuffed Pauline and the two had quarreled, increasing the shame Pauline felt when she had left.

Dressed in a faded calico dress covered with an apron, Elvira stood, her hair secured under a white cotton bonnet, damp tendrils framing her face. She was short of stature and of medium build like Pauline. Elvira greeted Pauline warily.

When Pauline asked, Elvira said August was in the fields and would not return until sundown. Pauline was pleased. She and her sister would have private time to talk while the children played.

Pauline helped her children down from the wagon as Elvira primed the backyard pump and washed her hands under the streaming water. Flora was not shy. She ran toward her aunt, wrapping her arms around Elvira's skirts, which Pauline noticed brought a tear to Elvira's eyes.

The Villiesse family cleaned up by the pump and used the Minsart outhouse before following Elvira into the farmhouse. Familiar aromas of sweat, pine, manure, and stew welcomed Pauline. A staircase led up to a loft split into two bedrooms: one for Elvira and August, the other still awaiting children. The first floor contained a large kitchen, a parlor, and a bedroom, which had belonged to August's older brother, Ignace.

While Ignace had served in the Twelfth Wisconsin Infantry during the Civil War, August and Elvira had married. They had initially lived on the farm owned by August's father. But shortly after Ignace's discharge, the two brothers had purchased the current sixty acres of farmland from Joseph LeCoque for $800. Pauline knew Elvira had been more than pleased when Ignace had sold his share of the farm to August in July of the prior year. Ignace had also treated Elvira like hired help, and Pauline had hoped his departure would have improved her sister's marriage. Unfortunately, it had not.

Inside the Minsart kitchen, the stone fireplace provided heat and the cast iron wood stove was used for cooking. A pine counter contained two holes fit for pails of water for washing dishes and garden produce. Above the counter, shelves held eating and cooking utensils. Centered in the room was a rectangular dining table with benches. Elvira placed five glasses on the table and opened a tin-lined wooden icebox holding a large block of ice. Elvira removed a pitcher of milk and filled the glasses.

Pauline's children eagerly gulped their milk down while Elvira told them about the new barnyard kittens. After Pauline gave her children permission to look, Flora excitedly grabbed her younger siblings' hands and ran to see the litter.

The door banged shut and Pauline's back straightened, assuming a serious posture in preparation for her serious talk. But before Pauline could broach the subject of her sister's infidelity, Elvira's words poured out. She told her sister how she had little to look forward to in her marriage, only the drudgery of being an unappreciated wife to a demanding man who was nothing to her "but a dog."

Pauline listened, surprised by her sister's outburst. Yet she had to admit, she could empathize with Elvira. What would Pauline's life be like if she only had herself for company, day-in and day-out? To wake each morning and put meals on a table for a man she cared nothing for, who treated her poorly. To wash and iron his clothes. To clean the house after he dragged in dirt and manure on his boots. To tend to the chickens and to milk the cows, morning and night. To churn the milk and to work in the garden. To make preserves and store the harvested root crops in the cellar for winter. To patch old clothes and knit her husband socks. All this, without the freedom to make choices for herself, and to never get any thanks in return.

Elvira said she knew why Pauline had come. Elvira said she realized she had disgraced their family due to her relationship with J.P. Soquet. But Elvira believed that unlike her husband, J.P. was a good man. She loved J.P., and he loved her. Those amorous feelings, Elvira said, had kept her going for more than a year. But that was no longer enough for either of them. Elvira said J.P. had saved $5,000 so they could run away together. Elvira wanted to conceive children with J.P. If Pauline could have babies, Elvira believed she could have them, too. August had to be the problem.

Elvira knew Esperance would never give J.P. a divorce. But Elvira said she and J.P. could live elsewhere. Nobody would know they were not legally man and wife.

Elvira's voice caught. She hesitated before asking Pauline what she thought she should do?

Pauline did not know what to say. How could her twenty-six-year-old sister love that forty-seven-year-old, cross-eyed man who rarely trimmed his grizzly beard? In Pauline's conversations with J.P. over the years, he seemed to be "an ill-favored sort of character ... not possessing a great amount of intelligence, and certainly none of the milk of human kindness," especially none directed at Pauline. He was a man who was shamefully unfaithful to his wife, and who was under suspicion after his previous wife's death. Pauline could not see what her sister saw in J.P. Soquet, to put it mildly.

The idea that he and her sister were engaged in criminal intercourse was disturbing. Even more so was this revelation that the two wanted to run away together. What about J.P.'s very pregnant wife? And what about J.P.'s children, who depended on him?

Their Belgian settlement maintained an honorable and just code of conduct.

J.P. and her sister had broken that code.

IMMIGRANTS' CHAMPION

XAVIER

XAVIER MARTIN paged through the May 24, 1873 *State Gazette* in his second floor Green Bay General Land Office, located at 81 Washington Street. At times the racket from the building site a block and a half away made it hard for him to think. The four-story Cook Hotel was currently under construction, proclaimed to become "one of the finest hotels north of Chicago."

Forty-one-year-old Xavier checked the pendulum clock on his office wall. Jean Philippe Soquet was due to arrive any minute. The Belgian farmer had sent word to Xavier requesting an urgent meeting, and the two men had confirmed today's date and time.

Xavier Martin (Courtesy Blodgett, Fay Willis via John Mertens)

Xavier had known J.P. Soquet for about sixteen years and believed him to be an industrious farmer who had "cleared and cultivated one of the best farms on Bay Settlement Road." But J.P. was "not a pleasant man to get along with." Before Xavier had moved to the city of Green Bay, he had lived near J.P. in the town of Green Bay on the Door Peninsula. There Xavier had served as postmaster, town clerk, school superintendent, and justice of the peace. In that last position, Xavier had dealt with J.P. more than once regarding charges of instigating brawls at local taverns.

Xavier was curious about J.P.'s urgent request.

On the *Gazette's* fourth page, Xavier located the two-column real estate advertisement he ran each week. He had more than $400,000 in listings (about twelve million in current valuation). Xavier's business was booming. Approximately 25,000 people lived in Brown County and nearly 4,600 in the city of Green Bay. Many county residents had emigrated from Europe with their large families of children who had matured and were ready to purchase property of their own. And Xavier, after years of hard work, was in a prime spot to benefit from the forthcoming boom.

Xavier turned back to the *Gazette's* front page. He focused on the article titled "Hell's Half-Acre" about the notorious Kansas Bloody Bender Family. There was even a schematic depicting the interior layout of the family's shanty where each murder had occurred. Readers, including Xavier, were intrigued by shocking murders. Green Bay had not experienced such gruesome news for some time. Xavier hoped that happy peace would remain.

As it was, Green Bay had plenty of news to occupy a busybody. He sighed and realized if his own tantalizing extramarital affair was ever exposed, it would cause its own kind of stir.

Xavier was in love, but not with his wife, Mary.

Xavier had met Mary Gray in Philadelphia when he was twenty-one, shortly after he, along with his parents and seven siblings, had emigrated from the Brabant Wallon Province of Belgium. There, a small noble class controlled the huge land estates where farm laborers worked the fields. Even when some of those husbandmen, like Xavier's father, had managed to purchase their own land, the acreage was rarely large enough to divide among the family's adult sons to provide each a living.

Francois Petinoit and Minne Petinoit (Photo 266, Belgian-American Research Collection, University of Wisconsin-Green Bay Archives Department)

That year of 1853, the Belgian crops were failing. Francois Petiniot, a friend of Xavier's father, had been conducting business in Antwerp. Inside a tavern, Francois found a pamphlet written in Dutch, which he could mostly read, describing America with land priced at $1.25 an acre. For the price of five-acres in Belgium, he could purchase about

100 acres in America. Francois convinced nine other small farming families, including Xavier's, to join his in immigrating to America. They were among the 325 passengers who boarded the Queenebec sailing craft departing Antwerp on May 18, 1853. The journey would be "long, tedious, and rough, attended with several terrific hurricanes, one of which carried off the mainmast of the ship."

On the voyage, some Hollanders had convinced the Belgian families to follow them to a state called Wisconsin, more than four times the size of Belgium. Xavier's family had decided to visit friends in Philadelphia first, however. A few months later, Xavier's parents and siblings left to join the other Belgian families in Wisconsin in a place they had named "Aux Premiers Belges" (home of the first Belgians). These families had settled in what would soon be called the Green Bay township per the recommendation of a Father Daems, who spoke their Walloon language.

Xavier had remained in Philadelphia to work at a cotton spinning mill while he "studied the English language and its literature" under a Professor Gardner of that city. That was when Xavier had met nineteen-year-old Mary Gray. A year later, they married with plans to start a large family.

Xavier opened his desk drawer and carefully removed the yellowed letter his father had written during Xavier's fourth year in Philadelphia. He treasured that letter as he did all of his father's correspondence. Three years had passed since Xavier's father, at age sixty-six, had unexpectedly died. This urgent request, authored in 1857, had asked Xavier and his wife to visit his countrymen in Wisconsin. When Xavier acquiesced, his arrival "made some noise," chiefly because the Belgian settlement knew Xavier had received an American education. Among the 15,000 settlers who had arrived, "not one could converse in [the English] tongue." Many wanted to learn the language but had found no one to teach them. Surrounded by forests, the settlers felt isolated on their newly cleared farmland. Xavier's brother, Constant, told him they needed a man among them to lead them out of their chaotic condition, one who spoke English.

Xavier slid the letter back inside the drawer and recalled that, after much consternation and inducements, he had agreed to be that man. He had educated the leading Belgian pioneers on the American system of local government and taught them English. Through Xavier's official capacity as school superintendent, he was instrumental in "establishing school districts, building school houses, and obtaining teachers." In his role as town clerk, he helped improve existing roads and construct new ones.

After five years of marriage, Xavier's wife had yet to conceive which had troubled their marriage. Each suffered from profound sadness, anger, and especially jealousy of the Belgian families in their community who seemed to have children to spare. That appeared to be the case for the Deterville family. Perhaps because they had more children than they could afford to raise, they gave up their six-year-old daughter Odile to the Martins who officially adopted her. When the citizens of Brown County elected Xavier to the office of register of deeds in 1862, Xavier and his family moved to Green Bay where they built a home on two Astor neighborhood lots.

Odile, still the Martins' only child, had graduated the prior year from Sale School near the top of her class of twelve students. She and John Swartz would marry in August and move to his birthplace in Goshen, Indiana. Without Odile's ongoing assistance to maintain the Martins' home, Xavier's wife had hired their live-in-servant, twenty-year-old Augusta Bliske, who had recently immigrated from Prussia but who already spoke English.

Augusta Bliske (Courtesy Blodgett, Fay Willis via John Mertens)

Xavier and Mary's marriage was emotionally detached, often leaving Xavier lonely. He also regretted deeply that they had never produced any children of their own. Xavier looked forward to conversations with Augusta, and their flirtations. It had started out innocently enough, but a deeper emotional connection had formed, and now he and Augusta were engaged in an illicit and intimate affair.

A knock sounded on Xavier's private office door. His office boy opened it and ushered J.P. Soquet and his very pregnant wife inside, the couple carrying in the scents of sweat, farm animals, and soil, disrupting Xavier from his reveries about Augusta.

When Xavier had arrived from Philadelphia sixteen years ago, J.P. Soquet had lived in the same neighborhood as Xavier's parents. Rumors had abounded about J.P.'s first wife, Marie Gillard. She and J.P. had emigrated from Belgium with their young daughter. The year before Xavier's arrival, Marie had allegedly fallen down a flight of stairs and broken her neck. J.P. had summoned neighbors, who assisted with caring for the body and the customary burial. But there had been no inquest to determine Marie's cause of death, and no witnesses other than his to what had happened. Xavier's family and other neighbors had speculated. Had Marie's death been an accident or had J.P. purposely pushed her down the stairs to end her life so he could marry the young neighborhood girl, Esperance Hannon, whom he had shown an interest in?

Esperance became J.P.'s second wife within weeks of his first wife's death, stirring further speculation which had continued ever since. Xavier's family was particularly interested because his youngest sister Celina was married to Frank Hannon, Esperance Soquet's first cousin.

Xavier eyed J.P. Soquet. He had never trusted the man. And new gossip was on the lips of the Belgian community concerning J.P.'s alleged affair with Mrs. August Minsart. Xavier wanted to judge J.P., but how could he condemn the man for falling in love with another woman and breaking his marriage vows? How could Xavier criticize the extramarital passions of Mrs. August Minsart and J.P. Soquet when Xavier was also engaged in adultery?

Speaking Walloon, Xavier offered chairs to the Soquets then asked how he could help them.

J.P. told Xavier he was worried. He and Esperance had never drawn up a will. If either one of them died, he wanted to make certain their farm, personal possessions, and savings would favor the survivor. J.P. said several women had recently died following childbirth, and he and Esperance feared that could happen to her.

Xavier had heard about the deaths of those Belgian women, perhaps caused by puerperal fever, better known as childbed fever. Xavier knew there were varying opinions on what caused the disease. Many still believed noxious conditions in the atmosphere were its cause. Others, like him, accepted new scientific ideas such as those promoted by Oliver Wendall Holmes, who believed the disease was so contagious "as to be frequently carried from patient to patient by physicians and nurses." Women who had recently given birth were the most susceptible, especially if they had experienced delivery trauma.

Xavier could tell Esperance was anxious as she stroked the bulge of her baby hidden beneath her skirts. He noted that while J.P. might be involved with another woman, here he was treating his wife with kindness and concern—just as Xavier would do with Mary.

Xavier assured the Soquets, as a notary public, he could author a legal will for them. Xavier wrote down the Soquets' wishes, and they signed the document. Xavier and his office boy added their signatures as witnesses and Xavier notarized the document.

After J.P. paid for Xavier's services, the couple stood to leave. Soquet smiled and slid his arm around his wife.

While Xavier had done his work with integrity, he felt a sense of foreboding as he watched J.P. usher Esperance out of the office.

SUSPICIOUS SUICIDE

Two-Story Log Belgian Home on Door Peninsula (Courtesy Belgian Heritage Center)

BENEATH THE LEAFY BRANCHES of an ancient beech tree, Pauline Villiesse and her twenty-three-year-old sister Fannie Vandenbusch discussed Elvira's troubling situation. Fannie, her husband, Peter, and their two-year-old daughter had arrived from Humboldt for a weekend visit. The two women sat on a bench in the backyard of Pauline's two-story log homestead while their husbands watched the children in the barn.

Only three weeks had passed since Pauline had traveled to Elvira's home, but in that time, the situation had changed completely.

Elvira's thirty-six-year-old husband, August Minsart, was dead.

Pauline and Fannie were shocked and unsettled.

Beside Pauline was her sewing kit, an empty basket, and another filled with clothing in need of mending before Monday's wash. Pauline told Fannie about her recent visit to their parents' home, where Elvira was now living. Their father, Alexis Coppersmith, brewed beer, which he drank to excess. When Pauline had visited, Elvira had been drunk. Slurring her words through bursts of tears, Elvira had claimed that August had taken his own life, but she had refused to elaborate.

Threading a needle, Pauline told Fannie, she had consoled Elvira, yet all the while Pauline had recalled how Elvira had wanted to run away with J.P. Soquet. August's sudden death, Pauline realized uneasily, had given Elvira that freedom.

While the laughter of their children carried from the barn, Fannie admitted she had misgivings about August's alleged cause of death. She and Peter had actually been called to the Minsart home on June 14 when Elvira's husband died. Their sister's neighbor, Mrs. Martin Simonar, had arrived at Fannie's house in such a state. The woman reported that Elvira had found August soon after his mid-day meal, unresponsive in the downstairs bedroom. After taking their daughter to a neighbor, Fannie and Peter had driven to Elvira's house. Mr. Simonar had answered the door. He said when he arrived about two hours earlier, August had already been stiff and cold, "in the embrace of death," and he appeared to have "died in great agony."

Martin and Christine Simonar Family (1890) (Simonar, Mrs. Carol J. (Gerald), The Simonart Descendants History and Genealogy, Luxemburg, Wisconsin)

It was hard for Pauline not to visualize her brother-in-law, especially when Fannie relayed how August had been lying on his face on the bedroom floor, dressed in dirty work clothes. Pauline looked down at Henry's grimy work shirt with the rip in the sleeve, which Pauline was mending. Pauline could not fathom her heartbreak of losing her kind husband.

She refocused on Fannie who said their sister had been silently sitting in a chair beside August. Fannie approached Elvira to comfort her. About then, J.P. Soquet arrived. He sauntered right into the bedroom and went directly to Elvira. Fannie's blood had run cold.

Pauline huffed, tying off the thread. She said she could not believe their sister's lover had the gall to make an appearance at that moment.

Then, Pauline wondered how J.P. had even known about August's death. She doubted that Mrs. Simonar would have alerted J.P. knowing he was shamefully carrying-on with their sister.

Like all their family members, Fannie knew about the illicit relationship. So, she said his unexpected arrival had been "sufficient to create suspicions of foul play."

Pauline placed Henry's work shirt into the empty basket and picked up a pair of Anton's dungarees, torn at the knee. Her consternation concerning August's sudden death seemed to be justified. Maybe J.P. had shown up because he was involved. Pauline thought little enough of him that part of her would not be surprised if that were the case. But the idea that their sister could be involved as well was shocking.

By then, Fannie said, Elvira's neighbors, Mr. and Mrs. Joseph Williams, had arrived at the Minsart house after Mrs. Simonar had alerted them. Fannie had tried to convince Elvira to lie down in the upstairs bedroom, but she had refused.

Pauline used a whip stitch on the coarse denim fabric, picturing Elvira, sitting beside her dead spouse, the one she claimed had been nothing to her "but a dog." What thoughts had been going through Elvira's mind? Had she been secretly pleased and relieved August was dead? That she had been freed from her miserable marriage. Did she fear the cost of her freedom?

Pauline shuddered at the shame of even the thought of it.

At that point, Fannie said she had noticed a change in August's face. It had turned black and blue. She had pointed out the discoloration to everyone in the bedroom, and Mr. Williams had immediately left the room with J.P. behind him.

Pauline tied off the thread as Fannie's words continued to flow, each one more unthinkable than the last. She said the two men had returned with Mr. Williams holding a corked "medicine" bottle. He said he had found it in the kitchen. When Mr. Williams removed the cork to sniff it, J.P. warned him not to do so.

Chickens clucked and cows lowed while Pauline and Fannie speculated, barely able to voice their unspeakable doubts. Had the medicine bottle contained poison? If the bottle contained poison, that could explain the mottled color of August's face. Had he taken the poison to end his own life? Or had another party given August the poison? That idea was not out of the question. Fannie had heard about a farmer in Sparta, Wisconsin, who had been poisoned by his wife. But if Elvira had poisoned August, why would she have gone to the Simonars' home before hiding or destroying the bottle containing the evidence?

Fannie said so much about that day had made her suspicious. Right after the discovery of the medicine bottle, their sister and J.P. had moved into the parlor, sitting together on the sofa, their heads tilted toward each other, their voices low. When Elvira announced August would be buried *that* night, Fannie had been astounded. And even more so when she realized J.P. seemed to be in charge. He was the one who directed the men to help load August's body into Elvira's wagon. Fannie shook her head. Such a grievous violation of their community's traditions.

Pauline was dismayed. Elvira should have stood up to J.P. and followed the established funeral customs. Women relatives or those close to the family should have prepared August for burial by washing and laying out his body. Another relative or family friend should have sat with the body for at least a day to ensure August had well and truly died. Only then should a burial have taken place with the body enclosed in a coffin.

But none of those customs were performed for August. And yet other than Elvira and August's ailing sister, Virginia Francart, who lived in the Green Bay township, August had no immediate family to speak for him. His father had passed away. His brother, Ignace, was working in the Wisconsin Northwoods. His two remaining brothers lived thousands of miles away, one in California, the other still in Belgium. So, it had been Elvira's responsibility to make certain August had dignity in death. This she had failed in miserably.

Fannie talked about the procession to Holy Cross Cemetery. She would never forget how J.P. and Elvira had driven the wagon carrying August's body as the sun dipped toward the waters of Green Bay, streaking the sky with red and orange. Fannie and Peter's wagon had followed behind, and together they had discussed the suspicious situation. The wagons of the Simonars and Williams brought up the rear. Everything was rushed; so rushed.

At the cemetery, J.P. paid a stranger to dig August's grave while a half dozen stragglers arrived, curious to witness an unannounced burial. Then, with "no semblance of religious form or decent rite," August's body was interned at about 8 o'clock that night and without a coffin. Fannie said she and Peter had stood by in shame and disbelief.

Pauline was stunned. How could their sister show such disrespect to her husband of eight years, a fellow Belgian countryman, and a Civil War veteran? How could their sister stand beside her lover as her husband's body was lowered into the ground? It was unimaginable.

Pauline told Fannie that J.P. was still in the picture, perhaps even more brazen than before. In the past week, he had visited Elvira at their parents' home even though his wife was due to deliver a child any day.

In Pauline's backyard, the two sisters tried to make sense of things. Perhaps August's death was due to natural causes. Or perhaps August had taken poison to end his own life. But Pauline and Fannie feared the cause of August's death was the result of foul play.

Could Elvira be a suspect in her husband's death?

Pauline shivered at the thought.

MOUNTING SPECULATION

XAVIER

AT A BRISK TROT, the horse-drawn carriage of Xavier Martin and his wife, Mary, entered the Preble township. The disconcerting news about August Minsart's mysterious death barely two weeks ago had spread through the Belgian community and reached Xavier's ears.

Now there was another death in the neighborhood.

Jean Philippe Soquet Home, Summer Kitchen and Barn in Preble Township (Photo used with permission of Ancestry.com member)

The Martins pulled up to the two-story stone farmhouse of J.P. Soquet. Beside it was a summer kitchen that contained a brick oven large enough to bake two dozen loaves of bread at one time. Beyond it was the barn. Xavier helped Mary climb out of the carriage for the upcoming solemn occasion. Tied to the hitching rail outside the Soquet home were several horses harnessed to buggies and wagons. A boy of about twelve approached Xavier and introduced himself as a neighbor. The boy offered to water the Martins' horse for a penny and Xavier agreed.

A black ribbon hung on the front door. Xavier and his wife stepped inside where a closed casket rested on a makeshift table inside the parlor. Bundles of rosemary and thyme were placed around the coffin to conceal the scent of decay.

A rush of sorrow shot through Xavier. Forty-two-year-old Esperance Soquet was dead. Her death was especially tragic since she had just given birth to an infant daughter. Now, the girl would never know her mother. The last time Xavier had seen Esperance, he had drawn up the Soquets' will in case something just like this happened. The coincidence of the timing disquieted him.

The casket was closed, as was the common custom. Embalming was not widely available in the Belgian farming community and the sight of Esperance's decomposing face would have disturbed those paying their respects.

The parlor was filled with neighbors and members of Esperance's family, all speaking in hushed voices. Xavier was proud that most Belgians were known for their "convivial disposition," but today the faces and attitudes of those present were subdued. Xavier's brother-in-law, Frank Hannon, was among those in the parlor and stood beside Xavier's youngest sister, Celina, and Frank's sister Adele. They were talking to Frank's aunt and uncle, the grieving parents of Esperance Soquet.

Near the casket stood J.P. Soquet and his children. J.P.'s eldest son, Gregoire Frederick, known as Fred, was around twelve. He stood beside his younger brother, Jule. Their stepsister, Mary, from J.P.'s first marriage, was about twenty and yet to marry. Genevieve, called Jennie, was about fourteen, the eldest daughter born to Esperance, and was followed by Elisabeth, Josephine, and Rose, ranging in age from ten down to four. The two oldest girls had inherited the daunting role of running the household with Esperance gone. They would be responsible for overseeing the house and barnyard chores, and caring for the rest of the children, especially the newborn, cradled in Jennie's arms. That was, unless the recent widower found a third wife.

Xavier searched the room for J.P.'s alleged mistress, the newly

Francois Hannon and Celina Martin Hannon (Photo 274, Belgian-American Research Collection, University of Wisconsin-Green Bay Archives Department)

Adele Hannon Minsart (Photo 273, Belgian-American Research Collection, University of Wisconsin- Green Bay Archives Department)

widowed Mrs. August Minsart, but Xavier did not see her. But he could overhear her next-door neighbor, Martin Simonar, whispering to Joseph Williams. Simonar was telling Williams he had talked to a *State Gazette* reporter the prior day. Simonar had told the newsman the Minsart neighbors did not believe August had committed suicide as his wife asserted. The neighbors believed Mrs. August Minsart knew "more than she cared to tell."

Xavier frowned when he heard what Simonar had shared with the press. For all anyone knew, August's death could have been from natural causes. Or perhaps, August's shame at knowing his neighbors had been talking about his wife's infidelity with J.P. had driven August to end his life, a thought which troubled Xavier. He glanced at his own wife. If Mary ever found out about his affair with Augusta, would Mary consider doing the same? Dear God, he hoped not ... But how could he know.

Xavier and his wife approached Esperance's parents and offered their condolences.

Mr. Jean J. Hannon accepted them and relayed all the sorrow and pain he felt with a waver in his voice. He said his daughter's labor had started last Sunday. All of her other births had been attended by a midwife. But for the most recent baby, his son-in-law—Hannon nodded toward J.P.—had retrieved Dr. Munro from Green Bay. After the doctor assisted Esperance in the delivery of little Clara on Monday, Hannon's wife arrived to help with the cooking and caring for her new granddaughter. On Tuesday, Esperance complained of "burning sensations in her throat and stomach." Both Dr. Munro and Father Daems treated his daughter over the next three days, but still she died on Friday evening.

Gottlerb Erdman was listening. His meaty paw squeezed Mr. Hannon's arm. Erdman said he could understand Mr. Hannon's grief. As Mr. Hannon knew, Erdman had recently lost his wife soon after childbirth. Dr. Munro had also been present at the birth of that child. Shortly after the delivery, Mr. Erdman said his wife complained of burning pains in her throat and stomach, then died a few days later. Mr. Erdman was convinced his wife had died from childbed fever like two or three other women in their neighborhood. Esperance's death was at least the fourth.

Xavier knew the deaths Mr. Erdman had referenced were the reason why the Soquets had made a will. Xavier wondered whether Dr. Munro had been the physician at each of those births. Could he somehow be the reason for these women's deaths? It appeared as if J.P. Soquet had taken precautions for his wife's delivery by engaging Dr. Munro, a physician, rather than a midwife, as she had always used in the past. But had J.P. brought the deadly source for childbed fever into their home? If so, had he done so unwittingly?

Family members transported Esperance Soquet's casket in a wagon to Holy Cross Cemetery for her internment. Xavier's rig and those of the other mourners joined the procession.

At the cemetery, Father Daems offered blessings for the deceased and sprinkled the coffin and grave with holy water. With a heavy heart, Xavier gazed at Esperance's children. The two boys and their sisters clung together, each overcome with grief for their dear mother.

As the coffin was lowered into the ground, each family member placed a handful of earth on top of the casket.

A short distance away Xavier noted an unmarked fresh grave, which he guessed contained the body of August Minsart. Xavier surveyed the gathered mourners.

While they were silent now, befitting the funeral, the Belgian community certainly had reason to talk.

Soon they would.

FROZEN EVIDENCE

PAULINE

Blacksmith Shop (1870s) on Door Peninsula (Courtesy Belgian Heritage Center)

FROST PAINTED THE WINDOWS of the Villiesse kitchen, and birch logs crackled in the large stone hearth, flooding the room with warmth. The soft glow of kerosene lamps provided additional light while scents of wet wool and roasted venison filled the air.

Over supper, Pauline, Henry, and Henry's younger brother, John, conversed amicably around the hand-hewn dining table on Friday, December 12, 1873. John was the guest of honor and a blacksmith by trade. He had just arrived by sleigh from the city of De Pere, five miles south of Green Bay, his eyebrows grizzled with ice. John's wet clothes were now drying by the fire. He planned to stay in town for a few weeks to work at the local blacksmith forge where he had initially learned his trade. In preparation for the following year, John and the owner would help Henry and other neighborhood farmers repair their equipment, such as plows, harrows, and scythes, and to forge new necessities like axes, wagon parts, and horseshoes.

Pauline and the children listened as the men discussed the economic uncertainty that had taken hold that year. Even after the tremendous amount of hay and wheat Henry had harvested, the best haul since the Villiesse family had owned their farm, Pauline knew they were just getting by. The Panic of 1873, as it would come to be known, had been triggered in September by the collapse of a major bank out east which had been heavily invested in the railroads. During the Civil War, Pauline knew many farmers had borrowed money to expand their operations. Banks were now demanding payment of those loans while crop prices had been driven down due to oversupply from record harvests, which weakened demand, and increased competition.

Uncertainty and fear permeated the conversation, but Pauline realized her family was better off than most. Henry was a proud man. Unlike many others in the Belgian community, he had refused to borrow money to purchase more land. Although the recent crop prices had dropped, Henry had produced more hay and wheat, meaning their year-to-year income was only slightly less. They could survive, but others faced graver risks.

Pauline gazed at her family gathered around the dining table. She was thankful the supper discussion had not centered on her sister, Elvira. Five months had passed since the death of Elvira's husband, August. In September, Elvira had discarded her mourning clothes, well short of the customary mourning year, and moved into the home of J.P. Soquet, heaping more shame on the family.

To Pauline it seemed that Elvira never failed to disgrace their extended Coppersmith family. At least, Elvira could no longer complain about her lack of children. She had taken on the responsibility for J.P.'s two boys and six girls.

Pauline, expecting her fourth child in May, smiled over at Anton whose gaze never left his Uncle John's bearded face, which was so much like Henry's. Pauline noted Anton's plate was scraped clean like his sisters. Pauline excused the children from the table. They eagerly pushed back their chairs to return to their gifts from St. Nicholas, received the prior week.

Pauline poured coffee for the adults as John leaned back in his chair, his face settling into a worried frown. He said he had new information to share about the death of their former brother-in-law, August Minsart. Pauline sat down on her chair; from his tone, she knew this would not be good. She had hoped the suspicious events surrounding August's death would become an old story, so her family could rest, but that was not to be.

John said that Ignace, August's brother, had recently arrived home from the Northwoods and discovered August was dead.

Pauline winced. She said she could only imagine Ignace's shock and sorrow at hearing that news, likely conveyed by Martin Simonar who would have also relayed the suspicious circumstances surrounding August's death: the medicine bottle, the color of August's face, and his rapid burial.

John agreed and said Ignace had contacted Brown County District Attorney John J. Tracy, who had ordered an investigation, which would be led by Justice Charles Kies. Kies had empaneled a coroner's jury of six men. Among them was John's friend, James Smith. His friend was to report to the courthouse the next morning to travel by omnibus to Holy Cross Cemetery with the other jurors, a physician, and Justice Kies. Once there, the disinterment of August's body would take place.

Pauline was stunned by John's news. There was no end in sight to her family's crisis. First there had been Elvira's shameful behavior, followed by the two suspicious deaths tied to their family, and now the authorities had launched an inquiry into one of those deaths. Pauline turned to her husband. She said she would go to Holy Cross Cemetery the next day to witness her brother-in-law's exhumation.

Bundled in furs and fleecy rugs, Pauline and Henry's brother traveled in his two-seater sleigh toward Bay Settlement. The fresh, bracing air was exhilarating as the horse quietly trotted along on the snowy ground. Since Pauline was expecting a child, Henry had asked John to accompany her while Henry watched the children.

The horse released a steamy gust of air as John used the reins to turn the sleigh off the state road. Up ahead, Pauline could see Holy Cross

Church. They passed it and reached the cemetery. Stationed alongside the road was the twelve-passenger omnibus harnessed to its team. A number of sleighs and wagons were there as well. The news about the exhumation of August's body had spread. Pauline wondered whether the grave could even be located beneath the snow. Elvira had never marked her husband's final resting place.

But as John helped Pauline down from the rig, she recognized Martin Simonar. He had been present at August's burial and would know the grave's general location. Simonar led an older gentleman attired in a beaver fur trapper hat and heavy wool coat to the spot. Pauline assumed the man was Justice Kies, known throughout the county as an avid hunter. Behind him followed six men, the jurors, including John's friend. Another man in a fur hat, gloves, and long black coat stood off to the side holding a leather satchel. Pauline heard Justice Kies call him Dr. Ayres. Neighbors of August Minsart, as well as his brother, Ignace, had also gathered.

Two grave diggers used spades to remove frozen chunks of earth from the topsoil. The frost depth was about ten inches, making for hard work. Below that the diggers used shovels. Pauline knew her brother-in-law had been buried without a casket. She wondered whether August's remains would even be recognizable, much less in one piece.

Amid Ignace's muffled sobs, the grave was opened. Revulsion and distaste sounded among the neighbors as the scent of the badly decomposed body spread. Pauline chose not to draw near as she did not want to view her brother-in-law's body in such a state.

Volunteers descended into the grave to help raise it, but they could not complete the task. Dr. Ayres placed his leather satchel near the rim of the open grave and climbed in. From the satchel, he selected a surgical knife and a large glass jar. It took some time before the doctor placed a number of specimens into the jar and sealed it.

Pauline's unease grew into nausea.

While the grave diggers covered August's remains, Martin Simonar caught sight of Pauline, his eyes alert as he approached. He asked Pauline whether she had talked to her sister, Elvira. He understood the recent widow and widower, Elvira and Soquet, were soon to be married.

Pauline flushed with anger and, most of all, shame. Once again, Elvira had failed to follow the established customs. Her mourning period—if you could even call it that—had only been a few months, not the customary year. Her sister's neighbor also knew about Elvira's impending marriage before anyone in the Coppersmith family. She turned away from Simonar without responding.

Pauline suddenly realized why her sister and J.P. were planning to marry so hastily. Pauline had underestimated J.P.'s intelligence. If something suspicious showed up in August's remains, J.P. would have secured a key protection for Elvira and himself: a husband and wife could not testify for nor against each other.

BEHIND BARS

XAVIER

ATTORNEY JOHN H.M. WIGMAN entered Xavier's office on the afternoon of January 26, 1874. At Xavier's invitation, Wigman, a Hollander, sat down and got right to the point. The former Elvira Minsart, now Mrs. J.P. Soquet, had been arrested for the murder of her former husband, August Minsart.

That revelation took Xavier by surprise. He had followed the news related to August's exhumation six weeks earlier and was curious what the analysis performed on the harvested specimens might turn up. By some means, *The De Pere News* had secured the findings and reported: "The presence of arsenic was found in the body of August Minsart." But Xavier had wondered if that news was true or just speculation on the newspaper's part to drive more readership.

Xavier Martin Office at 81 Washington St. (Postcard)

The rumor mill had exploded, not only about August Minsart's death, but Esperance Soquet's as well. Rather than childbed fever, many in the community had come to believe that J.P.'s second wife could have been poisoned too. The community wanted her body exhumed and examined as August Minsart's had been. But Xavier knew Brown County authorities could not act solely on community demands. In August Minsart's case, his brother, Ignace, had filed a complaint with District Attorney J.J. Tracy. A family member like Esperance's father, Mr. J.J. Hannon, would have to do the same if authorities were to exhume Esperance's body. So far, this had not happened.

Attorney Wigman told Xavier that J.P. Soquet had hired Wigman's firm to represent his wife.

Attorney John H.M. Wigman (Men Who are Making Green Bay 1897)

Xavier knew Wigman, at age thirty-nine, was one of the best attorneys in Brown County, as was his partner, thirty-eight-year-old Thomas Richard Hudd. Their fees reflected that fact. Wigman had initially worked in the Bay Settlement area as a teacher, town clerk, and justice of the peace. The attorney could speak fluent English, Dutch, German, and French. The latter was a benefit to the Soquets, since their native Walloon language was a dialect of French.

Attorney Wigman said the coroner's inquest into August Minsart's death should have commenced first. At the inquest, the six empaneled jurors, present at August's exhumation, would have received the official analysis findings and then issued their verdict stating whether he had died from natural causes or by a different means. But D.A. Tracy had jumped the gun and arrested Elvira Soquet before this process was complete.

Xavier inferred that the D.A. believed Elvira Soquet could be a flight risk. Afterall, the press had already reported the alleged analysis findings. But arresting Elvira also meant D.A. Tracy must have secured convincing evidence to tie Elvira Soquet to her former husband's death.

Attorney Wigman told Xavier that Elvira's preliminary hearing would commence the next afternoon, and he asked whether Xavier could translate at the hearing. D.A. Tracy had told Wigman that the county would pay Xavier for his services. In addition, Wigman asked whether Xavier could accompany his partner, Mr. Hudd, into the county jail prior to that hearing to act as translator with their client, Elvira Soquet. Wigman's partner only spoke English, and Wigman was unable to be there to translate.

Xavier agreed to both requests but with some trepidation. He realized the case would be complex, surrounded by an air of intrigue and public scrutiny. Xavier knew, in his role as translator, he would need to remain impartial, but it would be difficult not to be swayed by his personal opinions about the case.

·∞·

Attired for the frigid weather in a long wool coat, cape, and derby, Xavier Martin left his Washington Street office the next morning and headed toward the Brown County Courthouse on Cherry Street. A frightening yet thrilling personal problem occupied his thoughts. After that morning's breakfast, out of the hearing of Xavier's wife, his servant and lover Augusta Bliske had told him she was certain she was pregnant.

He was shaken, but also overcome with wonder. He had always hoped to have a biological child of his own. Now, that could be possible. He had told Augusta not to worry. He would figure something out. Yet Xavier *was* worried. If Augusta's pregnancy began to show, his wife would be suspicious. He worried, too, about his reputation in the community. What would Green Bay's businessmen think if they discovered he had impregnated his servant? What about his Belgian countrymen, who Xavier had helped by improving their community and expanding their knowledge about the American way? He was well-respected in the community, and this revelation risked it all. He knew an affair was not easily forgotten or forgiven.

Moreover, if Xavier's adulterous intercourse with Augusta was exposed, both of them could be arrested. Adultery had been illegal in Wisconsin since 1849. The state had enacted a law to make it a Class I felony, specifically related to extramarital affairs involving sexual intercourse. The law was applicable to the spouse involved in the affair and the third-party involved with the accused spouse. He and Augusta could each be sentenced to prison for up to three and a half years and each fined $400.

Every way he looked at the problem, it ended in ruin.

As Xavier trekked through the fallen snow, he weighed his options. He could pay for Augusta's illegal abortion. But how could he destroy the child he had helped to create with the woman he loved? Despite everything, he realized he and Augusta both wanted to keep the child.

He would have to provide Augusta the means to live elsewhere during her pregnancy. It would have to be a significant distance from Green Bay. Otherwise, rumors would follow Augusta—and those would surely lead back to him. Once the baby was born, he reasoned, he could figure out their next steps.

Xavier entered the first-floor jail vestibule of the three-story brick courthouse. He took a deep breath and forced his mind to focus on the job he had been hired for.

Thomas R. Hudd (Brady-Handy photo, Library of Congress)

Awaiting his arrival was the portly, curly-headed, Attorney Thomas R. Hudd, who had served as the Outagamie County District Attorney in the city of Appleton, thirty miles south of Green Bay. He had met Attorney Wigman there, who had moved to Appleton from the Bay Settlement area, and the two men had formed a partnership. Four years ago, the pair had moved their practice to Green Bay.

The jailer led Xavier and Attorney Hudd down the damp corridor toward Elvira's cell. Men stared out from behind bars, their voices raised, their fists banging. Xavier smelled the foul stench of urine and unwashed clothes.

Outside one of the cells, he was surprised to see a young man he knew to be a *State Gazette* reporter, scribbling notes on a pad as he talked through the bars to a prisoner. The jailer said the inmate was Patrick Flaherty, also charged with murder. He had been arrested the prior day for fatally stabbing a man outside a Belgian tavern. The jailer said, almost proudly, he now had two suspected murderers in his care, a rarity. The usual prisoners, he added, were the sort of men they had passed in the other cells, arrested for drunk and disorderly or for exposing themselves. He also had his share of female prisoners who kept houses of ill repute or the women who worked in those same brothels.

Elvira sat on a steel bedstead beside a washstand and toilet bucket. She looked up as Xavier introduced Attorney Hudd and himself.

Xavier looked into her pitiful eyes, and she tilted her head, a twitch of recognition tugging at her features.

When Xavier had been the Green Bay township postmaster, he had known most everyone in that Belgian community, including the Coppersmiths, Minsarts, and Soquets. He had not seen Elvira for at least a decade, but other than age lines creasing his face and graying hair, he looked the same. Elvira was not much changed either, though she was a young woman of nearly thirty now.

She began an emotion-filled plea for help. Elvira claimed she had not killed her husband. She was a grieving widow. J.P.'s children, her children, needed her. She had to get out of jail.

In that putrid corridor, amid the cacophony, Elvira's earnest words touched Xavier. He immediately believed that if she had poisoned her husband, she was doing an admirable job of hiding the "unnatural qualities" she had to possess to commit such an atrocity.

The Brown County Courthouse had been completed in 1868, six years after Xavier had moved to Green Bay. A visitor from the *Manitowoc Tribune* once stated, "The new Courthouse is an honor to the town both in architectural design and finish. The citizens may well be proud of it." Xavier was not proud only of the impressive courthouse he stepped into, but also of the impressive elected county officials who provided justice for Brown County. One of those was Justice Charles H. Kies.

Xavier entered Kies's courtroom to translate for Elvira Soquet's preliminary hearing. Justice Kies had been elected to the position the year after Xavier arrived in Brown County, although Kies had settled in the area a decade or so before the first Belgian immigrants. He primarily held jurisdiction over minor criminal and civil cases where he passed sentences. He conducted bail hearings, officiated marriages, and presided at preliminary hearings.

Today Justice Kies would determine whether there was enough evidence, or probable cause, to send Elvira Soquet's case to the Brown County Circuit Court judge for trial. The preliminary hearing would give Elvira's attorneys the chance to see the prosecution's evidence and cross-examine their witnesses. In turn, the prosecutor, District Attorney John J. Tracy, would have to convince Justice Kies there was a

Brown County Courthouse (A Souvenir of Green Bay 1903)

reasonable certainty that Elvira Soquet had committed the first-degree murder of her former husband, August Minsart.

J.J. Tracy was a thirty-one-year-old district attorney who had graduated from Dartmouth College and was a Civil War veteran. When he arrived in Green Bay, he secured the job of principal at Sale School, still the city's only public school, where Xavier's daughter had attended. While Tracy was principal, he studied law with Xavier's friend, Attorney John C. Neville. After Tracy had been accepted by the Brown County Bar, the two attorneys had established a partnership.

Two years ago, J.J. Tracy had run for the part-time position of Brown County District Attorney and won. The press deemed him to be "a rising young lawyer ... and an honest citizen ... who had gained distinction in his profession." The Brown County District Attorney annual pay of $1,200 supplemented the income Tracy made as a partner in the Neville & Tracy law firm.

Xavier stood beside the witness stand, his frame tall and thin while most of the Belgians in the spectator section were short and stocky, which was more the norm. Xavier would translate the three attorneys' questions into Walloon for the Belgian witnesses, then translate their responses back into English for those present to hear.

The Coppersmith family, seated in the courtroom to support Elvira, included her father, Alexis, and Elvira's sister, Pauline Villiesse. Xavier knew that most of the State's witnesses had been present at the Minsart home on the day of August's death. Those included the Simonars, the Williams, and Fannie and Peter Vandenbusch, who were the sister and brother-in-law to the defendant.

Xavier noted that J.P. Soquet was in the courtroom as well, seated beside his new father-in-law. J.P. seemed relaxed, knowing he could not legally be called to testify either for or against his wife.

The State and defense attorneys, with Xavier's help, conducted the direct and cross-examination of the Belgian witnesses. Professor Daniels from Madison, Wisconsin, then took the stand. He testified about the analysis he had performed on the tissue samples Dr. Ayres had extracted from August Minsart's remains. *The De Pere News* reporting was verified when the professor stated he had discovered a large quantity of arsenic in the tissue samples, estimating at least eight grams would have been present in Minsart's body at the time of death.

When District Attorney Tracy asked whether that amount of arsenic could have caused August Minsart's death, the professor said, "Yes." That amount of arsenic would be "sufficient to kill about ten men."

Xavier watched those in the courtroom, at least those who understood English, twitch in their seats, their eyes darting between Elvira and J.P. Soquet.

District Attorney Tracy called the name of the last witness, the victim's brother, Ignace Minsart.

That morning, inside Elvira's jail cell, Attorney Hudd had told Elvira that Ignace Minsart would be testifying. Xavier could tell that information had worried Elvira. She had told Mr. Hudd she and her husband had lived with August's brother for seven years. During that time, the two men had often angered Elvira. She admitted she had threatened to poison them. But those had been idle threats, nothing she had ever planned on carrying out. How could she do such a thing? She was just a housewife, she pleaded.

It was clear to all of them that Ignace's testimony would be damaging.

In the courtroom, D.A. Tracy again called Ignace Minsart's name.

The crowd rustled.

Xavier watched as August's brother attempted to take the stand but realized with surprise, he was too drunk to do so.

Incensed by the witness's disrespectful behavior, Justice Keis threatened to throw Ignace in jail for contempt.

As the crowd began to whisper, Elvira's attorney, Mr. Hudd, asked for a sidebar. He, along with Attorney Wigman and D.A. Tracy, approached the bench.

After much discussion, Justice Keis announced the attorneys had reached an arrangement. Elvira's attorneys, Mr. Hudd and Mr. Wigman, had agreed that Elvira Soquet *would* stand trial for the murder of her former husband at the March term of Brown County Circuit Court. In turn, District Attorney Tracy had agreed to two conditions: the deceased's brother, Ignace Minsart, could not testify at the future trial, and, until that trial, given Elvira Soquet secured a $2,000 surety bond, she could be released on bail.

At the unexpected turn of events, the Belgian witnesses filed out, confused by the outcome. Elvira was escorted back to her jail cell with Attorney Wigman's promise that once her husband returned with a $2,000 surety bond (about $56,000 in current valuation), she would be released on bail.

Xavier left the courthouse and wondered whether Elvira's attorneys had made a mistake in negotiating this agreement with D.A. Tracy. From Xavier's perspective, the testimony of the Belgian witnesses had not provided any direct connection to Elvira Soquet's participation in August's death. Even if Ignace Minsart had testified, Justice Kies might likely have discharged Elvira's case due to lack of evidence. Now, however, Elvira would be forced to stand trial.

Three days after Elvira's preliminary hearing, Xavier's brother Constant entered Xavier's office. He said he had drawn up a deed for J.P. Soquet's brother and sister-in-law, Constant and Mary Soquet. Four days after August Minsart's body had been disinterred, J.P. and Elvira had sold sixty acres of their 160-acre farm to J.P.'s brother for $4,000. But that morning, J.P.'s brother and his wife had apparently sold the same sixty acres back to J.P. and Elvira for the same amount.

Xavier guessed something was amiss. Perhaps, he reasoned, when J.P. had initially sold his sixty acres of farmland, he had been trying to get hold of $4,000 in cash. If he had known arsenic would be found in

August's remains, perhaps J.P. and Elvira Soquet had planned to use that money to flee. But before they could make their escape, Elvira had been arrested. Now J.P. wanted his farmland back from his brother since J.P. and Elvira were not leaving Brown County after all, and that tract of land could be used as surety to secure the $2,000 bond for Elvira's release on bail.

A week later, on February 3, 1874, Xavier's mind was finally clear of the problem of Augusta's pregnancy, which had been plaguing him. He had secured a flat in Milwaukee, Wisconsin, for his servant and lover Augusta Bliske. She had agreed to live in Milwaukee, 120 miles south of Green Bay, at least until their child was born, given Xavier would visit. Since he often went to Milwaukee on business, their plan should be entirely feasible. He was relieved to be in control of his life once again and truly excited about the upcoming birth of their child.

As Xavier paged through the *State Gazette*, his eyes landed on a news article. The coroner's inquest into August Minsart's sudden death had finally been held. The empaneled jury present at August Minsart's disinterment had issued their verdict:

> *That on or about the 14th day of June 1873, August Minsart, in the town of Humboldt, came to his death by being poisoned by a certain deadly poison called arsenic, inhaled and taken into his stomach, but by whose hands or by what means the said poison was administered, whether by his own hands or by the hands of any other person or persons, the jurors are unable to determine.*

Xavier folded the paper and placed it on his desk. District Attorney J.J. Tracy had quite the job ahead of him. If he could not find evidence to tie Elvira Soquet to August Minsart's death, the jury for her upcoming criminal trial would likely reach the same verdict.

FAMILY SECRETS

PAULINE

IN MAY OF 1874, Pauline nursed her new son beside the kitchen window. She and Henry had welcomed their fourth child, Jerome, four weeks ago. The sun appeared through a soft curtain of clouds, illuminating Pauline's view of her three children. They were taking turns on a swing made from tree bark while their father pushed them. Soon her extended family would arrive to meet the new baby.

Three months had passed since Pauline's sister Elvira had been released from the county jail on a $2,000 surety bond. Pauline rocked little Jerome and ruminated about Elvira who had visited the prior day. Elvira felt uncomfortable being part of family gatherings. In particular, those which included their sister, Fannie, who believed Elvira had handled August's death and burial in a disgraceful manner. Pauline believed the same but kept her feelings to herself.

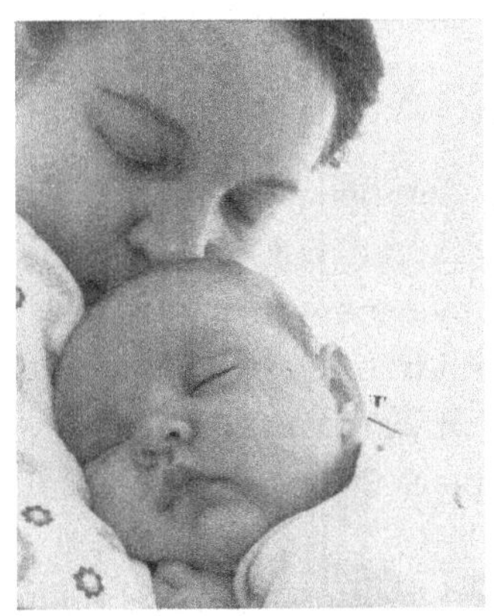

Amanda Villiesse Wevers (Current Descendent of Pauline Villiesse and her son Jerome) (Courtesy of Amanda Wevers)

Elvira had once again tried to explain the actions she had taken on the day of August's death, and Pauline had nodded along politely, despite her misgivings.

Elvira insisted there had been nothing sinister about August's death. Even though she and her husband had not gotten along, she would never have poisoned him, nor would she have wanted him to suffer. She had been in shock on the day of August's death, that was why she had not acted like herself. When J.P. had taken charge and helped her deal with their tragic situation, Elvira had been grateful. She implored Pauline to imagine if Henry had purposely swallowed poison and left her alone. How would Pauline have reacted?

Elvira knew she had blemished the Coppersmith family's good name, and that the upcoming trial would put an unwanted spotlight on their family again. Elvira told Pauline she was sorry. But what could she do other than to prove her innocence when her trial came to pass?

As Pauline thought over Elvira's visit, she burped Jerome on her shoulder and breathed in his newborn scent. She wanted to believe her sister, to give her a hug, to tell her everything would be alright. But ever since Elvira's affair with J.P. Soquet had begun, Pauline had found it difficult to embrace her sister or reach out for her hand.

Still, Pauline admitted she could not imagine how Elvira felt, living in the tension-filled environment of the Soquet home, not knowing day in and day out when she might go on trial. Brown County Circuit Court's March term had come and gone without Elvira's case being placed on the docket. According to the press, District Attorney Tracy continued to be "lamentably deficient" in discovering the slightest proof that Elvira had poisoned her former husband.

Elvira insisted that the lack of evidence supported her vehement claim: she had not poisoned August.

But Pauline still wondered.

She placed Jerome on her other breast. She believed Elvira was attempting to be a good stepmother to J.P.'s children. But Pauline knew Clara, nearing her first birthday, was coddled by her sisters and showed little affection toward Elvira. J.P.'s other children, except his eldest daughter, Mary, from his first marriage, had not warmed to Elvira. They told their stepmother that she could never replace Esperance, their real mother, whom they had dearly loved.

Pauline thought Elvira's current life seemed far more stressful than when she had been married to August. But Elvira, intent on keeping up the story of her happy marriage to J.P., had not revealed her own thoughts to Pauline.

Henry had told Pauline gossip continued to flow at the Dyckesville Stage House Tavern. Over pints of beer, while playing cards, or dice, or billiards, Henry said the menfolk would talk about Elvira's case and wonder: Who gave August Minsart the poison? Was it Elvira? Was it J.P.? Or did August poison himself? And where did the poison come from? Where was it procured? And who procured it?

The Stage House Tavern – Dyckesville (Courtesy Belgian Heritage Center)

They were the same questions Pauline was ashamed to have about her own sister.

Henry said the men had all agreed a skillful detective could answer those questions and set the case to rest. They could not understand how an alleged crime of that enormity could pass unnoticed. How human life in Brown County could be worth so little, how people could be allowed to die like dogs, simply because the State had failed to exert the necessary effort to secure the needed evidence.

Allen Pinkerton (Pinkerton National Detective Agency), President Lincoln, Major General McClernand (Library of Congress)

Pauline touched her son's petal soft cheek and smiled down at him. She did not totally buy into the menfolk's repudiation of authority. Pauline had heard that police forces in large cities like Milwaukee had detectives who performed investigative duties. But in the small city of Green Bay and the rural areas of Brown County, investigations were handled by the local constable or sheriff. Private investigators could be secured from companies like the famous Pinkerton National Detective Agency, but

Brown County had to secure the funds, which they had decided not to do. The suspicious death of a Belgian farmer did not draw the kind of attention that a more prominent citizen of a larger city might.

Pauline believed Brown County's district attorney had attempted to find the answers to the menfolk's questions using the county's limited resources. But the answers were not to be found. Arsenic was a common poison used to kill rats. It was found on nearly all Wisconsin farms. The poison could be purchased from a general store in a liquid or white powder form. It was tasteless and could easily be mixed, by anyone, into any sort of stew, porridge, or beverage.

Pauline doubted that August had taken his own life. That left her sister or J.P. as likely culprits, and Pauline's bet was on the latter. She believed J.P. was a loathsome man to allow her sister to take the blame for her former husband's death. To stand trial for something she had not done. To suffer the community disgrace, when J.P. could confess to the deed. But oh, no, J.P. would never do that. He was an unscrupulous man, apparently willing to destroy his wife's life to save his own skin and to place shame on the Coppersmith family in the process.

Pauline heard the front door open, followed by voices and footsteps. Her sister, Fannie, and brother-in-law, Peter, stepped into the kitchen from the entrance hall. They had already sent their daughter out back to play with her cousins.

As Fannie admired Jerome, Pauline's father and mother arrived with her youngest sister, twenty-year-old Flora, and Flora's husband, twenty-four-year-old William Lancelle. The two had been married for about one year. William was employed by Pauline's father to work on the Coppersmith farm. Henry came in from the backyard, and Pauline's mother volunteered to step outside to supervise her grandchildren so the rest of the family could visit in the parlor.

Once the seven adults had secured a coffee, beer, or cider, they all were seated on chairs and benches around the stone hearth. Fannie mentioned some interesting news. That morning, she and Peter had talked with John B. Gonion, the sexton who looked after Holy Cross Church and its cemetery. He had flagged down their wagon as it passed through Bay Settlement. Gonion knew Fannie's sister was Elvira, J.P. Soquet's new wife. The sexton said he had just walked by the grave of J.P.'s former wife, Esperance, and noticed it had been disturbed.

Pauline listened intently, startled by what she heard. Fannie said the sexton had known there had been talk about exhuming the body of J.P.'s second wife. But the sexton said the authorities would have alerted him if a coroner's inquest had been initiated to disinter Esperance's body as August Minsart's had been. The sexton believed someone else had secretly disturbed the grave.

Pauline noticed her father trade a nervous glance with William. Pauline was unsettled. As the eldest sister, her role included bringing leadership and wisdom, even questioning her family's actions when necessary. That role endowed Pauline with the boldness to ask her father whether he was somehow involved.

Alexis shook his head firmly. But he admitted that about three months earlier, soon after Elvira's preliminary hearing, J.P. and he had traveled to Green Bay together with a $2,000 surety bond to bail Elvira out of jail. On that long ride, J.P. had talked about his second wife, Esperance. J.P. said he understood the authorities were going to exhume her body.

Alexis looked over at Pauline, as he reluctantly recounted the rest of the conversation. He said he had asked J.P. if he was worried, if there was any danger in having her body exhumed. J.P. had admitted, he would be "in for it," since his wife had been poisoned with the same kind of poison found in August Minsart's stomach.

Pauline's body tensed, startling her sleeping son. The eyes of the family darted around, sharing worried glances among themselves. Pauline wanted to reprimand her father for not sharing that information earlier. But a cornerstone of her Belgian family culture was to respect one's parents and the decisions they made.

The news settled, and the family members began talking. Pauline quieted the group and asked her father whether he believed J.P. had confessed to killing his wife. Had J.P. somehow fed Esperance poison right after their new baby had been born? Pauline shuddered to think it. Even though she did not like J.P., it was hard to imagine anyone committing such an evil act.

Alexis had no answer. He said the family could interpret J.P.'s words in any way they chose.

An uneasy silence filled the room. Pauline clutched her baby tight and gazed over at Henry. She could not imagine any husband poisoning the mother of their newborn. It was beyond evil. Pauline took a deep breath and asked her father whether J.P. had mentioned Elvira's former husband, August, who had been poisoned with arsenic.

Alexis said he had not.

Pauline said what her family was all thinking, the unimaginable thing: Perhaps J.P. had not mentioned August since J.P. carried no responsibility for his death. Maybe Elvira was guilty of poisoning her spouse while J.P. was guilty of poisoning his. It was shameful to even mention the idea, but Pauline could no longer stand leaving these important questions unasked.

Everyone sat in stunned silence until Alexis spoke. He said he wanted to get something else off his chest. On the ride to Green Bay to bail Elvira out, he told them that J.P. had asked him to go into Holy Cross Cemetery and help him dig up Esperance's body. But Alexis said he had refused.

Pauline grimaced as her father turned to his son-in-law, William, and said he should tell everyone what J.P. had told him as well.

William could not look at his wife, embarrassed for having kept this information from her. He told them he had been at the Coppersmith house when J.P. had asked Mr. Coppersmith to accompany him to Green Bay to bail Elvira out. William said, while hitching up the horses for Mr. Coppersmith, J.P. had come out to the stable and offered him a pair of oxen if William would help "unbury his wife."

Flora glared at William as he continued. He had told J.P. that even if he gave him the entire city of Green Bay, he would not be tempted to participate in digging up the dead. But William said J.P. had not given up. He had asked about William's brother, if the same offer might entice him. When William told J.P. not to ask his brother, J.P.'s anger had flared. He had told William, if his wife was not "unburied" he was "in for it" since "his woman" had been poisoned.

Everyone was speechless.

Pauline knew her father and brother-in-law should contact the district attorney with the information they had. But that meant putting Elvira in danger of further scrutiny regarding her part in August's death. Also, reporting their sister's new husband to the authorities would bring additional shame to the Coppersmith family—perhaps too much for Pauline's parents to bear. She felt powerless and angry with no way to proceed. Even if Esperance's grave was opened by authorities, Pauline doubted her body would be there. Reporting J.P. and suffering that shame would likely be for naught.

Pauline had come to realize J.P. was no fool.

Pauline looked at her father and brother-in-law. They had kept secrets to protect Elvira. All of her family would continue to do so. That was what good Belgian families did. Pauline looked down at the innocent face of her son. She knew she would do whatever it took to defend and protect Jerome or any of her children, just as her father, Alexis Coppersmith, had done for his daughter.

·∞·

On the morning of September 28, 1874, about fifteen months after August Minsart's death, Pauline and her entire adult family, including J.P. Soquet, sat inside the Brown County courtroom of Justice Kies. At the defendant's table sat attorneys Hudd and Wigman with Elvira between them. Xavier Martin was also present to translate.

Pauline watched as District Attorney Tracy rose from his seat and spoke. His words caused a commotion among those in the audience who spoke English. The judge turned to Xavier Martin and asked him to translate D.A. Tracy's words.

Xavier said the D.A. had entered a *nolle prosequi* in the case of the State against Elvira Soquet, who had been charged with poisoning her former husband, August Minsart. The necessary evidence in the case was lacking, and the State was forced to discontinue the prosecution. The defendant was free to leave, and her $2,000 surety bond was discharged.

Pauline gasped at that unexpected news and glanced at Elvira. Utter relief was etched onto her sister's face. Pauline was relieved as well. Maybe the entire Coppersmith family could move on with their lives. They could maintain that August had taken his own life, and perhaps that was true. Pauline believed Elvira or J.P. had given August that deadly dose of arsenic, but she was willing to let it rest if it meant Elvira could walk free. She was thankful there was currently no way to prove it, a fact which might spare her family more shame. She was also grateful that nobody from the Hannon family had accused J.P. of any foul play related to Esperance's death.

Pauline and Henry followed the Soquet wagon out of the city of Green Bay. Had Pauline's sister and J.P. achieved the marital union they had desired by getting rid of their spouses? Pauline knew those dreadful deaths would come with a price, whether the worst proved to be true or not. Her sister, Elvira, and J.P. Soquet had lost the respect of the Belgian community. It would be difficult to win their respect back, especially when Pauline knew Ignace Minsart would not let the injustice against his brother go so easily.

ELECTION RAMIFICATIONS

XAVIER

MOST THEATRICAL TROUPES, minstrel shows, and opera companies booked space at Klaus Hall, situated on the second floor of 222 Pine Street in downtown Green Bay. Political rallies were held there, too, and the "rafters rang to the stirring oratory of such figures as United States Senator Tim Howe." On the evening of October 6, 1874, the senator would address about thirty leading city men, including Xavier Martin. The talk would center on the establishment of a Wisconsin Society for the Prevention of Cruelty to Animals.

Xavier had just returned on the Chicago & Northwestern passenger train from Milwaukee. He had conducted business and also visited his lover, Augusta, who was due to deliver their illegitimate child within the month. Xavier grappled with his complex emotions. He felt alive when he spent time with Augusta while simultaneously experiencing guilt and shame. He should tell Mary about his affair. But if he did, he knew his betrayal would destroy her and their marriage once and for all.

John C. Neville (Neville Public Museum of Brown County)

Below the seventeen-foot-high Klaus Hall ceiling, Xavier sat beside his friend, Attorney John C. Neville. The sixty-year-old attorney had arrived in Brown County in 1856, a year before Xavier. Neville was a native of Dublin, Ireland, and had immigrated to Pottsville, Pennsylvania, at age twenty-one where he had studied law and had been admitted to the bar. After he arrived in Green Bay, he built one of the most lucrative clientages in northern Wisconsin and had formed a partnership with District Attorney J.J. Tracy four years ago.

A week had passed since Elvira Soquet's first degree murder trial had been discontinued by Neville's law partner. Xavier wanted to broach that subject with Neville, eager to hear his thoughts on the case. But before Xavier could do so, the meeting was called to order.

Amid the smoky haze and scent of cigar and pipe smoke, U.S. Senator Howe described the injustice of animal cruelty and its effect on Brown County. He advocated for more humane treatment of animals such as horses, cows, cats, and dogs. He presented a recent story about a local farmer who had brought an old, decrepit, blind horse into Green Bay and left it uncared for while the farmer went off on a three-day drinking binge. There was currently no way to punish the farmer for the abuse of his animal. But in New York City, where the Society for the Prevention of Cruelty to Animals (SPCA) had been created eight years ago, the farmer could have been sentenced to jail time and received a fine.

U.S. Senator Timothy O. Howe (Wikipedia.org)

Convinced, those present appointed an executive committee to prepare articles of association for a Wisconsin SPCA that included the Honorable Tim Howe, Attorney John C. Neville, Colonel C. D. Robinson, Green Bay Mayor Alonzo Kimball, and Xavier Martin.

After the meeting, Xavier departed with Attorney Neville. Out on the street, the two men talked about the meeting, and Xavier brought up Elvira Soquet's case. Xavier asked how Neville felt about Elvira going free.

The Irishman explained that while District Attorney J.J. Tracy had entered a *nolle prosequi* withdrawing the charges against Mrs. Soquet, it did not represent a final judgment. This ruling did not mean she was not guilty nor that her charges had permanently been dismissed. D.A. Tracy could refile charges against Mrs. Soquet if new evidence came to light or if circumstances changed.

Xavier mulled over this facet of the law. He reckoned that D.A. Tracy now regretted he had initiated Elvira Soquet's first-degree murder case without finding proper evidence first. He said the attorney had his reputation to uphold. If Elvira was indeed guilty of her husband's murder, Tracy ought to pledge to the citizens of Brown County he would right that wrong during his final year as district attorney.

Neville simply nodded along.

·∞·

Three months passed. In that time, Xavier's lover, Augusta Bliske, gave birth to Xavier's first natural child, Rudoph Martin, and it was a joyous occasion. In addition to making trips down to Milwaukee to visit his lover and little boy, Xavier handled his local real estate business and translated at civil and criminal court proceedings connected to the Belgian community. But as Brown County's population had grown, its circuit court business had increased, causing court delays of nearly two years.

Xavier was dealing with his own delay. He had tried to corral the four men appointed to work with him to create the articles of association for the Wisconsin SPCA but had been unsuccessful. In January of 1875, he copied eleven sections of the New York SPCA statute, which could apply to Wisconsin. He invited Attorney John C. Neville and Attorney Thomas R. Hudd, who had been elected to the Wisconsin State Assembly, to help him finish the articles.

Attorney Hudd had recently suffered a tremendous personal loss. Falling lumber had seriously injured the spine of his little son, Freddie. Hudd's son had "lingered along, much of the time in pain, until death had relieved his sufferings." Xavier recognized Mr. Hudd's offer to help shape the Wisconsin SPCA bill, which he would bring to the Wisconsin Legislature, provided him a purposeful diversion to help him alleviate his grief.

During the January meeting in Xavier's office, the three men also discussed the time it took to get a criminal or civil case onto the Brown County Circuit Court docket. Neville and Hudd told Xavier the Brown County board had recently recommended the creation of a second county court, headed by a new justice who would be elected for a six-year term with an annual salary of $3,000. That second court would provide "speedy and permanent relief to Brown County citizens seeking redress through judicial proceedings." To that end, Mr. Hudd told Xavier, the Brown County Bar had held many meetings, and he had presented the bill for a second Brown County justice in front of the Wisconsin Legislature. The bill had passed both houses.

The next morning, Xavier opened the *State Gazette* and read the call for Mr. John J. Tracy, to become the Brown County attorneys' candidate for judge. The call stated the Brown County Bar "was united in their support of Mr. John J. Tracy" who "commanded their confidence and respect." He had "adequate knowledge of the theory and practice of the law" and a "judicial quality of mind." Twenty-two attorneys signed the call to give their support for the thirty-two-year-old district attorney, including seventy-year-old Morgan Lewis Martin.

Major Morgan L. Martin (1805–1887) (findagrave.com)

Virtually everyone in Brown County knew Morgan L. Martin. The old pioneer had studied law in Detroit, and at age twenty-two, arrived in Shantytown, which was now the village of Allouez within Brown County. The Wisconsin Territory had yet to be created and only about one hundred civilians lived in the area. M.L. Martin established a law office in Shantytown and was a member of the Michigan and Wisconsin Territory legislative councils. As president of the Wisconsin State Constitutional Convention, Martin helped frame the state's constitution, ratified in 1848 when Wisconsin became a state. Over the next decade, M.L. Martin served in the Wisconsin State Assembly and the State Senate. During the Civil War, he served as a paymaster and earned the title of Major. Now Martin had decided to retire from public service to enjoy his beautiful Hazlewood home on the Fox River, surrounded by his loving and accomplished family. His endorsement carried significant weight for Tracy.

-ꝏ-

Two weeks later, Attorney John J. Tracy's letter of acceptance to run for Brown County judge was printed in the *State Gazette*. Xavier met John C. Neville for a midday dinner at the Cook Hotel restaurant. Neither had any doubt that Neville's law partner would be elected judge given the endorsement and pledge from every one of his professional brethren. Also, no opposition had appeared. Neville reported that Tracy had formally withdrawn from their joint law practice. In addition, Tracy had resigned from the office of Brown County District Attorney. Wisconsin laws forbid Tracy from running for any judicial office while serving as district attorney.

Xavier and Neville finished their meal and stepped out into the sunshine on Washington Street. Xavier eyed a group of parading men "styling themselves as old settlers" in wide-brimmed felt hats, loose-fitting shirts, sturdy breeches, vests, and heavy leather boots. Their voices rang out, claiming a conspiracy was going on in Green Bay. That all the lawyers had combined to rob the people of their "sovereign prerogative" to select the new district judge themselves. These men loudly affirmed they would elect their own candidate in spite of the Brown County Bar's public support of Tracy. And their candidate was Major Morgan L. Martin.

Washington St., Green Bay, WI, from Pine to Cherry in 1876 (Courtesy Brown County Historical Society CBCH01-0142)

One of the parading men targeted Xavier and Neville with his comments. The man said the "old settlers" of the area represented a large portion of "the intelligence of the county," and they were determined to make Major Martin their candidate "whether he liked it or not."

Xavier knew that Martin had pledged to support Mr. Tracy, and he believed Major Martin would not accept the public's call to pursue the new county judge position.

But Xavier was wrong. On March 16, 1875, Martin's acceptance letter was published in the press: "The office [of county judge] is one of great responsibility, requiring qualifications of a high order and a maturity of thought and judgment attained only by years of experience; and should the people of the county confer the honor upon me, I shall accept it."

A meeting for the Society for the Prevention of Cruelty to Animals was held that week in Klaus Hall. Most of the city leaders were in attendance, although Xavier noted Major Morgan L. Martin and Attorney J.J. Tracy were not. Xavier was the speaker, and he announced the good news: With the Honorable T.R. Hudd's assistance, a bill to establish the Wisconsin SPCA had quietly passed in both houses of the Wisconsin Legislature. Anyone in the state who treated animals such as dogs, horses, mules, and cattle, badly, could be arrested, convicted, and punished. Everyone clapped and cheered.

Xavier was not surprised when the conversation switched direction to focus on the scandal brewing in the county. Neville said the call for Tracy had been prepared by one of Tracy's friends and had been circulated among the younger attorneys first who had signed the document, leaving two spaces at the top for the signatures of Major M.L. Martin and Neville himself, since both had been out of town. When Tracy's friend had presented the paper to Major Martin, he had unhesitatingly signed the call for J.J. Tracy to run for the newly created judgeship. Neville said he had placed his signature above Martin's. Now, four weeks later, after Mr. Tracy had relinquished his law work and district attorney position, Major Martin had publicly announced his readiness to run for the county judge position himself.

Neville said such an action was a disappointment to Martin's real friends, who were present in the hall today. The major's action had not indicated an impartial integrity which would enable a just and honest judge to resist personal interest solicitations.

Another member of the Brown County Bar stood. He pointed out Major Martin's lack of qualifications for Brown County Judge. He said Martin's acceptance letter had stated the office "requires qualifications of a high order and a maturity of thought and judgment attained only by years of experience," thereby implying, Major Martin held those qualifications and Tracy did not. But the man pointed out that Martin's career had primarily been spent as a Wisconsin Legislature member—not practicing law.

Attorney John C. Neville agreed. Major M.L. Martin had many good qualities, but Neville said the man was not as well read in the current practice of law as Mr. J.J. Tracy. Martin's long inactivity had left him without a thorough appreciation of the contemporary changes in law principles. If Major Martin was elected judge, Neville said his administration of the office would not attract the confidence of the Brown County Bar.

The men in the room, including Xavier, all mumbled their agreement. Mr. Neville said in closing, as if speaking to a courtroom jury, Brown County's true interests demanded the election of Mr. J.J. Tracy.

Despite the support for Mr. Tracy, Xavier left the meeting worried. He could tell his friend Mr. John C. Neville felt the pressure of being one of the attorneys who had signed the call for Mr. Tracy. In doing so, Neville's law partner of five years had been essentially forced to resign from his profession with the belief he would become the new county judge. If Mr. Tracy did not win the county judge position, he would likely fall from favor within the community. He would be left to fend for himself, to build a new client base, feeling as if he had been robbed of a job he had been all but promised.

On every street corner pole, on every tavern door, on every mercantile store bulletin board, and even on public outhouse walls, handbills and posters were plastered about the Brown County judgeship election. The other offices up for election drew little attention. Xavier was running for alderman of Green Bay's first ward. The *State Gazette* was behind him stating: "Of course [Xavier Martin] will have a large vote; for when did Xavier ever fail on that?" Xavier had no doubt he would win. How could he not, when he and only one other gentleman were running for the two Green Bay first ward aldermen positions? Nevertheless, Xavier would still enjoy receiving the most votes.

On the Washington Street door leading up to his office, two handbills were tacked. The first represented Xavier's own choice for county judge, Mr. J.J. Tracy. The handbill included the names of the Brown County Bar who had called him to run for the position, including Mr. Morgan L. Martin's name printed in capital letters, big and black, above the names of the twenty-two other attorneys.

The other handbill supported Major Morgan L. Martin. Xavier frowned as he read:

> *To the Foreign-Born Voters of Brown County: Twenty-two lawyers of the city of Green Bay have undertaken to tell the voters and taxpayers of Brown County who they must have for Judge. Twenty-two aristocrats, who live upon the misfortunes of the people, who fatten upon the wages of strife and wickedness, tell us that we must have Mr. Tracy, and they attempt to force this monstrous doctrine of privilege down our throats by hired advocates and scandalous handbills. Are we prepared to accept that decree? Are we only cyphers and slaves that we must be treated so basely? It was just such class privilege, such heartless aristocracy that drove us from our native lands. Is it to follow us and govern us and oppress us always? Mr. Martin was our friend when we were poor and houseless. Next to Divine Providence we owe to him our sacred holies and daily bread. Mr. Martin, we know to be an experience lawyer and an honorable and able man. Let us shame the impudent pretensions of the shameless crew and declare that we will have Mr. Martin, and not the lawyers' candidate, for Judge.*

Xavier knew this fight would be divisive, and he feared its impact on the community.

∞

Election day arrived on Tuesday April 6, 1875. Xavier was elected alderman representing Green Bay's first ward. When the day drew to a close, there was no clear winner for the Brown County judge position. The votes of every town, village, and city in the county would have to be carefully recounted and tallied.

Inside Klaus Hall the next day, both candidates and their supporters were present when county clerk Mr. J.J. Meade arrived with the final count. Xavier stood with Mr. John J. Tracy's supporters as the county clerk mounted the stairs to the stage.

The crowd hushed.

The county clerk announced, nearly every Brown County man registered to vote had cast their ballot: 2896 votes for one candidate and 2692 votes for the other. The winner of the 204-vote majority was Major Morgan L. Martin.

Major Martin's supporters cheered while J.J. Tracy's voiced their shock and disappointment.

Hazelwood (Morgan L. Martin home) (Courtesy Brown County Historical Society)

The county clerk posted the results on a board showing the tally by Brown County voting district. Xavier crowded in to analyze the votes. The first ward, where he lived within the Astor neighborhood, had supported Major Martin. Not surprising, since the Major's Hazelwood home was located there as well as the homes of his lifelong friends.

Most of the Belgians situated on the southern Door Peninsula had also voted for Major Martin rather than Mr. Tracy. Xavier realized Jean Philippe Soquet and his father-in-law, Alexis Coppersmith, would likely be among them. As district attorney, Tracy had gone after Mr. Coppersmith's daughter and J.P. Soquet's wife. Now the two Belgian men had retaliated at the ballot box.

Xavier doubted whether Elvira Soquet's case would ever go to trial without Tracy as D.A. or county judge. In addition, Wisconsin Governor William R. Taylor had commissioned Elvira's attorney, Mr. John H.M. Wigman, to serve out Mr. J.J. Tracy's unexpired Brown County District Attorney term.

Xavier was pleased by his own victory, but the whole event filled him with concern.

SHEER DESTRUCTION

PAULINE

PAULINE'S HUSBAND Henry was in the fields on April 4, 1877, preparing the ground for planting and fertilizing. Flocks of ducks flew over the kitchen garden where Pauline worked, their wings beating to a cacophony of quacks, whistles, and honks. Pauline's strong arms and hands loosened the soil to pull weeds. She enjoyed getting her hands in the dirt and working beside her nine- and eight-year-old daughters, Flora and Celinda. Seven-year-old Anton was in charge of entertaining Jerome, now three, and the newest addition to the family, Philomene, barely two. As Pauline worked and conversed with her children, she thought about her sister, Elvira.

Three years had passed since the State's case against Elvira had been dismissed. But August's brother, Ignace, would not let the injustice rest. Most of the Belgian community had moved on from their gossip and finger pointing, relieving the Coppersmith family from the high scrutiny. Pauline had tried to move on as well. Although, whenever she drove past Holy Cross Cemetery, she could not help but wonder whether Esperance Soquet was still in her grave.

Pauline finished her work in the garden. Her sixty-two-year-old mother arrived to watch the children while Pauline joined Henry in the fields. Like other Belgian farmwomen, Pauline knew how to use a hand plow pulled by a team of horses. She wore a bonnet with a long curtain of fabric attached to the lower edge to shield her neck from the sun. Traditional wooden *sabots* were on her feet.

Desiree Meuron Coppersmith – Pauline's mother (Courtesy of Brian Schultz on Ancestry.com)

Later that night, after Pauline's five children said their prayers, she tucked them into the large bed they all shared in the upstairs bedroom. Elvira, she knew, had hoped to have a child with J.P. Soquet. That had not come to pass, but Pauline was pregnant again.

Pauline crossed the hall and dimmed the lantern before entering the bedroom she and Henry shared. He snored, exhausted from his dawn to dusk labor. Pauline quietly undressed and poured water from the washstand pitcher into its bowl, then used a dampened sponge and lye soap to clean herself. She pulled a flannel nightdress over her head. Pauline's mother had burned logs in the parlor fireplace and the one in the kitchen throughout the day. But in the bedroom, the chill had found its way through loose panes and log chinks. Pauline released her hair from its bun and used her cramped and tired fingers to make a thick braid. She slipped into bed, snuggling under the quilts beside Henry, his body providing its familiar warmth. She felt tired and at ease, a feeling of life being as it should.

·∞·

The acrid smell of smoke jolted Pauline awake. A crackling sound mixed with pops and hisses seemed to be coming from downstairs. Pauline shook Henry's arm, urging him to get up, telling him she believed the house was on fire. The two bolted out of bed in their nightclothes. Pauline's bare feet hit the cold, hardwood floor. All Pauline could think about was the children. She hurried into the hallway and was met by a thick wall of smoke. Pauline opened the door to the children's bedroom. Flora, her eyes wide, sat huddled on the bed with her four siblings. Their panicked cries filled the smoke-filled room.

Pauline scooped up the two youngest. Henry picked up Anton then grabbed Flora's hand, instructing her to grab Celinda. Struggling under the weight of her children, Pauline lumbered toward the staircase. She thanked God it was still intact. Heat rose from below, the air scorching Pauline's skin and burning her throat.

Henry led the group down the stairs toward the front door. Pauline looked inside the parlor as she passed. Flames licked at the curtains and had ignited the timber walls. A loud crack echoed through the room, followed by a shower of sparks spraying out from the fireplace opening. The chimney had to be on fire. Fueled by adrenaline, Pauline followed

Henry out to the safety of the front yard, the cold air stinging her cheeks. Pauline knew she and Henry should have cleaned the chimneys that spring by dropping weighted bundles of brush down the flues to dislodge the debris. Now that neglected task had caused all this. Later, she would feel regret, but that moment was reserved entirely for gratitude that the children were okay.

Henry placed Anton on the ground and dashed toward the barn, returning with four feed buckets. Pauline and the older children formed a line from the water pump. Pauline filled the buckets and they passed them down to Henry who threw the water onto the burning timbers, attempting to contain the fire.

Neighbors arrived to pitch in, but the fire spread rapidly, engulfing the house in flames. Pauline's only consolation was that the wind had died, so sparks and embers from the house had not ignited the barn as well.

Grief-stricken, Pauline clustered together with Henry and their children. The Villiesse family's sanctuary was gone. All that remained were the smoldering remnants of their home and the nightclothes on their backs.

·∞·

After the fire, Pauline's family moved in with her parents, but she knew it was a huge imposition. In the backyard of her childhood home, Pauline, Flora, and Celinda sowed seeds into the Coppersmith kitchen garden for vegetables such as carrots, peas, leaf lettuce, and beets. It was the least Pauline and her daughters could do. The clip clop of horse hooves made her look up, and Pauline was surprised to see her sister, Elvira.

Covered in dust, Elvira jumped down and smacked her rumpled skirts with her hands. She said she had heard about the fire and ran to embrace Pauline, but Flora reached her aunt first. She wrapped her arms around Elvira's skirts, and Flora started to cry. Elvira stroked her niece's head, saying soothing words, while Pauline stood next to them. The tragedy could perhaps bridge the gulf between Pauline and her sister.

Their mother, Désirée Coppersmith, opened the back door and welcomed Elvira. Désirée told her daughters to come into the kitchen for a chat. Elvira took a detour to the root cellar. She returned with a mug filled with beer and the three women settled on chairs around the kitchen table.

Pauline admitted she had been trying to count her blessings—her family had survived the fire, and so had the barn and the animals—but they had lost their home and everything in it. She regretted she and Henry had not cleaned the chimney. She regretted she and Henry had not been as forward thinking as Elvira's husband, J.P. Soquet. Three years before Elvira had married him, the Soquet house had burned to the ground, but the house had been insured. Madison Mutual's settlement rebuilt the new stone home Elvira lived in.

Pauline said it was hard to believe her family had survived the Fire of 1871 only to have a chimney fire demolish their house six years later.

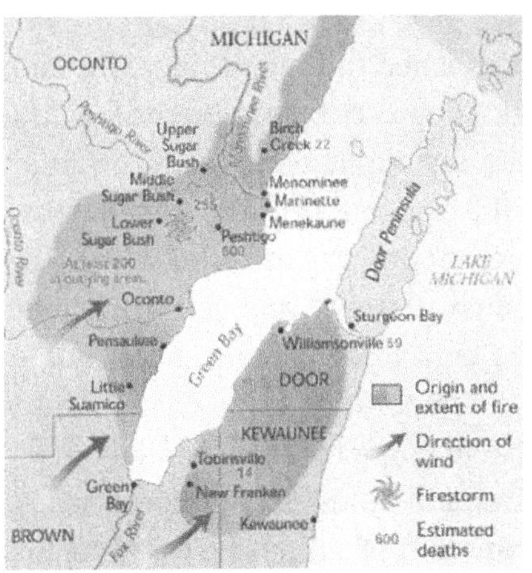

The Great Fire of 1871 (Courtesy of the Peshtigo Historical Society)

The Fire of 1871 was the first time Pauline had experienced utter fear for her children's lives. Flora was three, Celinda, two, and Anton barely one. Little rain and snow had fallen that year, causing an extreme drought. Simple brush fires fueled by the wind had ignited the forests surrounding the waters of Green Bay. On October 8, the fires could not be contained and spread rapidly, burning a ten-mile by sixty-mile span through the Belgian settlements on the southern Door Peninsula. Houses, barns, mills, taverns, churches, and schools were all destroyed. Domesticated animals roasted to cinders inside fenced-in yards. Pauline and Henry believed the world was coming to an end and the fire would destroy themselves and everyone they loved.

The fire had miraculously spared the lives and property of the Coppersmith and Villiesse families. But others in the Red River settlement had not been as fortunate. A farmer whom Henry and Pauline knew had jumped into a well with two of his children. The three survived while his wife and their three other children perished. The fire claimed more than 200 lives from the Belgian community and left close to 5,000 homeless and destitute. From all over the world, Pauline remembered how people had responded, sending clothing, bedding, food provisions, farm implements, and money.

Pauline's eyes met those of her sister and mother. Pauline said she realized her family's loss was minor compared to the loss so many people had experienced back in 1871. But Pauline could not help but feel the way she did. Their neighbors had provided used clothing to help her family get back on their feet. But they had no home, no furnishings, no sentimental mementos to gaze at, nothing to remember the special occasions from their lives. Before the Panic of 1873 and the ongoing Long Depression, which had no end in sight, Pauline's neighbors would have helped her family rebuild. But now the Belgian community had nothing to spare. It was all they could do to keep their own farms operating and families fed.

Elvira took a last swig of beer and pushed the mug aside. She said she did not want Pauline to give up all hope. Two years earlier, Elvira had sold the sixty-acres of Minsart farmland back to its original owner, Joseph LeCoque, for $1,500. But she had kept the home, barn, outbuildings, and forty uncleared acres. Elvira was thankful Wisconsin statues allowed a wife to own her own property and sell it without "the concurrence of her husband." Elvira offered the Minsart home to Pauline and her children, to live in temporarily, at no charge, until Henry had the means to construct a new home for their family.

Overcome by Elvira's generous offer and kindness, Pauline reached out and touched her sister's hand, something Pauline had not done for five years. Pauline would not hold back her love any longer. Despite it all, Elvira was her sister. Their love was strong. They stood by each other, like the good Belgian family they were.

Their mother rose and placed her hands on Elvira's shoulders and gave them a tender squeeze. She said she would step out of the kitchen so the sisters could talk privately.

Once their mother had left, Elvira acknowledged her sister would have a difficult time caring for her five children without Henry's help. But Elvira reminded Pauline that the Minsart home was only two miles from the Soquet home. Elvira planned to assist Pauline. Elvira also admitted she could use her big sister's help in return. Living in the Soquet house was challenging for Elvira. Although she got along with Mary, J.P.'s eldest daughter from his first marriage, the other children had rejected Elvira. Jennie, J.P.'s eldest daughter from his second marriage, had recently left home to join a convent. But before leaving, Jennie had told Elvira her main reason for doing so was to escape her stepmother's cruelty.

Jennie Soquet (eldest daughter of J.P. and Esperance Soquet) (Photo used with permission of Ancestry.com member)

Pauline knew her sister believed in child corporal punishment such as spanking, slapping, and even whipping. For most parents, corporal punishment was a standard part of child-rearing, although Pauline did not agree. She was convinced a good talking to was more constructive. J.P.'s second wife, Esperance, appeared to have believed the same as Pauline. Pauline could understand why the Soquet children believed their stepmother was cruel when she punished them in this way.

Elvira said her marriage was a struggle, too. J.P.'s initial obsession and attraction to Elvira had gone to the wayside. Elvira confessed to Pauline that J.P. had not turned out to be anything like Pauline's Henry. But when Pauline prompted her sister to elaborate, Elvira claimed she had spoken out of turn. Her problems were minor compared to Pauline's.

The two sisters sat in the kitchen where they had grown up, when both had been bursting with young girls' dreams of love, marriage, and children. Pauline realized her family life with Henry and their children had surpassed her imaginations, while Elvira's life had failed, dismally, not once, but twice.

Elvira's coarse and calloused hand squeezed Pauline's.

Pauline knew she had found her little sister, and she hoped nothing would ever separate them again.

LAMENTABLE WOES

XAVIER

THE PENDULUM CLOCK inside Xavier Martin's real estate office approached ten o'clock on the evening of July 9, 1877. The open windows let in a breeze and the sound of piano music from a nearby saloon. Xavier sat at his desk lit by a kerosene lamp, a decanter of whiskey within reach, a filled snifter in his hand.

Xavier eased back in his chair and reflected over recent years. Three had passed since his brother, Constant, had joined Xavier's real estate firm—about the time when most rumors concerning the suspicious deaths of Esperance Soquet and August Minsart had faded. Attorney Wigman had been elected to a second term as Brown County District Attorney. As Xavier had predicted, the State had not refiled any charges against Elvira Soquet. Yet Xavier still had suspicions about Mr. and Mrs. J.P. Soquet and the two deaths that had cleared the way to their union.

Xavier knew August's brother, Ignace, still held onto hope that someone would come forward with new evidence. He roomed at the nearby Bodar House on Main Street and worked as a laborer. Xavier believed Ignace's grief and passion for revenge had robbed him of any joy in his life. At the city saloons, he would rail about the injustice dealt to his brother whom he was convinced had been poisoned by Elvira or J.P. Soquet.

But Xavier was only distracting himself with the Soquets' scandal. His real problems were the double life he was living and his financial issues.

After his brother had joined Xavier as an equal real estate partner, hiding his affair from Constant had become impossible. Xavier's time away had impacted the Martin brothers' business, so much so, that Xavier had moved Augusta to Oshkosh, Wisconsin, fifty miles south of

Green Bay. There she had given birth to Xavier's second son, Albert. But soon after, his wife Mary discovered that Augusta and Xavier had been "posing as man and wife" in Oshkosh.

Xavier swirled the amber liquid around in the glass and closed his eyes, recalling the moment when his wife had shown up at Augusta's Oshkosh house. Xavier had opened the door. Horrified and humiliated at seeing his wife, Xavier had sent Augusta and the boys upstairs. His wife had spewed accusations until Xavier had admitted that the children were his. Xavier remembered feeling something he had not expected: relief. His wife had finally discovered he had a second family. The secret was out.

He had expected that Mary would insist on a divorce. How could any woman want to stay married to a man like him, one who had fathered two children with his lover? But his wife was not like other women. Instead, Mary had begged Xavier to sever his intimate relationship with Augusta. Mary wanted to fix their marriage. She would forgive Xavier, if he promised to end his affair and to live a "pure life."

To spare both of his families' shame, Xavier had agreed to do so. But it had not taken long for him to break his promise.

Xavier looked out onto Washington Street where gas lights illuminated the pedestrian traffic weaving between the saloons. He shook his head, ashamed of his actions. He had treated his wife so poorly. She wanted their marriage to last, and he did not care.

When Xavier had been the Green Bay township justice of the peace, he had learned the ins-and-outs of Wisconsin divorce law. Prior to 1840, securing a divorce had been regarded as a husband's exclusive right. A man's authority over his family could not be questioned. But Wisconsin divorce law had changed due to the plight of women battered, physically and mentally, by their husbands. Women as well as men could now file for divorce on the grounds of cruel and inhuman treatment.

Xavier knew the rule was just, but it placed him in a quandary. Mary had every right to claim cruel and inhuman treatment. He did not. There were other ways to secure a divorce such as desertion or a voluntary separation of five years, but Mary had not deserted him, nor had they been separated for any length of time.

Unless Mary filed for divorce, Xavier was stuck in his loveless marriage. He felt trapped because more than ever, he felt certain he wanted to be with Augusta.

Aside from relational and legal trouble, Xavier's double life had also placed him in dire financial straits. For nearly four years, he had supported two families while continuing to make personal real estate investments. He had overextended himself and could not make the monthly payments on his mortgages. His creditors wanted their money. The only way he could get out from under his predicament had been to file for bankruptcy. He had provided proof to a judge that he owed more than $300 to his creditors, and Xavier had promised to surrender his entire estate and effects to those same creditors. At the end of the bankruptcy process, Xavier would be back where he had started two decades ago upon his arrival in Brown County: square one. That his personal problems would become public knowledge, that he had lost all that he had fought to acquire...the shame was too much.

His wife knew that bankruptcy proceedings had commenced. Xavier unfairly blamed her for some of his financial problems due to the way she managed their household. He encouraged her to leave him, to return to her parents in Pennsylvania, but Mary refused to go.

Xavier took a nip of whiskey and felt its burn. What a mess his life had become.

Uncle Frank's Block between Pine and Cherry (Courtesy Neville Public Museum of Brown County)

He stepped out onto Washington Street and headed south toward home. He passed Uncle Frank's block and reached Cherry Street. One block to the west was the Fox River. He could hear the splash of water against Marshall's Dock, the creak of mooring lines, and the thuds of cargo being loaded onto boats. Suddenly, muffled cries and shouts for help came from that direction.

Xavier abruptly changed course and rushed toward the river, where an odor hung heavy of decaying algae and fear.

Behind the Cook Hotel, the shipmates of the Menominee paddlewheel steamboat had secured her to Marshall's Dock where bundles of shingles were stacked to be loaded. One of the stevedores told Xavier a man had fallen into the river. Another workman had immediately thrown a plank to the man, but the victim's grip had slipped, and he had disappeared

Cook Hotel (Postcard circa 1870s to 1890s)

Denessen Steamer with Shingles on dock (Courtesy of Belgian Heritage Center)

under the dark water. A shipmate from the Menominee had jumped in and was repeatedly diving under the water in search of the man.

The Menominee Captain dropped large hooks on chains and began to drag along the bottom of the slip in hopes of rescuing the victim. Another man launched a rowboat and was using a pike pole to search for the body.

The boatman yelled: his pike had snagged something. He struggled to lift a limp body from the water. Xavier watched as the lifeless man was laid out on the dock. A doctor arrived and attempted to resuscitate him, but it was too late.

No one knew how the workman had ended up in the water. While carrying shingles on his back, perhaps he had stepped too close to the edge of the dock and lost his footing. The noise of falling shingles had drawn attention to the incident, and another workman had raised the alarm.

Xavier watched as a workman lifted a lantern toward the deceased man's face: it was Ignace Minsart.

Xavier was stunned. With Ignace dead, who would fight for August now?

Had Ignace slipped on the dock? Or, perhaps, had someone been hiding in the shadows, someone who wished him dead, someone who had given him a blow to the head and pushed him into the water.

Xavier gazed across the dark river. He wondered where J.P. Soquet was that night.

ACCUSATIONS AND FISTS

PAULINE

ON THURSDAY, November 29, 1877, Pauline and Elvira's families gathered for Thanksgiving inside the large kitchen of the Soquet limestone house. Five months had passed since Elvira's former brother-in-law, Ignace Minsart, had drowned, though the sisters did not speak of it. With him, Pauline knew the talk about the poisoning death of August had died as well.

That morning, Pauline and her two oldest daughters arrived early at the Soquet home to prepare the Thanksgiving feast with three of Elvira's stepdaughters. It was a special time together, but also a way for Pauline to express her gratitude to her sister. Pauline's family was slowly getting back on their feet after their Red River home had burned down, thanks to Elvira.

For the past eight months, Pauline and her five children, ranging in age from two to nine, had resided at the Minsart house in Humboldt. Pauline's husband continued to work their Red River farm while staying in a makeshift living space inside the barn. The proceeds from the recent harvest had been good but were still not enough to rebuild the Villiesse home and provide furnishings for their family of seven. Pauline and Henry had decided their current living situation would need to continue for at least another year.

Henry had arrived that week to spend the winter lull with Pauline and the children before returning to Red River in the new year with his brother, John, to repair the farm equipment in preparation for the planting season.

Standing in the Soquet kitchen, Pauline exchanged a smile with Elvira, treasuring the sisterhood they had renewed. But as the cooking progressed, Pauline was disappointed in her sister. Elvira did not pitch in. Instead, she ordered all the women around, directing their duties. Pauline could tell her sister's behavior irked Elvira's stepdaughters and Pauline's girls, too.

Pauline set her annoyance aside as the food was served. Belgians revered the act of eating, and their adopted Yankee Thanksgiving tradition was an excuse to feast with family. But instead of turkey and pumpkin pie, their hearty meal included traditional Belgian food like they served at the Kermiss, the three-day Belgian holiday held each August to celebrate a successful harvest. Everyone ate favorites such as *trippe*, a pork, cabbage, and onion sausage; deep-fried meatballs called *boulettes*; a cooked cabbage and bacon mixture called *jut*; a cured and seasoned cottage cheese known as *kaset*; and Belgian fruit pies for dessert. J.P. and Elvira kept the beer flowing. Henry and J.P. told *fauves*, or tall tales, and sang songs like they were in a local tavern, enjoying the *joie de vivre* of the moment.

Kermiss in Dyckesville in 1940s (Courtesy Brown County Historical Society – BCHS-DUG01-3161-cc & BCHS-DUG01-3161-cc)

When everyone was stuffed, Pauline's husband and J.P. retired to chairs by the hearth to smoke their pipes. The older boys went out to the barn. Pauline, her two eldest daughters, and J.P.'s three eldest cleared and washed the dishes and pans. Pauline frowned as her sister filled another mug of beer and joined the men.

After the last dish was put away, Pauline approached Henry. She could tell he was in a mellow mood, while J.P.'s demeanor had turned foul. Pauline wondered what had changed. She bent down and placed her arms around Henry's neck. She told him the children needed to get to bed. It was time for them to leave.

J.P. stood on wobbly legs. He said he would have none of that. He gazed down at Elvira, lolling in a chair, and announced she was lazy. She never did any work and left all the chores to his daughters and guests.

Elvira was nothing like his last wife who had been a good worker and a "good woman." Pauline watched as Elvira, having had far too much to drink, stumbled to her feet and faced J.P. She said he was a cruel man who did not deserve her. Their marriage was nothing like the marital bliss he had promised.

Pauline wanted no part of the Soquets' quarrel, especially when they were both drunk. She yanked Henry's arm and said it was time for them to leave.

Henry stood as Elvira continued to rage. She spit out that if J.P. was so unhappy with her, he should not have "poisoned his wife and poisoned her husband."

In the brittle silence, a jolt of shock passed through Pauline. Her sister had actually accused J.P. of murdering Esperance and August. Elvira seemed to have forgotten Pauline and Henry were present.

Pauline looked over at J.P. His eyes had narrowed into a cold and hard stare. His mouth had tightened. So had his fists. He denied Elvira's accusations and, with no warning at all, punched her in the face. Elvira's hands flailed, trying to protect herself as J.P.'s fists continued to swing, hitting their mark.

Pauline cried out while Henry tried to pull J.P. off his wife.

J.P.'s eldest daughter came running. With a firm voice, Mary instructed her father to calm down. He was making a fool of himself in front of company. He was scaring the children. She told him to go outside to cool off.

J.P. eyed everyone in the room and abruptly left through the back door.

A chill settled in Pauline's core. She didn't think the abuse she had just witnessed was the first J.P. had dealt to her sister. Watching his violence sickened her. Pauline had never cared for J.P. Now she despised him.

While J.P.'s eldest daughter tended to her stepmother, Pauline and Henry loaded up the wagon with their five children. She couldn't face her sister right now, not with what Pauline had just witnessed and what Elvira had said.

On the short ride back to the Minsart house, Pauline and Henry discussed Elvira's accusations and J.P.'s reaction. Three years earlier, Pauline's father and brother-in-law had revealed their encounters with J.P. and his request to help him dig up Esperance's body. J.P. had said he would be "in for it," if the authorities disinterred his wife, since Esperance had been poisoned with the same poison found in August's stomach.

Pauline realized Elvira's recent accusation confirmed what J.P. had told Pauline's father and brother-in-law: J.P. had poisoned his second wife. It was what they had all suspected and feared. But Elvira had also accused J.P. of poisoning her former husband, August Minsart. Had J.P. acted alone? Or had Elvira been a partner to that crime?

Henry turned the wagon toward the Minsart barn. Pauline knew she had to stop speculating about August's death. There was nothing to be done. But the death of Esperance Soquet was a different matter. Rumors had never faded about the suspicious death of J.P.'s first wife, Marie: that J.P. could have pushed her down the stairs. Had J.P. gotten away with his first wife's death and now his second wife's death as well? It was all more than suspicious. In a grip of sudden terror, Pauline feared for her sister's life, J.P.'s third wife.

·∞·

A fire in the hearth warmed the Minsart home as Pauline and her two eldest daughters made bread. Pans were filled for the first rise and the yeasty scent filled the kitchen. Anton was splitting firewood outside while Pauline's two youngest sat on the kitchen floor clanking pots and pans with wooden spoons. Henry was mucking the stalls where the horse and cows were kept. A cold draft of air filled the room. Pauline looked up to see Elvira entering through the back door, her face bruised and battered from the prior evening's altercation with J.P.

Pauline sent her girls and their little siblings to the parlor so she and her sister could talk.

Elvira, her jaw set tight, said she wanted to retract what she had said the night before. Of course, J.P. had not poisoned Esperance and August. His wife had died from childbed fever and August had taken his own life. Elvira realized her drunken behavior had ignited her argument with J.P. When she had been married to August, she had been responsible for all the household chores. In the Soquet home, J.P.'s daughters shared the workload with her. Elvira knew she had become lazy. To apologize, she had told J.P. she was committed to pulling her weight. She had promised him an outburst like the prior evening's would never happen again.

Pauline frowned. Elvira seemed to have prepared this statement in order to set things right, to appease someone. Pauline gazed at her sister's bruised face. Elvira seemed to have accepted she deserved J.P.'s abuse. Pauline knew no one deserved this, certainly not her sister.

Pauline asked Elvira whether J.P. had ever hit her before. Elvira did not answer, so Pauline asked again. Elvira's shoulders slumped. She admitted J.P. had hit her before. But she assured Pauline, she had been responsible for bringing on his wrath.

It was well known that J.P. Soquet liked his beer and liquor, which often caused heated discussions in local taverns and ended with fists. He had even earned the title of "The Bay Settlement Bruiser" for his frequent clashes. When he returned to his farm, soaked to the gills, it came as no great surprise to Pauline that he occasionally used his fists on Elvira as well. She wanted to convince her sister that his dangerous behavior was no one's fault but his.

Pauline told Elvira about her growing sense of worry. If J.P. was dissatisfied, Elvira had to be careful. J.P.'s fists could have killed her if Henry had not been there and J.P.'s daughter had not stepped in. Pauline implored Elvira to leave J.P. before that happened.

Pauline could not quite bear to say it, but she thought it: *before he could do to her what he had done to his first wives.*

Instead of responding, Elvira hung her head.

Pauline hesitated, then asked whether Elvira had told the truth. Why would she have purposely riled J.P. up by accusing him of poisoning Esperance and August if those aspersions were not true?

Elvira covered her bruised face with her hands.

Pauline touched her sister's shoulder and simply asked: Did J.P. poison Esperance and August?

Elvira finally choked out: Yes.

Pauline released an angry gust of air. She had been right. J.P. had indeed poisoned his wife, the mother of his children, the one whom they were still grieving for. Elvira had also confirmed J.P. had poisoned August. But Pauline feared he had not acted alone in the death of Elvira's husband, a fact that shamed Pauline as much as it made her despise J.P.

Pauline had the truth about Esperance's death. But what could she do with this knowledge unless Esperance's body was exhumed as August's had been? Further confounding her was that Pauline believed Esperance's casket was likely empty. When Pauline asked Elvira whether

Esperance's body was still in her grave, Elvira insisted she had told Pauline enough and would say no more.

Elvira's sad eyes met Pauline's. She said that nothing would make any difference. She was married to J.P. She could not testify against him and lock him away.

Pauline shook her head firmly. She said that was not necessarily true.

·∞·

Henry and the children dropped Pauline and Elvira off in front of the Denis General Store where they and two other passengers climbed aboard the daily stagecoach to Green Bay. To hide her bruised face, Elvira wore a hat with a veil of dark netting. On the ten-mile journey, as light snow fell, the two sisters whispered about Elvira's situation.

They disembarked at the Reis Hotel on Main Street and climbed onboard an omnibus that traveled between city hotels and train stations. Pauline and Elvira climbed off at the Cook Hotel. Ice had formed along the Fox River's edge, and men were using pickaxes to remove frozen mud heaps along the street. The two sisters walked the last block and a half to Xavier Martin's office.

Washington St. and Cook Hotel (Courtesy Neville Public Museum of Brown County)

Three years had passed since Pauline had seen Mr. Martin in the courtroom, when he had translated at Elvira's dismissal hearing.

Xavier offered Pauline and Elvira chairs and asked how he could help them. His eyes widened when Pauline's sister lifted her hat's dark netting to reveal the pitiful condition of her face. Purple bruises covered Elvira's cheeks, and her left eye was virtually swollen shut.

Pauline prompted her sister, and Elvira's words trickled out. She told Xavier that her husband, J.P. Soquet, did not know she had come to Green Bay. Elvira wanted to keep it that way. She needed advice from someone who knew her background, someone who hopefully did not believe she had poisoned her former husband.

Pauline listened as her sister told Xavier about her dismal marriage, her inability to conceive a child, and the resentment she suffered from

J.P.'s children for trying to take the place of their beloved mother.

Pauline was not surprised when Elvira did not accuse her husband of poisoning Esperance or August outright. On the way to Green Bay, Elvira had told Pauline she feared retribution from J.P. if her accusations became public knowledge. Elvira believed Xavier Martin was an honorable man and would be discrete. Yet she could not take any chances. Until she was free from J.P., she preferred to keep his responsibility for the deaths of their spouses between Pauline and herself.

Pauline had grudgingly agreed to honor Elvira's wishes. She could see the tight spot her sister was in, and she feared for her safety.

Pauline gazed over at her battered sister, patiently waiting for her to broach the most important topic. But it seemed as if Elvira could not say the word *divorce*, so Pauline did. She asked Xavier what Elvira needed to do to secure a divorce from J.P. Soquet.

Xavier said he was not trying to be disrespectful, but based on the condition of Elvira's face, he assumed J.P. had hit her, so she would have no problem claiming cruel and inhuman treatment. Xavier offered to orchestrate a meeting with Elvira's former attorneys, Mr. Hudd and Mr. Wigman, to initiate a discussion about divorce.

Pauline watched her sister consider Xavier's words. Elvira finally said she "wanted to be boss in her own property and live by herself." She explained to Xavier that she had sold the Minsart farmland, and she controlled the proceeds. Elvira said she could use a portion of that money to purchase a small house in Green Bay where she could eventually live. It would have to be a good distance from the Soquet home for Elvira to feel safe.

Pauline felt heartened when Xavier told Elvira he could help her purchase a Green Bay home within her means. Until Elvira was ready to move in, for a small fee, Xavier said he could handle leasing out the house and collecting the rental payments.

Everything was falling into place. Pauline nudged her sister, encouraging her to take the next steps: to purchase a house and to initiate her divorce action.

Instead, Elvira stood. She thanked Xavier and paid him for his counsel. Elvira said she still needed time to think about his propositions. She began walking out, while Pauline sat there, stunned. She finally stood as well, a sinking feeling in her belly.

It was Elvira's decision whether to move forward. Pauline had done as much as she could. But was it enough? She was afraid that Elvira would wait too long and end up like the first and second Mrs. J.P. Soquet.

GROUNDS FOR DIVORCE

XAVIER

Xavier Martin 728 Crooks St. Home (Courtesy Brown County Historical Society BCH01-0129-cc)

ON A DAY in late May of 1878, Xavier Martin left his office early. Instead of heading directly to his home on the corner of Monroe and Chicago, Xavier zigzagged through city blocks, looking over his shoulder, until he reached the intersection of Jackson and Crooks. On the southwest corner was the home at 728 Crooks Street that Xavier had purchased about a year ago for his lover, Augusta Bliske. A month later, he had transferred the title into her name, so the home and the land it sat on had not been included in Xavier's bankruptcy action, initiated a few months later.

One of his creditors, the former Green Bay mayor and current postmaster, A.W. Kimball, had been authorized to inventory Xavier's property, auction it off through the sheriff, and disburse the proceeds to each of Xavier's creditors. Those men had agreed to exempt the Green Bay Astor neighborhood home Xavier and his wife owned, including its "necessary household and kitchen furniture."

Xavier scanned Crooks Street before darting through an opening in the tall hedges bordering the backyard. Under a large maple tree, Augusta sat on a bench. She looked up and smiled at Xavier while nursing their newborn daughter, Pauline. Love overwhelmed him. That was why his promise to Mary—to live a "pure life"—had not lasted long. Baby Pauline's brothers, Rudolph, four, and Albert, two, stopped their play and rushed toward Xavier. Their exuberance made him grin. Xavier lifted Albert up into the air while his older brother waited his turn.

Xavier spent a few hours with his second family and departed the same way he had arrived, his eyes surveying the street. The plank sidewalks were empty, but in the house across the street the window curtains moved slightly. He was always worried.

In less than ten minutes, he reached the home he shared with his wife. The close proximity of the two homes added to his risk of being exposed. But Xavier believed he was being discreet.

Mary was waiting, her cheeks blotchy, her eyes red from crying.

Xavier felt a sense of dread.

She said a neighbor had told her that their former maid, Augusta Bliske, lived on Crooks Street and had recently given birth. Mary asked Xavier whether the child was his.

To lie would be fruitless. Xavier admitted Augusta's three children were all his. He loved them, and yet he was ashamed to face his wife with this confession.

Mary staggered and collapsed onto a chair. Through fresh tears, she told Xavier she had always "discharged her duties toward him as a good and faithful wife." During their twenty-three years of marriage, she had done everything in her power to please him. She had done all the customary housework, all the chores in the stable attending to his horse, even though he had been "well able to procure and pay for hired help." After she had caught him with Augusta in Oshkosh, he had promised to live "a pure life." Mary had believed "he had kept his promise and had not had any intercourse with Augusta." But the birth of her third child was all the proof Mary needed that Xavier had broken his word and treated her with cruelty.

"This is no type of marriage between myself and you," she said. Mary told Xavier she would not share a bedroom with him any longer.

Humiliated but also ashamed to feel relief, Xavier said he fully understood her decision. He was sorry for the pain he had caused Mary and encouraged her to file for divorce. In the meantime, he would move to the Cook Hotel to give Mary space.

To stay with Augusta and his children would have been ideal. But Xavier knew whatever neighbor had alerted Mary to the birth of baby Pauline might also report his full-time presence at the Crooks Street home to the authorities and have him arrested. Xavier turned abruptly and ascended the stairs to gather a few belongings. He knew he had been a terrible husband to Mary. She deserved better.

Mary had finally realized that too.

·∞·

A month passed. The July heat sweltered. Xavier stepped out of the Cook Hotel onto Washington Street and headed north. His wife had yet to take any divorce action, and Augusta was putting up a fuss. She and his three children needed Xavier's undivided attention, she said.

Xavier climbed the stairs to his second-floor office. Inside the reception area was Elvira Soquet. Seven months had passed since she and her sister, Pauline, had met with Xavier. Even in the summer heat, Elvira wore the same black hat with dark netting. The veil could not hide the fresh bruises on her face. Xavier hoped Elvira's visit meant she had decided to move forward with a divorce.

Green Bay Horse & Buggy (Courtesy Brown County Historical Society BCHS-MOO01-105-lr-w_WM)

He ushered her into his private office and offered Elvira a chair. She informed Xavier that she had made up her mind. She wanted to purchase a Green Bay house like they had discussed. She believed she was ready to leave her husband. But first she needed a place to live.

Xavier felt a surge of hope for the battered woman. He said he would drive Elvira around that day and show her some properties. Xavier grabbed a sheet of his portfolio listings which fit her criteria and the keys for those properties. They traveled in Xavier's rig. In front of each property, they paused for a few moments to allow the air to clear from the dusty streets before they climbed out.

Elvira eventually selected a small one-story clapboard home on Main Street. It was next door to a meat market and two blocks east of Whitney Park where neighborhood cows often grazed. The house was currently rented, but Elvira told Xavier she would not ask the tenants to move out until her divorce was in process. She wanted a bit more time before she would ask Xavier to help her secure a divorce attorney. He wondered what she needed time for, but he did not ask.

That same week, Elvira returned with the necessary cash and paid Xavier in full for the property. She also decided to collect the rent herself. Xavier commended Elvira for taking that first step to leave J.P. Soquet. But he wondered what would happen when her husband was eventually served divorce papers. Xavier did not believe J.P. would take that request lying down.

When Elvira had initially been arrested for August Minsart's death, J.P. Soquet had not been qualified to testify for or against his wife due to marital privilege. If Elvira secured a divorce, and she had firsthand knowledge tying J.P. to either or both of their former spouses' deaths—and Xavier suspected she did—J.P. would no longer have the protection of a silenced wife. He admired Elvira for finally taking this step, but he worried whether she recognized the thin ice she was treading.

Another month passed. Thursday, August 8, 1878, was a sultry day, ninety-six degrees in the shade and at least that in Xavier's stuffy office. The windows were barely cracked, however, due to intense winds scattering trash, dust, and, according to the *State Gazette*, even coupled freight cars. Strong gusts had moved four cars six rods down the track.

The door to Xavier's private office opened and a man entered, the cross ventilation causing papers to rustle on Xavier's desk. The man said he was a representative from attorneys Hudd and Wigman and handed Xavier a large envelope. The man said Xavier had been served and departed.

Xavier opened the envelope and breathed a sigh of relief. At last. Inside was the official divorce complaint from his wife, Mary Rebecca Martin.

Xavier carefully read the complaint. It ordered him to pay $50 to Hudd and Wigman within ten days to enable his wife to carry on with the divorce action. But at the next words, Xavier's face burned with shame. He was prohibited from committing any "acts of violence" toward his wife, or using "abusive epithets" toward her, or "interfering with her property" until the determination of the action.

Despite all he had done to her, he would never have considered acting in this way.

Xavier removed an additional document: his wife's sworn statement. He skimmed the pages. The portion that dealt with his wife's money distressed him. He was not in a position to provide what she requested.

A few years back, Xavier had told Mary he would invest $425 of her own money. He purchased twenty acres of land near East River and a year later sold it for $1,100. His wife told him to put the proceeds into Xavier's bank account, although her intention was that they both would use the money. Mary's statement claimed she had never received any of that money, which Xavier knew was true. When the delinquent mortgages had weighed on him, he had used that $1,100 to satisfy creditors.

At that time, his decision had kept his family afloat and in their home. He had tried to explain that to Mary, but she had known that decision was evidence of his prior lack of faithfulness to her. Of course, she was right.

The document went into detail about his cruel and inhuman treatment. It discussed his five-year affair and adulterous intercourse with Augusta Bliske, which had produced three children.

In summary, his wife demanded judgment that their bonds of matrimony be dissolved, the money she had given Xavier be returned, the title to their home be allocated to her, and that Xavier be ordered to provide her a reasonable amount of ongoing support. Last, she requested that Xavier be responsible for all costs related to her divorce action.

It was a hefty list of demands.

A month or so later, when Elvira Soquet walked into Xavier's office, he believed she was finally ready to file for divorce, to take her fate into her own hands, as his wife had done. But Xavier was mistaken. Elvira wanted him to draw up a deed. She was selling the forty acres of forested land, formerly owned by her late husband, to her current husband, J.P. Soquet, for the price of $440. Xavier did not probe her for her reasons and witnessed and notarized the deed.

When Elvira left, without bringing up her marriage or her decision to end it, Xavier was frustrated. He knew the longer she remained in her marriage, the more danger she was in.

Two months later, on October 18, 1878, Xavier entered the 728 Crooks Street home he had purchased for Augusta Bliske. In the front room, Xavier's two boys lay on their bellies paging through a picture book. Baby Pauline watched from a blanket on the floor, her legs shaking with excitement, a rattle gripped in her hand. Augusta was in the kitchen by the stove. Xavier wrapped his arms around her and announced he had great news. That morning, Brown County Judge D.H. Ellis had permanently dissolved Xavier and Mary's marriage.

At those words, he felt the mother of his children relax against his chest a contented sound emitting through her lips.

Xavier explained that Augusta's home would now be his as well. His former wife had been awarded the Astor neighborhood house and nearly all its furnishings. Xavier had managed to negotiate certain items in the settlement, which would be useful to Augusta and him. Those included his bookcase and books, a sofa, five chairs and a table, a clock, a writing desk, a student lamp, a hair mattress with bedding, and a coal stove.

Augusta turned to face Xavier, her smile wide.

He said he would need to pay Mary's court costs of $65 and the taxes for his former home, but only for the current year. He had not been ordered to repay the $1,100 of his wife's money. The Green Bay sheriff had verified Xavier had no assets to sell. Last, he was to provide Mary with a modest monthly support payment for the rest of her life. Even Augusta agreed that seemed only fair.

Xavier pulled Augusta into his arms. His former wife of twenty-three-years had given him his freedom. He and Augusta could finally marry and live legally together as "man and wife." For the first time in years, Xavier felt at ease.

Xavier & Mary Martin Chicago and Monroe home circled and Xavier and Augusta Crooks St. home in Triangle (Brown County Plat Map 1889 Southern Part of Green Bay)

PART II

TEMPERATURE ON THE RISE

(1879-1887)

TRUTH REVEALED

PAULINE

ON MONDAY, February 26, 1879, Pauline drove a sleigh over to the Soquet house. It was two miles from the Minsart home, where she and her children had lived for two years. Snow gusted and eddied across the fields. Henry had spent the past month in Humboldt with her, and Pauline believed she was pregnant again. While their situation was complicated, a new baby would be such a blessing.

The prior spring, she and Henry had lost two daughters likely to scarlet fever: newborn Adeline and nine-year-old Celinda. The disease had spread to nearly every family on the Door Peninsula and had claimed many lives. Celinda had been such a bright and promising girl, beloved by all, while baby Adeline had barely had a chance to live. Every day, Pauline grieved the loss of her two children. A new baby would bring her some much-needed hope.

Pauline halted the horse in front of the Soquet farmhouse. She climbed down from the sleigh as J.P.'s twelve-year-old son Jule approached, a shovel in hand. He had cleared snow off the plank walkway leading up to the house.

Jule tied up Pauline's horse, and she approached the front door. Henry had been kind enough to stay home with the children so that she and her sister, Elvira, could attend the funeral of Father Daems. He had been a spiritual adviser to Pauline's family, a counselor, a healer, and a "Father indeed." Following a serious illness, the caring priest had died at the Bay Settlement rectory at age fifty-three. Henry was fifty-two; that thought made Pauline take pause.

J.P.'s eldest child, Mary, answered the door. She was twenty-six and unmarried. Mary said Elvira was getting ready upstairs. Pauline hung her cloak on a hook, and she and Mary joined J.P.'s other daughters in the kitchen. Mary, along with Josephine, fourteen, and Rose, nine, were in the process of making candles. The scent of melting animal fat filled the room as they repeatedly dipped braided cotton wicks into the tallow bubbling in the large pot on the stove. Their sister, Elisabeth, who was sixteen, had recently wed. She and her husband, Sam Bebeau, had moved to Michigan where Sam worked in a mill. On the far end of the kitchen, their father idled on a chair by the hearth, drinking coffee. Clara, age five, sat on his lap.

Mary gave Pauline a cup of coffee. She reluctantly sat down in a chair near J.P. as he shooed Clara away. Pauline despised the man her sister had married five years ago. Pauline knew those feelings were mutual. It was difficult for Pauline to converse with the man who physically abused her sister, the man who Pauline believed had poisoned his former wife, the man who she believed was at least an accomplice in the death of her sister's husband. Pauline continued to plead with Elvira to leave J.P. Although Elvira had purchased a small house in Green Bay, she continued to rent it out, and she had taken no further steps.

That was because, at age thirty-two, Elvira was pregnant for the first time. Elvira's face had glowed when she had revealed her pregnancy news to Pauline. Elvira believed a new baby would change everything, and she had set aside any thoughts of divorcing J.P. Pauline had attempted to be happy for her sister. But how could she feel true happiness when the child's father was J.P. Soquet.

Sitting beside J.P., Pauline listened as he criticized her sister. He continued to sing the same tune, complaining that Elvira was lazy. He said his previous wife, Esperance, had been a hard worker, a good wife, and a good mother. Pauline's heart sunk. Unable to stop herself, she retorted: "[You] had a good chance to keep [your] wife; and [you] should have kept her."

J.P. raised his fist.

Pauline bolted from the chair and joined his daughters.

·∞·

Layered in warm clothing and wrapped in thick blankets, the two sisters traveled in Pauline's horse-drawn sleigh over the snow-covered Bay Settlement Road. The route provided a sweeping view of farmland extending steeply down toward the frozen waters of Green Bay. At last report, the ice was "three feet thick and as clear as crystal."

Pauline traveled north toward Holy Cross Church and joined the multitude of people headed that way in sleighs, perched on wagons fitted with runners, or trudging on foot.

Holy Cross Church (Courtesy of the Sisters of St. Francis of the Holy Cross Archives)

The sisters felt fortunate to find seats in the church, which was filled with the scents of incense, beeswax, and the huddled crowd. Hundreds of mourners stood outside. A few rows up from Pauline, she could see Xavier Martin sitting beside his brother, Constant.

The walnut casket holding the remains of Father Daems rested on a high bier in front of the altar. Dozens of diocese priests held lighted tapers in the darkened chancel. Amid the congregation's muffled sobs and sniffles, Pauline listened to the comforting drone of the Latin funeral mass. At its end, three priests, each speaking one of the languages of the settlers, eulogized the Christian character of the pioneer priest. Pauline and Elvira listened intently to the priest who spoke in Walloon.

Father F.E. Daems (Courtesy Belgian Heritage Center)

Once the service concluded, six priests carried Father Daems' coffin outside into the fast-falling snow. The sisters joined the procession of men, women, and children toward the gravesite inside the new Holy Cross Cemetery. The church bell rang a solemn peal and the German Cornet Band played a mournful dirge as the priests lowered Father Daems' coffin into the ground.

Xavier Martin approached Pauline and Elvira and asked after the two women.

Elvira excitedly told Xavier she was expecting her first child. She and J.P. had reconciled, and she looked forward to a bright future with her husband and their child.

Pauline kept her mouth shut. Her sister seemed to believe the lies she was telling.

The two sisters settled back into Pauline's sleigh for the return trip. Pauline snapped the reins and the horse took a few steps before easing into a slow trot. Icy snow pelted Pauline's face as she carefully brought up the death of J.P.'s former wife. Pauline said she understood Father Daems had been called to Esperance's bedside in the last few days of her life to doctor to her and to give Esperance her last rites. Father Daems, Pauline said, would have had firsthand knowledge concerning her illness and any symptoms leading up to her death. But that knowledge was now buried with the priest inside his plot, just down the road from Esperance's remains inside the old cemetery.

Pauline glanced over at her sister and dared to ask whether that last assumption was true. Was Esperance Soquet still buried in her grave?

Elvira did not respond.

Pauline's shoulders braced against the bitter cold. She needed an answer. She relayed what the sexton had told their sister, Fannie, five years ago: that Esperance's grave had been disturbed.

Elvira closed her eyes and rocked on the seat.

Pauline asked again: Was Esperance still in her grave?

"No," Elvira whispered and looked up. She took a deep breath and finally confessed: In the spring of 1874, soon after J.P. had bailed her out of jail, she had accompanied him to Esperance's grave in the dead of night. J.P. had found a man named J.B. Rose who had agreed to stand watch while she and J.P. had performed the grizzly job of removing his wife's body from the casket. Elvira said J.P. had carried the badly decomposed corpse away in a gray blanket and buried it by a grove of plum trees on a neighbor's land. But Elvira said, her teeth chattering, J.P. had moved Esperance's remains again, likely onto the Soquet property, to protect them from ever being found.

Elvira's gaze met hers. She said Pauline was the one person she could trust with this dark secret.

Pauline felt physically ill while Elvira seemed relieved. Pauline tried not to judge her sister. Soquet had likely threatened to beat Elvira, or worse, if she had refused to help.

Her sister had not had any choice, Pauline reasoned.

FALLEN STAR

XAVIER

THRONGS OF PEOPLE lined Pine Street on Saturday, June 12, 1880. In the breeze, scented with brewery yeast, manure, and sewage, American flags flapped outside homes and businesses. Street vendors hawked candy and peanuts. Excited voices filled the downtown blocks in anticipation of the parade to celebrate the visit of former President Ulysses S. Grant and his wife.

Xavier Martin stood beside Augusta, his young wife, not yet thirty. Augusta gripped a wicker pram holding six-month-old, Freddie, and two-year-old, Pauline. Little Pauline kept calling out "Papa," and Xavier would tousle her curls. Vying for a good viewing spot, Xavier grasped the small hands of Rudy and Albert, ages six and four. Atop their heads the boys wore sailor hats with rounded crowns and narrow brims, the current craze.

Xavier caught a glimpse of his former wife, Mary, standing across the street beside her new husband, Justice Octavien J.B. Brice, three years her junior. Brice had lost his wife, and he had wed Mary six months after the Martins' divorce. Xavier was pleased that Mary looked happy. It was what she deserved.

To be heard above the din, Xavier bent down to tell his boys about General Grant's leadership during the Civil War and his two terms as United States President. He also told them about the General's train trip to Green Bay, which had nearly ended in disaster. According to the *State Gazette*, while traveling at a speed of sixty miles per hour, a strap had snapped inside the train's engine, releasing scalding steam into the cab occupied by the train engineer and the fireman. The automatic brakes had shut the engine down, and the two men had escaped from the cab unharmed. The train superintendent had walked four miles to the nearest train station and telegraphed for a replacement engine. Xavier told his boys the General and his wife had arrived just in time for last night's welcome party with city dignitaries, followed by a Fox River steamboat tour, and today's parade.

His boys clapped at that news.

Xavier knew the General's decision to make a stop in Green Bay was quite an honor for the small city. The Grants were completing a world tour, and they had visited dignitaries such as Pope Leo XIII and Queen Victoria. The city across the river, Fort Howard, which was slightly larger than Green Bay, felt snubbed. The two cities had a longstanding rivalry based on cultural and socioeconomic differences. Green Bay contained most of the professional men and served as the government seat. Fort Howard was home to most of the recent immigrants employed at the city's sawmills and factories.

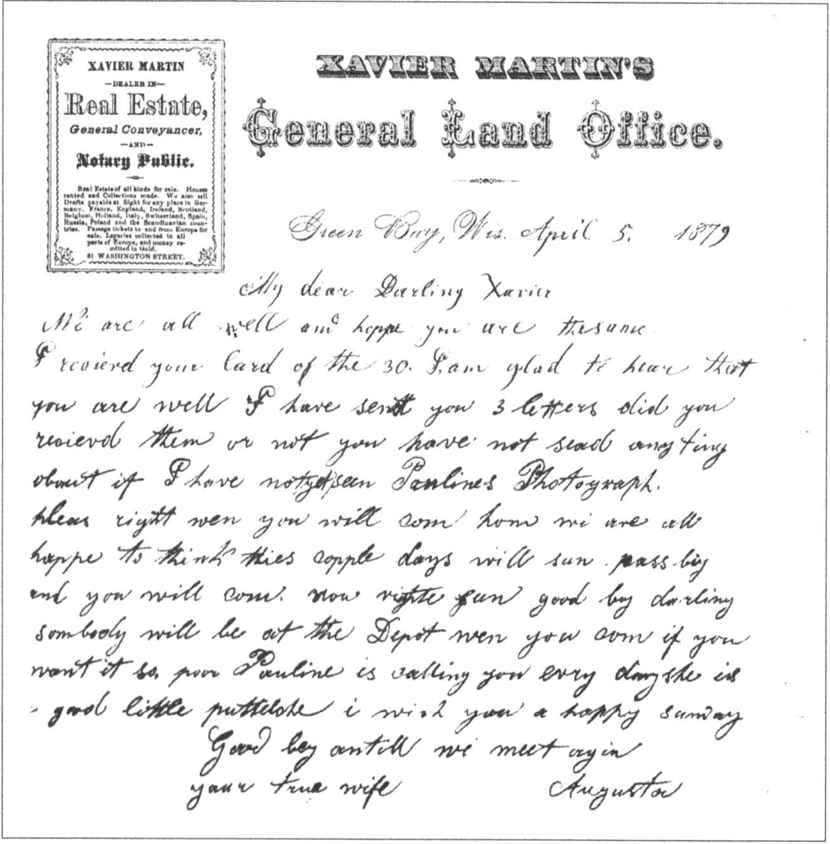

XAVIER MARTIN
—DEALER IN—
Real Estate,
General Conveyancer,
—AND—
Notary Public.

Real Estate of all kinds for sale. Houses rented and Collections made. We also sell Drafts payable at Sight for any place in Germany, France, England, Ireland, Scotland, Belgium, Holland, Italy, Switzerland, Spain, Russia, Poland and the Scandinavian countries. Passage tickets to and from Europe for sale. Legacies collected in all parts of Europe, and money remitted in Gold.
81 WASHINGTON STREET.

XAVIER MARTIN'S
General Land Office.

Green Bay, Wis. April 5. 1879

My dear Darling Xavier
We are all well and hoppe you are thesame
I recieved your Card of the 30. I am glad to hear that
you are well I have sendt you 3 letters did you
recievd them or not you have not seand anyting
obout it I have notyetseen Paulines Photograph.
pleas right wen you will com home wi are all
happe to think thies copple days will sun pass by
and you will com. now righte sun good by darling
sombody will be at the Depot wen you com if you
want it so. poor Pauline is calling you evry day she is
a good little puttelohe i wish you a happy sunday
Good bey antill wi meet agin
your true wife Augusta

Augusta letter to Xaiver (Courtesy Blodgett, Fay Willis via John Mertens)

Xavier's family cheered when the German Cornet Band marched into view. Smartly dressed in uniforms and tall cylindrical shako hats with visors, the energetic band played cornets, euphoniums, tubas, and trombones. The Drum Corp followed with snare and bass drums along with high-pitched fifes. Xavier watched his boys' rapt and curious faces and shared proud glances with Augusta.

Xavier was glad to be home. In April, he had traveled on horseback along the Des Moines River in southern Minnesota and in northern Iowa to examine some land, which he had purchased for resale. During that time, he and Augusta had written letters back and forth via post offices in Sherburn, Minnesota, and in Jackson, Iowa. He had loved her salutation of: "My dear Darling Xavier" and her closings of "Your True Wife ... Augusta" or "My true love to you."

The uniformed Bay City Light Guards marched by, and the elegant carriage everyone was waiting for came into view at last. It was "drawn by a team of spanking black horses." The open carriage held General Grant seated beside Xavier's friend, Attorney John C. Neville, Green Bay's newly elected mayor.

President Ulysses S. Grant (Library of Congress)

Xavier's boys waved. Mayor Neville and the General waved back to them and the crowd. Behind Grant's carriage came his wife's. She was seated with Senator Howe and Mrs. Torry.

The Civil War veterans marched next. Among them were a number of Belgian countrymen Xavier recognized.

When the Civil War draft conscription law was passed in 1862, all able-bodied Belgian men between the ages of eighteen and forty-five who had signed a Declaration of Intent to become U.S. citizens were eligible to be drafted. Xavier was among that group, but his name had not been drawn in the first round. By the time his name was selected in 1864, the conscription law allowed those drafted to hire a substitute. Xavier decided to take that option and would forever carry guilt. Alexander Delain, the Belgian man Xavier had paid to serve, had died in battle.

Among those marching veterans, Xavier realized, should be the two Minsart brothers, August and Ignace. Both had survived the battlefields only to have returned to Brown County where each had died by disturbing means. As Attorney J.J. Tracy marched by, Xavier wondered whether the man harbored suspicions about Elvira Soquet, the woman he had prematurely arrested for August Minsart's death. No matter of her guilt, Xavier still hoped Elvira would file for divorce from J.P. Soquet, who may have participated in both of the Minsart brothers' deaths, though Xavier had no evidence for his suspicions.

Ever since Tracy had resigned as the District Attorney of Brown County, believing he would win the judgeship position, Tracy's star had failed to rise. The lawyer scrambled to find clients after losing the election. One of the first had been John McCormick, who was arrested for scamming a number of citizens out of $20,000 during a Spanish Monte card game. Tracy had defended the nefarious man against the new District Attorney, John H.M. Wigman.

After McCormick's trial, which Tracy lost, he placed his name on the Republican ballot for the Wisconsin Assembly. During the party's informal ballot, he received the fewest votes of anyone running. Tracy tried again in October of 1875, this time attempting to get his District Attorney job back. At the Brown County Republican convention, his party conducted an informal ballot. Out of the three potential candidates, Tracy again received the fewest votes. In fact, he only received one—his own. In March of the next year, Tracy ran for Green Bay City Attorney, but he lost that election as well, this time to a Mr. O.B. Graves.

Soon after, as alderman, Xavier had presented a resolution to retain J.J. Tracy as counsel to assist City Attorney Graves in handling a dispute between the cities of Fort Howard and Green Bay. The prior summer, a schooner had damaged the Walnut Street Bridge, which spanned the Fox River. Due to their rivalry, the drawbridge had not been repaired by either city, neither willing to take on the entire work they believed the other should be partly responsible for. After some maneuvering and with J.J. Tracy's help, the funds to fix the bridge were secured from taxes provided by both cities. After that positive press, Attorney Tracy's confidence was buoyed and he ran for the office of City Attorney again. But again he lost, this time to the incumbent.

As Fire Engine Number One passed, horse hooves clattering, bells ringing, and steam pump hissing, Xavier could not help but feel sorry for Attorney J.J. Tracy. Ever since the county judgeship fiasco, he had suffered never-ending humiliation. But Xavier knew what humiliation felt like. He had dealt with his fair share during his bankruptcy and divorce, yet he had recovered and risen to new heights. During the past year, Xavier had actually made forty-two real estate sales at an "aggregate amount of $28,523," (about $1 million in current valuation).

Fire Engine Number Two and its hose cart brought up the rear, the engine's mechanical siren wailing and firemen riding the rails. Xavier and his family followed the parade procession to the Armory grounds near the East River. General Grant climbed onto the stage with Mayor John C. Neville. While the mayor delivered the welcoming speech, Xavier held Albert up on his shoulders. Rudy got his turn when General Grant gave his remarks, which were followed by "three hearty cheers" from the crowd.

Grant and Mayor Neville entered the Armory where the General and his wife would welcome the immense crowd. The Light Guards controlled the steady stream of humanity pouring inside, single file. The Martin family finally reached the General and his wife who shook Xavier and Augusta's hands. General Grant bent down and shook Rudy and Albert's hands as well, giving them quite a thrill.

Outside the Armory, Xavier noticed several Belgian countrymen and their families milling around, including J.P. and Elvira Soquet. She was holding a babe about the same size as his six-month-old Freddie. At Father Daems funeral, Elvira had mentioned she was expecting. Xavier was gratified to know she had given birth to a healthy child, but he doubted whether the Soquets' marriage had improved.

THRESHING AND THREATS

PAULINE

A WARM GLOW transformed the dark sky into soft pinks and oranges on the morning of September 22, 1881. Pauline drove the wagon, her twelve-year-old son beside her, as they approached the Soquet house. The crisp air enhanced the scents of manure, silage, and decomposing leaves. The wheat on the Soquet farm had been cut and shocked. The dried bundles stood tall in the fields. Threshing day had arrived.

For more than four years, Pauline and her children had lived about two miles from her sister, Elvira. But not for much longer. Henry had finally rebuilt their Red River homestead. Not of brick and stone, like in the old country, as Pauline had hoped, but once again of logs sealed with chinking to keep the weather and pests out. The log construction was far cheaper but not fireproof. Henry had convinced Pauline they would take every precaution so their house would not burn down a second time. After so long, they were both ready to be home together.

She and the children were due to move back to Red River by Thanksgiving, and Pauline was counting the days. She could not wait to sleep beside Henry's warm body each night, to see her children celebrate Christmas in their new home, to watch the winter wheat in the Villiesse fields come alive in the spring. Pauline had so missed having her family all together under one roof, to feel the heartbeat of their shared home.

Pauline and Anton's wagon reached the Soquet home. A neighbor lady had offered to help Pauline's eldest child Flora watch her siblings, including the new baby, Delia, and two-year-old George. Elvira's little boy, named Henry, for Pauline's husband, had arrived the same year as George. Watching the two cousins grow up together had been a joy for

Pauline and Elvira, and they both felt a bittersweetness at separating the two.

Pauline and Anton stepped down from the wagon onto the Soquet property. Two and a half years had passed since Elvira had admitted to Pauline that J.P. had secretly disinterred and hidden his second wife's remains on his property. That fact still made Pauline uncomfortable. She looked down at her feet and wondered whether she was unknowingly standing on Esperance Soquet's final resting place.

J.P. and his son, Jule, crossed over from the barn. J.P.'s eldest son Fred had left home the prior year, right after he had helped plant the winter wheat, first by plowing the Soquet fields, then by spreading the seed with a horse-drawn grain drill. According to J.P., Fred had not wanted to be a farmer, and he had left to pursue work at Smith's Mill in Michigan.

Belgian farm boy (George Wautlet, Photo 22, Belgian-American Research Collection, University of Wisconsin-Green Bay Archives Department)

Fred's departure had seemed odd to Pauline. He had been J.P.'s primary worker on the farm. The general expectation in Belgian farming families was that a son should remain home until he turned twenty-one or was married, so his labor would help the family financially. With Fred's departure, Pauline knew J.P. needed extra help, and he had hired August Vandenack, who lived down the road. He arrived in a buckboard as did the Joseph Everard family, their wagon pulled by a team. J.P. and Everard were threshing partners, and their fields would be worked together.

Two other neighbors arrived to pitch in: Joseph Williams and Martin Simonar.

Elvira stepped out of the house. She held little Henry's hand and joined Pauline and Anton. Elvira said Soquet's daughters were finishing the daily chores of milking the cows, separating the milk from the cream, and feeding the calves.

Pauline knew her sister doted on little Henry, and J.P. was jealous of the attention Elvira lavished on the boy. Little Henry's birth had not helped the Soquets' tumultuous marriage. Pauline knew J.P. still abused her sister. Pauline continued to plead with Elvira to leave her marriage and to take Henry with her. But Elvira felt J.P. would come after *his* son, and she could not bear to lose him.

President James A. Garfield (Library of Congress)

While everyone waited for the threshing team's arrival, the adults likely discussed President Garfield's tragic death. The whole country was in mourning. Less than four months into Garfield's presidential term, on July 2 of that year, he had been shot in Washington, D.C. by Charles J. Guiteau, a mentally unstable office seeker. Garfield's medical treatment had failed and ended with his death two days ago. The adults standing in the Soquet front yard were all immigrants, and two presidents in their adopted country had died by assassination since their arrival, Abraham Lincoln in 1865 and now President Garfield. This was a very sobering thought.

Their pensive mood shifted into one of excitement as the black steam-powered engine, belching smoke, came into view. It lumbered down the road with the threshing machine behind it. The engineer tooted the whistle in greeting, and Henry cheered.

Two Everard boys left to pitch bundles from the fields onto the wagon. Anton and Jule were paired up to do the same. The two wagons

Belgian Threshing Day (Courtesy Belgian Heritage Center)

would bring the bundles back to the neighborhood men, who would run the racks of bundles into the steam powered threshing machine. J.P. Soquet and Joseph Everard would load the kernels of grain removed from the husks into bushel baskets. Each grain wagon would hold up to fifty-two bushels of wheat.

Pauline and the other women would prepare the workers' meals. She surveyed the group gathered. The same scenario would play out in Red River on the Villiesse farm where neighbors relied on each other. Even if people had their differences—Pauline eyed J.P.—they put those issues aside to get the job done. It was the Belgian way.

Inside the house, Pauline peeled potatoes beside J.P.'s eldest daughter, twenty-eight-year-old Mary, who always kept to herself. In confidence, Elvira had told Pauline that Mary was dealing with her own abuse issues, although Elvira had refused to elaborate. Pauline could only imagine what Elvira meant. Was J.P. beating his eldest daughter? Or could his abuse be of a sexual nature? Pauline shuddered to think it, but she did not put the revolting supposition past J.P.

It amazed Pauline that one man could destroy so many lives and get away with it. Yet, Pauline was ashamed to admit, she was as much to blame as anyone else for not stopping him.

·∞·

The Soquet and Everard threshing day had been a success. At about midnight, Pauline sat beside Anton's bed in the first-floor bedroom of the Minsart house. The kerosene lamp was turned low so as not to wake his two sleeping brothers. The three girls were in a bedroom upstairs across from Pauline's. Next to Anton's bedside, a sick bucket stood which he had used more than once, and the room smelled of vomit. The combination of hard labor, sun, and heavy food had not sat right with Anton. He was paying the price for their hard day's work.

Others might be suffering as well. During that evening's feast, the men had consumed ample beer and so had Elvira. And for some, the celebration had not ended at the house. J.P., Elvira, and Joseph Everard had decided to take a load of wheat to the Denis General Store and spend some of the proceeds at its adjoining saloon.

Through the outside wall of the sparsely lit bedroom, Pauline heard the crunch of gravel followed by muffled male voices. She split the window curtains and peered into the blackness. The night was dark with a new moon. The voices grew louder and fists pounded on the locked back door.

Pauline approached, her steps hesitant. Beneath her nightdress, her heart rioted against her ribs. She placed her ear to the door and raised her voice to ask who was there.

J.P.'s angry voice answered, demanding she open the door. He knew "his woman" was inside. He had come to take her home.

Pauline told J.P. that Elvira was not there. He should leave, before he disturbed her children.

The sound of boots kicking against the wooden door made Pauline back away. Her mouth turned dry and her hands began to shake. A sharp crack sounded, followed by ripping metal. The door came flying in, banging against the wall.

J.P. staggered inside, holding a whiskey bottle. Everard followed in the same inebriated condition.

Joseph Everard
(Courtesy John Mertens)

Pauline stumbled back, her eyes wild, her

mind and body filled with a primal instinct to protect her children and herself.

J.P. kept shouting that Elvira had to be inside the house. Some man had to have brought her here from the Denis saloon. J.P. had looked for her at Frank Greenwood's saloon and Alex Robson's place, but he had not found her, nor had she returned home. He knew Pauline was hiding her.

Lurching toward Pauline, J.P. dropped the whiskey bottle. It shattered into pieces and his cross-eyes turned feral. He entered the parlor and pitched a chair, then another. Everard joined in.

Anton emerged from the bedroom, unnoticed by J.P.

Pauline instructed her son to run next door and to tell Mr. Simonar to bring the neighborhood constable.

Anton ducked out through the open door while J.P. smashed two windows and a lamp with the leg of a chair. Tearing through the parlor and kitchen, J.P. bellowed that Pauline and Elvira were nothing but prostitutes.

Pauline's fear twisted into rage. Nobody could insult her like that, especially J.P. Soquet. In Everard's listening range, Pauline charged J.P. of being an "assassin." That he had poisoned Elvira's husband and his own wife. And, "scoundrel" that he was, J.P. had unburied Esperance to protect himself. Pauline minced no words.

Incensed, J.P. picked up the broken neck of the whiskey bottle and swung it toward her face.

Pauline lifted her forearm as the ragged glass ripped through her nightdress sleeve, slashing her skin from her wrist down to her elbow. Pauline gasped in pain. Blood dripped onto the floor and the sharp taste of bile filled her mouth.

Pauline could hear the muffled cries of her daughters from up above and the whimpers of her sons in the first-floor bedroom. She had to shield her children from harm. Pauline backed toward the kitchen to secure a knife, using her ripped sleeve to stanch the flow of blood from her arm.

In the moments after the cut, at hearing the sounds of the children, J.P. and Everard seemed to sober a bit.

Pauline's ragged breath calmed as J.P.'s eyes flicked between Everard and her. J.P. suddenly looked worried. He promised to give Pauline $35 if she would "keep still" about the poisoning claims and his wife's exhumation. He would "take a load of wheat to town on the morrow" and provide her the proceeds.

Pauline realized the situation had changed. She was now in control. Her information about J.P.'s crimes had given her power and leverage. As she considered his desperate proposition, the neighborhood constable entered through the open door followed by Pauline's son.

The constable eyed the two men and asked Pauline about the situation.

Pauline knew this was her chance. She could report Soquet for that evening's crimes as well as his old poisoning crimes. But his bribe of $35 represented a small fortune. It would provide Pauline's family great assistance when she and the children moved back to Red River. Besides, Pauline realized, by accusing J.P. of those old crimes, renewed scrutiny could surface concerning her sister's part in August's poisoning death.

So instead of telling the whole truth, clutching her bleeding arm, Pauline only explained to the constable what had transpired that evening. But as he handcuffed J.P. and Everard, Pauline wondered why she continued to protect her sister. If Elvira had not ditched her husband at the Denis saloon, J.P. would not have arrived at Pauline's house and placed her and her children in harm's way. Now that J.P. would be locked up in the county jail, awaiting his arraignment for assault and battery, in addition to breaking and entering, Pauline realized she had saved her sister again.

When Elvira returned home from who knows where, J.P. would not be there to assault Elvira as he had Pauline.

POWDER KEG

XAVIER

XAVIER MARTIN and his eldest son, seven-year-old Rudy, stepped out of their Crooks Street home on Tuesday, October 18, 1881. Xavier was headed to the Brown County Courthouse while his son was en route to school. Xavier had been hired to translate at J.P. Soquet's preliminary hearing for the charges of assault and battery and breaking and entering. Xavier was surprised that J.P.'s sister-in-law, Pauline Villiesse, was the complainant rather than J.P.'s wife, Elvira. Four years had transpired since Pauline had accompanied her sister on that meeting to Xavier's office to explore Elvira's options for divorce. It appeared as if J.P.'s abuse had widened beyond his wife and tavern brawl victims.

Finally, someone was willing to do something about it.

Sale School – first Green Bay Public School (Wikipedia)

Xavier walked side-by-side with Rudy, his son's schoolbooks strapped together and slung over his shoulder. They reached Monroe Avenue. Rudy turned right toward Sale School, the Green Bay public school known as "Old Brick." He was in first grade and would attend the same school through twelfth grade.

Xavier continued on the plank sidewalk toward the section of the city that had burned out about a year ago. A few homes had been rebuilt while others were still under construction. The scent of wood smoke rose from new chimneys.

On the day of the fire, Monday, September 20, 1880, Xavier had left home after eating breakfast with his family. Fierce winds battered him as he completed the mile walk to his office. At about 3 P.M., Xavier heard church bells ringing and cries of "Fire!" He hurried down the stairs as wagons raced past. Xavier stopped a man traveling on foot to ask what had happened. He said the old Astor Planing Mill was on fire.

The mill, just north of Mason Street Bridge, was only a few blocks from Xavier's own Crooks Street. The wind suddenly changed its direction, blowing diagonally toward the finest homes of the city, including his own. Xavier ran like a madman until he reached Crooks Street. He looked

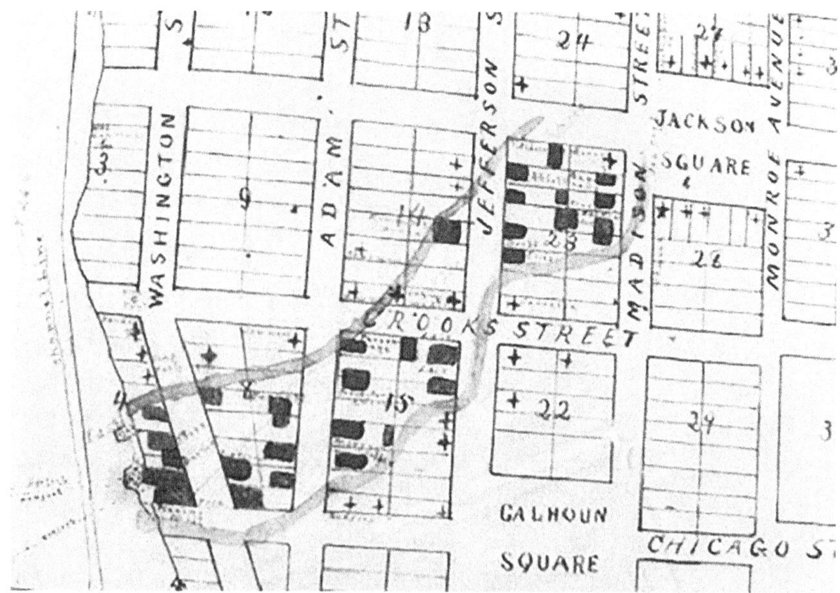

Fire Survey Map for Great Fire of 1880. (Courtesy of The Lavinia Goodell Wisconsin State Law Library) *Atkinson v. Goodrich Transp. Co.*, 60 Wis. 141, 18 N.W. 764, 765 (1884). Case brief, Exhibit A.

to the east and stood there in horror. The cupola of the First Presbyterian Church was on fire, scattering embers over the parsonage, which had started to burn. Xavier made the rash decision to turn onto Crooks Street. He dashed past the burning church and parsonage as crashing timbers exploded. Through the billowing smoke, he continued to run, his leg muscles screaming from the exertion.

First Presbyterian Church (Courtesy Brown County Library)

Distant fire engine bells clanged as Xavier traveled five more blocks to reach his 728 Crooks Street home. He bent over, panting, and thanked God his house was undisturbed. He turned around and gazed back over the path he had run. The fire had spread in a northeast direction, burning down homes along Adams and Jefferson Streets. Xavier worried about the wind, whether it might change direction again and send destruction toward his home.

Elie and Phoebe Martin (Courtesy Blodgett, Fay Willis via John Mertens)

He rushed into his house and found his wife and children all safe inside. Xavier gathered them up and drove his family to his brother Elie's house south of the Mason Street Bridge before returning to the devastated neighborhood. Houses and trees along Adams, Jefferson, and Madison smoldered in the fire's wake. Household effects lined the streets. Xavier and other volunteers loaded goods onto wagons to aid those who had escaped from their blazing residences.

The fire was controlled by around 7:30 that night. Xavier and his family had suffered no damage, but about one hundred businesses and homes had burned down, including those of Dr. Munro, Attorney J.J. Tracy, Dr. Benjamin Brett, and Judge Ellis. Only one life had been lost.

One year later, Xavier gazed up ahead. Reconstruction of the First Presbyterian Church, where he and his family attended, was still in progress. Augusta was a devout Christian, as was he. Xavier had been baptized Catholic, but he had abandoned that faith in Belgium to follow the Protestant pastor Cacheux. Until the completion of the new church, the congregation of First Presbyterian would worship inside Klaus Hall.

Xavier turned north onto Jefferson Street and arrived at the courthouse. Inside Justice Van Buren Bromley's courtroom, Xavier took his seat near the witness box. He eyed the defendant, J.P. Soquet, who looked like a powder keg, ready to explode. But unlike last year's fire, which the city had managed to contain, no brave soul nor the court system had discovered a means to permanently diffuse J.P. Soquet's dangerous and violent behavior. In fact, his temper seemed to be only getting worse.

Xavier had followed the news related to the Belgian farmer's skirmishes in saloons. Little had changed from twenty-some years ago when Xavier, as justice of the peace, had dealt with J.P. There was also the unreported abuse J.P. had levied on his wife. The farmer's cycle of violence seemed to be repeating more frequently as his anger and jealousy boiled. After each arrest, J.P. received a $10 fine. That was apparently little to him, because following each arrest and release, nothing seemed to change.

Xavier admired J.P.'s sister-in-law, Pauline Villiesse, as she took the stand. Through Xavier's translation, she relayed her story of J.P.'s break-in and assault at the Minsart home. Pauline was a strong woman, and Xavier wondered if she was the only one who had ever stood up to J.P. Soquet.

The next witness was J.P.'s partner in crime, Joseph Everard, who testified about the break-in and assault. He said J.P. had been mad at his wife, Elvira, not at Mrs. Villiesse. When Everard was asked about that evening's conversation between J.P. and Mrs. Villiesse, Everard said he had been too drunk to remember. Xavier watched as Everard's eyes darted toward J.P. as he spoke. Unlike Pauline, Everard seemed to be terrified of J.P.

After all the testimony, Justice Bromley determined there was probable cause to hold J.P. Soquet over for trial in Brown County Circuit Court. Until those proceedings, J.P. would remain in jail unless he secured $500 ($16,000 in current valuation) to be released on bail. Xavier was pleased. That amount of money would take some time for J.P. to secure. In the meantime, the women in his life would be safe.

·∞·

About a year later, on September 21, 1882, Xavier walked back to his office after a noon meal with Jules Parmentier. Over the weekend, the two friends, in addition to a dozen other prominent Belgians from the city, had taken a ride on the Henry F. Brower tugboat loaded with cases of beer and a picnic supper for their monthly déjeuner. In a light-hearted mood, Xavier turned onto Washington Street and tipped his bowler to Attorney J.J. Tracy, whose law office was located in the Post Office Block, a short distance from Xavier's.

Xavier climbed the stairs to his real estate office and entered the reception area. Inside was Mrs. J.P. Soquet, the bruises on her face unsuccessfully hidden beneath her hat's black netting.

Xavier's carefree attitude dissipated.

Months ago, Xavier had noted that Joseph Everard had been fined $10 for his part in the crime of breaking and entering into the home of Pauline Villiesse. But Xavier had not seen any mention of a trial or fine attributed to J.P. Soquet. It appeared as if Elvira's sister had mysteriously dropped her charges against her brother-in-law. Xavier shook his head. What a mistake—one that Elvira Soquet had apparently paid for.

Xavier escorted Elvira into his office. She said J.P. had used his fists on her that weekend, which had scared her little boy. J.P.'s oldest daughter had gone for the neighborhood constable. Per Elvira's complaint, the first she had ever initiated against her husband, the constable had arrested J.P. for assault and battery. But the next day, Justice Killian had only fined J.P. $10 plus court costs.

Elvira said she could not live like that anymore. The justice system would not protect her. Next time J.P. used his fists, Elvira feared he might kill her. But her biggest concern was for her child's safety. J.P. often caned little Henry on his backside and legs with a birchwood switch for no reason other than to upset Elvira. She was ready to begin a divorce action and to secure custody of her little boy. But Elvira wanted an attorney other than Mr. Wigman or Mr. Hudd. Her husband, she believed, would have undue influence with them, seeing as J.P. had paid the pair so well for his many arrests.

Xavier suggested Mr. J.J. Tracy, who had been the District Attorney eight years ago at Elvira's preliminary hearing. Elvira questioned whether Mr. Tracy would be the right attorney to help her since he had had her arrested for her former husband's poisoning death. Xavier reminded Elvira that Mr. Tracy had not found any evidence to tie Elvira to August's death. When he added the thought that perhaps this meant Mr. Tracy had considered J.P. might be the party responsible, Xavier noted Elvira averted her eyes.

Xavier offered to send his office boy to Mr. Tracy's office to see whether he would be willing to talk to Elvira that day. Elvira's face clouded, which frustrated Xavier. He could tell she was vacillating again.

Elvira admitted that before she had given birth to Henry, she should have filed for divorce. Everything would have been easier. She could have moved into her rental home in Green Bay, and J.P. would likely have let her. But now they shared a son. Without J.P.'s permission, she could not simply move out of the house with Henry. And once she filed for divorce, J.P. might win custody of her child, which she could not bear. She felt her life was hopeless.

Xavier was distressed when Elvira stood and walked out of his office.

Two months passed. Xavier had not heard from Elvira. Nevertheless, he had contacted Attorney J.J. Tracy who had agreed to represent Elvira Soquet if she decided to proceed with a divorce. Then, on the morning of November 15, 1882, Xavier read the *State Gazette*; J.P. Soquet was in the news again.

According to the article, J.P. and another Preble farmer named Milquet had been in Green Bay the prior day and had sold a quantity of wheat. Part of the proceeds had been used by Soquet to purchase a demijohn of rye whiskey. On the return trip, the two men had quarreled and come to blows. Milquet got the worst of it, but when J.P. got home he "raised the devil" by whipping his wife and young child. The newspaper's informant claimed Mrs. J.P. Soquet would be filing a complaint, and a warrant would be issued for her husband's arrest.

Xavier hoped Elvira Soquet would come calling again—before it was too late.

COMPOUNDED MISERY

PAULINE

THE WINTER LULL in Wisconsin farming arrived in early December of 1883. Thirty-nine-year-old Pauline stepped into the musty Minsart home with her husband Henry and their seven children ranging in age from one to sixteen, including their newest addition, Frank. Two years had passed since Pauline and the children had left this place to return to Red River where Henry had built their new log house. Pauline was relieved that she and her children had been removed from the daily friction of the Soquet home.

Pauline walked through the first-floor rooms and shivered. She could still picture her last encounter with J.P. Soquet in this house when he had assaulted Pauline with the broken whiskey bottle. Pauline had taken Soquet's $35 afterward to "keep still" about the poisoning deaths of August and Esperance and the latter's disinterment. Pauline wished she had not accepted J.P.'s bribe or dropped the charges against him. But Elvira had implored her to do the latter. Elvira had feared, once J.P. secured the $500 of bail money, he would have retaliated against her.

In the kitchen, Pauline could see her breath as the children raced around, checking out each room, calling out memories from their time here. Pauline's family planned to spend a week in the home, based on Elvira's urgent request. She had sent it and the house key through Pauline's sister, Fannie, whose family had joined Pauline's for Thanksgiving the prior week. Elvira had told Fannie the conflict in her home had escalated, and Elvira needed to talk to Pauline. Pauline, after all, was the eldest sister in the family, so she came. She did not want to let Elvira down.

Also, Elvira's request worried Pauline. About five months prior, following the violent Milquet incident, J.P. had pled guilty to the charge of assault and battery for abusing Elvira and their four-year-old Henry. J.P. had only been fined $25 plus court costs. Clearly, the fees were no deterrent, because three months later, Elvira had filed assault and battery charges against J.P. again. The court had fined him the same small amount.

The flawed judicial system rankled Pauline as Henry and Anton carried in wood and kindling for the stove and fireplace. Last week, over the Thanksgiving dinner, Fannie had also relayed that Elvira had recently met with Mr. Xavier Martin and an attorney, the one who had prosecuted Elvira's case more than a decade ago. Fannie did not know what the three had discussed, but Elvira had told Fannie that Pauline would know.

Pauline did know. But if Elvira had followed through and served J.P. divorce papers, Fannie would have heard by now. Everyone in the Belgian community would have, too.

Elvira's inaction, going on for six years, frustrated Pauline to no end. Tomorrow, Pauline would insist her sister proceed with her divorce. For good measure, Pauline would accompany Elvira to the attorney's office to get the divorce paperwork done. Before J.P. was served, Pauline would ensure that Elvira and Henry were in the Villiesse buckboard headed back to Red River. Pauline knew their parents would take Elvira and their grandson into their home.

On this visit, Pauline was determined to change her sister's life once and for all.

The next morning, Henry and Pauline's four eldest children shrugged on coats and left for the Soquet home. Henry and two sons planned to help J.P. and Jule mend fences. Their two oldest daughters went to visit with the Soquet girls. But Mary, Soquet's eldest daughter, made the reverse trip to the Minsart house with Elvira and little Henry. He joined his cousins, George, Delia, and Frank, on the bedroom floor to play with wooden farm and forest animals that Henry had whittled.

The three women took seats at the kitchen table. Pauline's resolve was as strong as ever. She was eager to relay her plan to her sister about how Elvira and little Henry could get away from J.P. for good. But before Pauline could speak, Elvira told her stepdaughter to tell Pauline about her troubling situation, that Pauline would know what Mary should do.

Pauline was caught off guard, but she shifted her focus to Mary.

J.P.'s eldest daughter balled up a handkerchief in her trembling fist. Through tears, she confided in Pauline about how her father repeatedly visited her bedroom. How J.P. had made her do things with him that only a husband and wife should do.

Pauline was shaken by Mary's confession, even though she had feared as much. She was certain J.P.'s shameful acts would send him to hell. But would they send him to prison?

Pauline knew how difficult Mary's situation was. Unlike physical abuse that left bruises, sexual abuse was often impossible for the naked eye to discern. J.P. would absolutely deny her accusations. For Mary to accuse him of incest, she would suffer the community's gossip, which would be mortifying for her. Her father's home had been *her* home for thirty years. She had nowhere else to go. There was nowhere she could be safe.

A knock sounded on the door. Pauline stood and opened it. The local constable was on the stoop. He handed Pauline a court order he said had been signed by Judge M.L. Martin. The constable said he had first stopped at the Soquet farm and had been told by Mr. Soquet that his daughter, Mary, would be at the Minsart home. The constable said he was to transport Mary to the Brown County jail.

Pauline was stunned. She looked down at the document, which she could not read. The constable told Pauline the court order stated Mary was to be examined by two court appointed physicians to determine whether she was insane, such was the complaint of Mary's father J.P. Soquet. Only after Judge Martin received those results would he determine whether Mary would be released from jail.

Pauline fumed as Mary bravely stood. Vile words flew from Elvira's mouth, condemning her husband.

Pauline knew there was nothing the three women could do, however. J.P. was wickedly clever. Before his daughter had had the opportunity to report her sexual abuse to the authorities, J.P. had filed his own complaint, claiming his daughter displayed insane behavior. Women were often at the mercy of men, especially relatives, who sexually abused them. J.P. had most likely claimed *she* had been the predator, making sexual advances toward him, her own father. Seduction and sexual derangement were two of the many reasons a doctor could deem a woman insane.

Pauline seethed with anger as Mary and the constable departed. Pauline's plans for the day had gone terribly awry, especially when Elvira, her boots pounding, sailed out of the house with Henry in tow to confront her husband.

Pauline felt a growing sense of dread.

The next afternoon of December 6, 1883, Pauline's sister and little Henry returned to the Minsart home. Elvira seemed defeated, her face lined with resignation as she dropped onto a kitchen chair. That morning, Elvira said, Judge M.L. Martin had adjudged Mary insane based on the two physicians' reports. J.P.'s eldest daughter had been transported to the Oshkosh Northern Hospital for the Insane.

Northern Hospital for Insane (Postcard)

Elvira swayed on her chair, moaning. She said she had lost her only ally in the Soquet home. Mary had been the lone Soquet child who had come to Elvira's aid when J.P.'s temper had flared. Now, Elvira and her little son had no one in the family to defend and protect them. If anything, J.P.'s son and other daughters seemed to be out to get Elvira, especially eleven-year-old Clara, who despised Elvira. In her father's eyes, Clara could do no wrong, while Henry, without any provocation, suffered J.P.'s beatings.

Elvira gazed up at Pauline. What was she to do? Her home life was the worst it had ever been. She had to protect her child. Yet she feared by doing so, she might do something she would regret.

Pauline tried to quiet her revulsion so she could help her sister. She placed a hand on Elvira's shoulder and told her to go home. In absolute secrecy, she was to pack a few belongings for Henry and herself. Tomorrow, the pair would travel back to Red River with Pauline. Once Henry was safe with their parents, Pauline would accompany Elvira to Green Bay to finalize Elvira's divorce paperwork with Attorney J.J. Tracy. They devised that he would wait to serve J.P. the divorce papers until Elvira had returned to her parents' home.

Pauline reiterated to her sister: follow the plan; you'll be safe. To herself she added: *And end the shame of our family's involvement with J.P. Soquet once and for all.*

Elvira wiped the tears from her cheeks, sparks of hope in her eyes. She would do everything Pauline suggested.

∞

Over supper, despite the plight of J.P.'s eldest daughter, a lightness swelled inside Pauline's chest. By tomorrow morning, her sister and little Henry would be safe from J.P.'s abuse. Pauline settled the children for the night then she and Henry began to organize their belongings for their return journey.

Violent knocking breached the front door.

Henry opened it and Elvira stumbled in sobbing. In her arms was little Henry, terribly battered, a dribble of blood at the corner of his mouth.

Pauline was stunned and sickened.

Elvira implored Pauline to go for a priest, one who would pray for her child, one who could heal her little boy.

Pauline and Henry hurried Elvira into the kitchen and helped her place the child on the dining table. Pauline checked his pulse. Nothing. She placed her fingertips to his lips but felt no breath. She leaned over and placed her cheek to her nephew's small mouth, cold to the touch.

Pauline stifled a sob and looked up at her husband. The last time she had felt this helpless was when their two daughters, Celinda and baby Adeline, had died of fever.

She knew Henry was dead. So did Elvira. But neither could say it.

Elvira's chest convulsed in sobs. She whimpered that J.P. had discovered her plans. He had found the carpet bags she had packed. He had stormed through the house chasing her and Henry. Elvira heard her little boy scream. When she had found him at the foot of the stairs, she had scooped him up and run, all the way across the neighbors' fields to her sister's house.

Elvira scooped Henry up again and wailed. Her voice coursed with pain and rage.

Pauline could only listen, deadened by shock.

Pauline and her family decided not to leave until little Henry's funeral. Pauline, awash in sadness, sat beside her husband in their wagon, which was loaded up for their return to Red River, their children seated in back. The Villiesse family followed the funeral wagon carrying little Henry's casket along Bay Settlement Road.

Just like the deaths of J.P.'s first and second wives, the authorities had held no inquest to determine the cause of death for Elvira's four-year-old. None of the Soquet children had accused their father of any wrongdoing, and Elvira had not witnessed what had occurred. Pauline knew so many children died by accidental death or by infectious disease. The death of Elvira's little boy had not raised any alarms.

Pauline, however, could not help but wonder how Henry had ended up at the bottom of the stairs. Had Elvira's child fallen on his own? Or had his father, while on his rampage, shoved Henry down the stairs?

Pauline stood by the grave. She felt Elvira's immense grief over losing her only precious child. Pauline's blurry eyes took in the panorama of J.P. and his children, Elvira distanced from them. J.P. had his arm around Clara.

Pauline's intention to positively change her sister's life had failed. Things were worse now, in ways, more horrendous than she could have imagined.

Pauline had still begged her sister to return to Red River with her family. But Elvira had refused. She seemed consumed by hate. Standing by her son's small grave, Elvira eyed eleven-year-old Clara, as little Henry's casket was placed into the ground.

Elvira had told Pauline that J.P. deserved to suffer. Pauline agreed. But when Elvira had added she knew just how to make that happen, Pauline saw something sinister in her sister's eyes. Henry's death had sent Elvira over the edge. Pauline was not sure she knew her sister anymore.

CHILD PROTECTION

XAVIER

THE JULY 4, 1884, celebration was in progress at Green Bay's Riverside Park. Amid lush green vegetation and hot and humid air, Xavier's family sat on blankets along the East River. An excursion boat that traveled between three local parks, all holding celebrations, pulled up to the dock and passengers climbed off.

Xavier's family had watched the Fourth of July procession and listened to music by Kimball's Silver Band. The Honorable T.R. Hudd had given a rousing speech, after which the Oneida Indians played an exciting game of lacrosse for the crowd using wooden sticks and deer-hide balls. Awaiting the evening's fireworks, Xavier and his family were finishing up a picnic packed by Augusta as the Vandenack brothers approached. Xavier knew the pair of Belgian farmers, August and Louis, who lived in the Preble township.

Xavier Martin (Courtesy Blodgett, Fay Willis via John Mertens)

August Vandenack asked whether he and his brother could talk privately to Xavier. It would only take a moment.

Xavier agreed and the three men walked a few steps away from his family. August, holding his straw hat in his hands, began. Since everyone knew Xavier was the person to talk to about cruelty toward animals, August thought he might also take an interest in a case of cruelty toward a child. He said he had worked for Jean Philippe Soquet for some time, handling the cows and working in the fields. August said he needed to unburden his conscience. He wanted to tell Xavier about the family situation of eleven-year-old Clara Soquet, who Vandenack believed was J.P.'s favorite child. August said Clara's stepmother, Elvira Soquet, made "the child [do] all of the work of the house and some work in the field, making hay." Last week, he had seen Mrs. Soquet "hit the girl in the face with her hand." It was a "severe blow," and Mr. Vandenack was worried.

Xavier was disturbed at hearing the man's claims. Not only about the "severe blow" to the child's face, but her work in the fields. Making hay was no easy chore, especially not for a young girl. It was usually done by hand with scythes, followed by manual raking into haycocks, allowing it to dry, then gathering it with forks and hoisting it into the barn.

August's brother, Louis, told Xavier he had also heard that Elvira Soquet had recently knocked her stepdaughter "down sixteen-foot stairs."

Xavier flinched.

Louis said Mrs. Soquet was in the habit of beating the child with "any articles she could lay her hands on."

August said the young girl's abuse had started about seven months ago, following the death of Mrs. Soquet's four-year-old son, Henry.

Xavier was taken aback at that last news. He had not heard about the death of Elvira's son, who was the same age as Xavier's boy, Freddie. He glanced over at his son's sweet face.

August Vandenack said the neighbors suspected the little Soquet boy had died at the hands of his father, that he had pushed him down the stairs. August and Louis had heard that J.P. had ordered his daughters to sew his four-year-old son up in a sack, so when family and neighbors had paid their respects, the child's bruised body had not been visible.

Xavier was horrified and struggled to absorb everything he was hearing. He knew Henry was Elvira's only child, her miracle child, and he mourned the fact that the boy was now in God's hands. Xavier knew such grief would leave an indelible mark on any parent. He again glanced over at his own children, safe and sound.

Xavier was angered that no charges had been brought by the local constable concerning Henry Soquet's obviously suspicious death. That no neighbors or family members had reported anything until now. It was the same old story. The Vandenack brothers had likely been afraid of J.P. They had known what he was capable of and they had feared for their lives and those of their family. Once again, there was no definitive proof that J.P. had caused his youngest son's death. Only common sense told Xavier it was true.

Xavier wondered whether Elvira was exacting revenge on J.P. by abusing her husband's youngest daughter. It seemed likely. Xavier needed to protect Clara Soquet.

He knew parents held the primary accountability for their children. Reasonable corporal punishment was widespread, and the government rarely interfered with the parental prerogative to punish their children as they saw fit. But changes had taken place in some states, and New York once again had led the way.

Back in 1874, the high-profile case of eight-year-old Mary Ellen Wilson had led to the creation of the New York Society for the Prevention of Cruelty to Children (SPCC). Mary Ellen had been severely abused by her foster mother. Neighbors brought the girl's abuse to the attention of Henry Bergh, the head of New York's SPCA. With the help of those neighbors' testimony, Bergh had removed Mary Ellen from the foster home and had taken her foster mother to trial. A jury convicted the woman of assault and battery, and the judge sentenced her to one year in prison.

Based on that court case, the New York Society for the Prevention of Cruelty to Children had been founded, the first organization of its kind. Wisconsin had created its own Child Protection Act soon thereafter. Now a child could be removed from their abusive family.

Xavier thanked the Vandenack brothers for their information and concern. He settled back on the blanket with his family. Xavier lifted his and Augusta's two youngest onto his lap, Evelyn, three, and Richard, one. Xavier wrapped his arms protectively around their small bodies. In the Martin family, each of their six children were considered precious. Sadly, not so in the Soquet family.

As fireworks exploded overhead and the crowd celebrated America's independence, Xavier vowed to secure young Clara Soquet's independence from her abusive family.

∞

The next morning, Xavier walked directly to the Brown County Courthouse, hoping to find Judge Morgan L. Martin inside his chambers before court. Xavier was in luck.

At age seventy-nine, the Honorable M.L. Martin had held his position for nine years. After Xavier explained the Soquet situation, Judge Martin stood and selected a Wisconsin law book from a shelf. He opened the book on his desk and located the Child Protection Act. Using that as a reference, Xavier swore, under oath, the following complaint:

That Clara Soquet, now residing with her parents J.P. Soquet and Elvira Soquet in the Town of Preble in [Brown County] is seriously endangered in her life, health, and safety by the continuous neglect, abuse and criminal treatment by her said parents in whose custody she now is ... That the said Clara Soquet is of the age of about eleven years.

Following Xavier's sworn complaint, Judge M.L. Martin summoned Clara Soquet, August Vandenack, and Louis Vandenack to appear in his chambers. Those individuals would each be called in separately and questioned by the judge under oath. Xavier had filed the complaint, but he would also be present to act as translator as each Belgian witness testified, a duty he continued to perform.

Clara Soquet was called in first. Her father had brought her to the courthouse, but he was sitting outside the judge's chambers so he could not intimidate his daughter while she provided her statement.

Clara Soquet (Hannon Weed) (Photo used with permission of Ancestry.com member)

Clara said she was eleven and did not remember her mother. She had been to school every day for one and a half years including last year. She had frequently been ill-treated and abused by her stepmother who had struck Clara with "sticks of wood on her back." Within the last ten days, Clara's stepmother, Elvira Soquet, had thrown Clara down the stairs twice. "For one year past," she said, "I have been compelled to do the washing for the family of four persons." Her father had sometimes interfered to protect her, which had resulted in a quarrel between her father and stepmother, and Clara's ill-treatment had continued.

The two Vandenack brothers each repeated to the judge under oath what they had told Xavier.

Xavier sat alone with Judge Martin and the court reporter for his testimony. He swore he was acquainted with the family of J.P. Soquet, having known its members for many years. "That the family is notoriously bad."

The judge called J.P. Soquet to provide a statement of his own. Soquet said his child Clara "is not properly treated by [my] wife," and J.P. "could not control his wife's cruel treatment of the child." J.P. conceded Clara should be given into the custody of "some proper person."

After Judge M.L. Martin had heard all the evidence, he entered an order to remove Clara from J.P. and Elvira's care. He assigned her to Peter Miller's custody, and he was to find her a good home. J.P. Soquet was ordered to supply the necessary clothing for Clara, not to exceed $30 per annum.

Xavier left the courthouse reassured that Clara Soquet would be in a better family environment, yet he was still concerned about Elvira's motive for treating Clara so cruelly. Xavier recalled the meeting he had finally arranged between Elvira and Attorney J.J. Tracy, prior to Thanksgiving of last year. Tracy had discussed Elvira's odds of winning her child's custody if she initiated a divorce. Tracy had told Elvira the court would likely give her custody due to Henry's age. Wisconsin had recently adopted Britain's Tender Years Doctrine, which presumed a child under the age of ten was best cared for by the mother.

But those odds had not been good enough for Elvira. She had said she could not take the chance and had decided not to move forward, which she now likely regretted deeply.

Elvira's son was dead, perhaps at his father's hands. Unthinkable. If Elvira proceeded with a divorce, winning custody of her boy would no longer be an issue.

But Xavier realized gravely, the repercussions from today's hearing *could* be an issue. What would J.P. do to Elvira when he arrived back at the Soquet farm without his favorite child?

CHARITY EXPECTATIONS

PAULINE

PAULINE WIPED THE SWEAT from her brow in the hot July heat. A fresh blend of green and earthy aromas circulated in the welcoming breeze. Summer insects buzzed, birds called, and leaves rustled as she and her girls Flora and Philomene, now sixteen and nine, picked ripened tomatoes, cucumbers, green beans, and summer squash. They squatted over the Minsart four-quadrant garden rather than their Red River kitchen garden.

That was because in mid-March, Pauline and Henry's log home had burned down for the second time.

Pauline was devastated and defeated. She and Henry both knew they should have taken out a loan to purchase fire resilient brick, rather than rebuilding their home with logs and chinking. Or they should have insured their log home. But they had felt the pressure of time and expense, and the desire to be back together had made them hasty. Now the Villiesse family had lost everything for a second time.

The loss was crippling, far worse than the first fire. Henry was fifty-seven and suffering from rheumatism. He was "almost wholly unable to do any work." There would be no way for Henry to rebuild their home this time, and they still had seven children to feed. Henry had been forced to sell the farm. But Pauline's sister, even in her state of all-consuming revenge, had recognized the dire straits Pauline and her family were in. Elvira had once again offered the Minsart home to Pauline's family. Henry and their two eldest sons, Anton and Jerome, now fourteen and ten, were employed by the LeCoque family next door to help with the animals and to work in the fields.

Pauline's sister, Elvira, was currently in the chicken coop collecting eggs with Pauline's youngest children, George, Delia, and Frank, now five, four, and two. These little children brought out the best in Elvira, especially George. He reminded Elvira of her Henry, whom she had buried seven months prior. Pauline had discovered, over those months, that her sister lived in a dark world. She had sought retribution by beating her husband's youngest daughter and even attempted to kill Clara by pushing her down the stairs where Henry had died. Pauline hated to admit her sister had become a "bad woman," even though Elvira was helping Pauline's family. Pauline understood Elvira's grief, yet she was ashamed of her sister.

But Pauline's family desperately needed Elvira's help.

Pauline climbed to her feet, her back aching. She washed her hands at the pump, splashed cool water on her face, and cupped her hand to take a swallow. Pauline filled a jug and entered the house to make a pitcher of lemonade. She was thankful the court had removed Clara from the Soquet home. The day after that judicial decision, Elvira, covered in bruises from J.P.'s fists, had moved into the Minsart house with Pauline's family.

Pauline could not turn her sister away. The house belonged to Elvira. And despite everything, Pauline knew she had to stand by her sister. It was what Belgian families did.

Elvira stepped into the kitchen with a basket of fresh eggs. Pauline's three youngest followed. Pauline still could not believe her sister had

Belgian Farm Woman (Zelia Wautlet, Photo 16, Belgian-American Research Collection, University of Wisconsin-Green Bay Archives Department)

suffered no consequences for abusing J.P.'s daughter, other than his fists. Pauline was glad but perplexed. Elvira had not been arrested nor had she been required to pay a fine. Wisconsin law believed the removal of the child from the unsafe home was penalty enough. But in this case, Clara's removal had hurt J.P. Soquet, because he loved the girl.

Elvira had indeed gotten her revenge.

Pauline cut and squeezed some lemons and added sugar to the jug of water. She stepped out onto the back stoop and called her daughters in to get a glass of lemonade. Pauline's eyes scanned the fields to the west. The Soquet home was on the near horizon. Even in the July heat, that fact made Pauline shiver. She believed J.P. would not let her sister's actions against his youngest daughter go unpunished. The beating Elvira had already received from J.P. would not be nearly enough to satisfy his rage. Of that, Pauline was certain.

The girls came inside and sat around the table with their little siblings to drink their lemonade. Elvira complained she needed something stronger. She cleaned up and told Pauline she was headed to the Dupont tavern to enjoy herself. Pauline watched from the window as Elvira drove away in the wagon.

Pauline was getting ready for bed when she heard the rattle of Elvira's wagon returning. Moments later, fists pounded on the door accompanied by her sister's shouts. Pauline quickly descended the stairs. Apparently, Elvira had forgotten her key again. To stop the ruckus, which had awakened the children, Pauline opened the door for her inebriated sister. Henry had followed Pauline down the stairs in his nightshirt and boots. He went outside to take care of the horse.

Elvira ranted about J.P. He had shown up at the tavern, and they had quarreled. She had threatened to reveal everything she knew about their former spouses' deaths. J.P. had grabbed her arm and shook her. He said he did not care if she told the authorities. No one could prove anything against him. And she was still his wife. She could never testify against him.

Elvira stumbled, her glassy eyes meeting Pauline's, the smell of liquor on her breath. She slurred her words, talking about J.P., how it was high time for her to divorce him once and for all so she could put her scoundrel of a husband behind bars.

Pauline had heard it all before.

But then Elvira began to sniffle, her bravado evaporating. She said her life was hopeless. She was trapped. If she divorced J.P., that devil would find a way to put her "behind bars as well." Or he might even kill her. Elvira released a pitiful cry.

Pauline knew Elvira's words could be true.

The parlor served as Elvira's bedroom. Pauline helped her sister undress and get into bed. She dimmed the kerosene lamp. Speaking quietly, Pauline told Elvira she had no choice, she had to divorce J.P. She had to think about her future. Elvira was thirty-seven, still a young woman. She could move into the Green Bay rental house she had purchased years ago and start over. Pauline's family could rent a house nearby. Elvira was an excellent seamstress. So was Pauline. Just think about it, Pauline whispered. The two Coppersmith sisters could start a business together, and Henry could find less strenuous work. All of them could start a new life.

Pauline had said it all before, but the dream still held a little spark of hope for her. She gazed down at her sister, whose eyes had drifted shut. Sadness welled up in Pauline. She smoothed Elvira's tangled hair knowing she had likely not heard a word Pauline had said. Pauline loved her sister. She did. But to go on like this was too much for Pauline to bear.

In the fall of that year, Pauline took walks in the nearby woods where rotted logs covered in moss rested between pine saplings and cottonwoods. She would come upon startled deer, their gaze briefly locking with hers before they fled. She would walk along the trampled path, her dark thoughts dragging her deeper and deeper into the dark woods.

Her sister's behavior had not changed. Elvira had sucked so much joy out of Pauline's life. Her sister's marital situation was in shambles and her drinking uncontrolled. Nearly every night, she cavorted at local saloons.

·∞·

Six months passed. On the morning of March 1, 1885, Pauline realized Elvira had not come home. Pauline waited until about noon, then she walked over to the Simonars' home. She knew Martin had picked Elvira up in his wagon the prior night to go to Anton Dupont's tavern in the town of Scott.

Simonar was in the barn, hoisting hay into the cows' feeding troughs with a pitchfork.

Pauline asked him about Elvira's whereabouts.

Simonar said that when he had been ready to leave the tavern shortly before closing time, Elvira had still been having a merry time and had refused to leave. He had arrived back at his farm at around midnight. Soon after, on his way to the house from the barn, Gustave Dupont's sleigh had emerged from the dark. He had told Simonar he had offered to drive Elvira home from the tavern. But as they had approached the Minsart house, she told him to drive on and drop her off at the home of Peter Maus.

Maybe, Simonar said as he provided each animal a scoop of grain, Pauline would find Elvira there.

Pauline was relieved to know where her sister might be, but she was also concerned that she had likely spent the night with another man while still being married.

Pauline headed back toward the Minsart house as the sleigh of Gustave Dupont drew up beside her. He repeated Simonar's story then explained what had happened once he had dropped Elvira off at the home of Peter Maus.

Because it had been so late, Gustave had decided to take the short route back to the town of Scott through the frozen fields of J.P. Soquet. Gustave had just driven onto the Soquet property when Jule Soquet stepped out of the house and grabbed the reins of Gustave's team. Then "old man Soquet" appeared with a shot gun. J.P. had apparently seen Gustave pass earlier in his sleigh with his wife, and J.P. wanted to know what the two had been up to.

At that point, Gustave said he had jumped down from the sleigh and tried to wrestle the gun out of J.P.'s hands. When J.P. fell to the ground, Gustave had hopped back in the sleigh and managed to escape.

Pauline could only shake her head. She asked Gustave whether he was filing charges.

He said he had just done so. He had reported the matter to the Brown County sheriff and filed charges of assault and battery against J.P. and his boy.

The winter sun glinted off the frozen fields as Pauline marched back to the Minsart home. She found Henry in one of the outbuildings grooming their horse. Pauline said she could not put up with her sister and J.P. any longer. Their family had to move out.

Henry's steady voice calmed Pauline. Although he agreed the situation with Elvira was far from desirable, Pauline's sister was still providing their family with a home at no cost. He promised that once their eldest daughter, Flora, married her beau, Joseph Geyer, who lived in Green Bay, the Villiesse family would move to the city as well.

Pauline reluctantly agreed to stay.

∞

Eighteen more months passed. In that time, the Statue of Liberty was installed in the New York Harbor where Pauline's family had arrived from Belgium twenty years ago. It stood as a symbol of democracy and freedom. But in the Minsart house, in Wisconsin's Humboldt township, Pauline felt no sense of freedom.

She had been tied to her sister's issues for too many years. The ever-mounting shame had no end. J.P. had continued to stir up the neighborhood, time after time, never receiving more than a fine. Even when J.P. and his son, Jule, had threatened Gustave Dupont with a gun, the two men had only received fines. J.P. was a menace to everyone who crossed his path, but primarily to Pauline's sister.

In early October, 1886, Pauline and Henry moved their family to a Green Bay rental house at 1288 Main Street. One night soon after, in the home's backyard, Pauline gazed up at the stars and nearly full moon, their light dim compared to how they shone in the night sky of the country. The evening sounds were different, too. Instead of the calls of screech owls, the chirping of crickets and frogs, and the wind rustling in the trees, Pauline listened to the clatter of horse hooves, the rumble of wooden and iron-rimmed wheels, and the neighbor's barking dog.

Pauline had given her sister so many chances to fix her life, but Elvira had not taken them. Without Pauline and Henry's presence in the Minsart house, maybe Elvira would take matters into her own hands. Pauline knew if she were Elvira, she would not be living anywhere near J.P. Soquet: he owned a gun and was not afraid to use it.

NO WIN SITUATION

XAVIER

XAVIER REACHED the Post Office Block in the first week of November of 1886. He climbed the stairs to Attorney J.J. Tracy's second floor office. Xavier hoped the upcoming divorce discussion with Elvira Soquet would not fail miserably as the others had. Elvira and J.P. Soquet had been married for thirteen years. Xavier knew of no family more troubled than theirs within the Belgian community or, for that matter, in all of Brown County.

Xavier was ushered into the attorney's personal office where Elvira Soquet was already seated. The gas lamp on Tracy's desk hissed as Xavier removed his cloak.

In the past decade, Elvira had come to Xavier three times to initiate divorce proceedings against her husband. Attorney J.J. Tracy had been present at one. Three times Elvira had stopped those actions for various reasons, which had baffled Xavier. Now, she told him, as he translated for Tracy, she was determined to follow through.

As before, Elvira said, "She wanted to be boss in her own property and live by herself." But she could not stay in the Minsart home that she still owned. Ever since her sister's family had moved out, about a month ago, she had been afraid to live in the country by herself. Her husband was only a short distance away. She wanted to move to Green Bay and live in the Main Street home she had purchased from Xavier eight years ago, but the house currently had renters. Therefore, once Elvira secured her divorce, she planned to live with her parents in the Green Bay township until her renters' lease reached its term.

This time, Xavier believed that Elvira seemed serious about dissolving her marriage. He hoped, for her sake, he was right.

·∞·

On November 22, 1886, Elvira's attorney, John J. Tracy, filed divorce papers on her behalf, and J.P. Soquet was officially served. The Brown County court ordered J.P. to pay Elvira's attorney $50 to allow him to proceed with the divorce. J.P. was also ordered to provide Elvira $4 a week for support and "not to molest or interfere with his wife."

During the first two weeks of December, the weather was unnaturally warm. Instead of snow, unfettered streams of rain filled Washington Street, which oozed with the foul scent of mud mixed with manure.

Xavier arrived at his office. Since his election to the position of Green Bay tax assessor two years prior, he had enjoyed its annual salary of $500, which supplemented his real estate business. With his new responsibilities, he found he needed more space. Two offices on his building's second floor had been combined into one, and this provided him a conference room for meetings such as the one being held that day.

On one side of the rectangular table, Attorney J.J. Tracy sat beside his client, Elvira Soquet. On the opposite side, J.P. Soquet was seated beside Attorney Thomas R. Hudd. Xavier took a seat beside Elvira to act as translator.

Xavier gazed at the gathered group. He realized that thirteen years earlier, each person at the table had been present in the Brown County Circuit Court for Elvira Soquet's preliminary hearing for her first husband's poisoning death. But at that time, Mr. Hudd had represented Elvira while J.J. Tracy, serving as the Brown County District Attorney, had prosecuted her. So very much had changed since then.

Xavier was in a unique position. Unlike the two attorneys, he could understand everything the Soquets said. Mr. Tracy slid over some paperwork, which Xavier told Elvira and J.P. they were to sign in order to proceed with the divorce. Elvira turned to Xavier, worry lining her face. Her voice vulnerable, she said she had second thoughts.

Xavier released an audible sigh and thought: *Not again... It's too late.*

Elvira told him she did not want to sign the paper. She was afraid J.P. would "kill her or poison her, the same as he had done formerly."

Xavier was stunned by Elvira's words, which J.P. had obviously heard. Xavier believed Elvira had been referring to the deaths of both of their former spouses, Esperance Soquet and August Minsart. Xavier had his own suspicions about those deaths, but he was shocked to hear her levy this accusation out loud.

Xavier wanted to reason with Elvira, but he had to remain impartial. They sat in silence. After a few moments of indecision, while rain assailed the office windows, Elvira signed the paperwork with an "X." She faced her husband and shoved the document across the table toward him. Raising her voice, she threatened to send J.P. to the "state prison for the rest of his days."

J.P.'s eyes narrowed as he calmly signed the document and said, "When he would go, she would go too."

Attorney Tracy had not understood the substance of the Soquets' conversation as he announced: the couple's divorce hearing was scheduled for January 5, 1887.

Xavier translated, and the two attorneys added their signatures to the paperwork. The meeting ended without Xavier finding an opportunity to tell Mr. Tracy and Mr. Hudd about the content of the Soquets' exchange.

Xavier stood by his office window. Elvira's claim disturbed him: that J.P. would "kill her or poison her, the same as he had done formerly."

The Sunday following that meeting, fresh pine boughs scented the sanctuary of the new First Presbyterian Church, dedicated four years ago. Xavier, his wife, and their six children filled up nearly an entire pew. Gold and white fabric draped the walls for Christmas, and candles provided warm and reverent lighting. Behind the pulpit, Reverend L.J. White preached, but Xavier thought only about Elvira Soquet's startling statements. Communion was served. Due to the rise of the temperance movement, unfermented grape juice was passed rather than wine, along with cubed bread.

First Presbyterian Church (Postcard)

During the church social after the service, Xavier talked to his good friend, Attorney Charles E. Vroman. Charles had graduated with a law degree from the University of Wisconsin and had arrived in Green Bay in the early 70s. He and Attorney George G. Greene had created a successful law practice. Before being elected to his current position of Green Bay City Attorney, Vroman had served as the Brown County District Attorney for four years. Xavier and attorneys Vroman and Greene went on an annual ten-day fishing trip to Thunder Lake.

Charles E. Vroman History of Brown County Commemorative Biographical Record

Xavier told Vroman about the Soquets' recent divorce meeting and their disturbing exchange. Vroman suggested, as city attorney, he could meet with Elvira Soquet while Xavier translated.

Sometime before December 31, the three met inside Xavier's office. Sitting across from the two men, Elvira, without any hesitation, confirmed part of Xavier's conjecture: that in June of 1873, J.P. Soquet had murdered Elvira's former husband, August Minsart.

Xavier translated, exchanging a look with his friend, as Elvira continued. She said J.P. had mixed poison into some "griddle cakes," and he had fed them to her former husband "who was then sick abed." Elvira said August had died two hours later.

After Elvira left Xavier's office, he and City Attorney Vroman talked about Elvira's alarming revelation. Yet Xavier recognized they had not taken advantage of their one-on-one meeting. Xavier said they should have asked Elvira about the death of J.P.'s second wife, Esperance. Both men realized Elvira had been solely focused on her former husband's death. They speculated whether she had been trying to get something on the record to protect herself.

Xavier recalled the exchange in his office between Elvira and J.P. when she had threatened to send her husband to "the state prison for the rest of his days." And J.P. had responded, "When he would go, she would go too." Once Elvira's divorce was finalized, and both spouses could testify against each other, both Elvira and Soquet could claim the other had poisoned August with the "griddle cakes."

But after so many years, Xavier wondered how anyone could find enough evidence to prove whose claim was true?

-∞-

Xavier arrived at the Brown County Courthouse on January 5, 1887 to translate at Elvira and J.P. Soquets' divorce hearing. He stamped his boots on the inside door mat before entering the vestibule. The first snowfall had occurred right before Christmas. The prior evening, three more inches had accumulated.

At the plaintiff table sat Elvira's attorney, Mr. J.J. Tracy. Mr. Hudd and J.P. Soquet were seated at the defendant's table. In the spectator section, Elvira Soquet's sister, Pauline Villiesse, was present. Xavier sensed Pauline had been waiting a long time for this day.

Xavier took his seat near the witness box. All eyes focused on the rear doors of the courtroom, awaiting Elvira Soquet's arrival.

Xavier's gaze drifted over to J.P. Soquet who displayed a nonchalant demeanor. J.P.'s attitude was similar to the one he had exhibited in Xavier's office in mid-December, where Elvira had threatened him. Although J.P.'s eyes had narrowed, he had been composed when he had threatened her back.

Xavier pondered the reason for J.P.'s calm deportment as the bailiff called court to order. The judge entered the courtroom and settled behind the bench.

Mr. Tracy apologized to the judge. He said his client, Mrs. J.P. Soquet, had yet to arrive. As everyone waited, the tension mounted.

The judge finally told Attorney Tracy to proceed without his client.

Tracy presented Elvira's case for her divorce from Jean Philippe Soquet as Xavier translated for J.P.'s benefit.

Attorney Hudd did not put up a fight on J.P.'s behalf.

The judge granted Elvira Soquet's divorce and ordered the defendant, J.P. Soquet, to pay his former wife's court costs and any litigation expenses she had incurred. The latter included Mr. John J. Tracy's attorney fees and those for Mr. Xavier Martin's translation services. Elvira had not requested any financial settlement nor ongoing support.

Court was adjourned.

Xavier stopped to talk to Pauline Villiesse on his way out. Neither could understand why Elvira had not been present to celebrate her release from J.P. Soquet.

Both were unsettled by her absence.

SECRETS SHARED

PAULINE

IN A SLEIGH buffeted by northerly winds, Pauline and Henry traveled past snow covered fields on their way to the Minsart house. A week earlier, in early-February, the U.S. Congress had passed the Interstate Commerce Act of 1887, enthusiastically welcomed by small farmers across the nation. Railroads, which had been exploiting small farmers with unfair rates and discriminatory pricing, would now be regulated by the Interstate Commerce Commission. That was certainly good news for the entire Coppersmith family.

Still, for Pauline, the Act's passage had taken a back seat to her worries about her sister, Elvira. As Pauline's anxiety had grown, she had convinced Henry they needed to drive out to the Minsart house to see for themselves whether Elvira was still living there—just two miles from J.P. Soquet.

Six weeks had passed since Attorney J.J. Tracy had secured Elvira's divorce. Pauline had recently discovered her sister had not collected the January and February rent from the occupants of her Green Bay Main Street house. That was not like Elvira.

The last time Pauline had seen her sister was in mid-December, after she had left the divorce meeting in Xavier Martin's office which J.P. had also attended. Elvira had admitted to Pauline that she had not controlled her temper. After Elvira had expressed her fears to Xavier Martin that J.P. would "kill her or poison her, as he had done formerly," she had threatened J.P., and he had threatened her back.

Those words had created a dangerous situation for Elvira, one that Pauline had thought about each day since.

Now, as Pauline and Henry turned down the road toward the Minsart house, her worry increased. Smoke percolated from the chimney of the Simonar home, curling over hand-split shingles, but not from the Minsart home. Henry halted the sleigh in front of the two-story log house. The drive leading toward the barn was not visible beneath the undisturbed snowfall. The plank walkway to the front door had not been shoveled. The house looked deserted.

Even so, Pauline gingerly stepped out of the sleigh and crossed the yard in her boots. The front door was locked. She knocked and waited, the taste of dread on her tongue. She knocked again. Only the sound of dripping icicles along the eaves filled her ears. Pauline peered in through the small windows on either side of the door, but the muslin curtains obscured her view. She hiked around to the back door. It, too, was locked. She no longer had a key. She wondered if she should ask Henry to break a window. But she doubted anyone was there.

Pauline returned to the sleigh and asked Henry to stop at the Simonar home. Martin was out by the barn. He told Pauline the last time he had seen Elvira at the Minsart house had been in late December. He and his wife had assumed Elvira had moved in with her parents following her divorce. Elvira had shared those plans with Simonar's wife.

As much as Pauline disliked the idea, she knew she and Henry had to stop at the Soquet home to ask after Elvira. Henry offered to talk to J.P. so Pauline would not have to. She watched as J.P. answered the door and talked to Henry before he returned to the sleigh. Henry said J.P. and his two children, Jule and Rose, were the only ones living in the house. Josephine had married Fred Beno, and they lived with Fred's parents on their nearby farm. J.P. had told Henry he had no idea where his former wife could be, but he hoped she would stay away.

His words distressed Pauline. Her sister would never be safe from J.P.

She and Henry stopped at the home of her sister, Fannie. She and Peter had not seen Elvira for some time, but that was not unusual. Elvira did not always attend mass at Holy Cross Church, the place where Fannie would normally run into Elvira. Perhaps, Fannie said, Elvira had moved in with their parents. Fannie's speculation matched the Simonars'. Pauline's heartbeat calmed. Maybe, just maybe, Elvira was safe with their parents.

Pauline and Henry decided to head directly up the Door Peninsula toward Pauline's childhood home. On the way, Pauline asked Henry to stop at Anton Dupont's tavern in the town of Scott, which she knew

Elvira had frequented. Perhaps, Elvira had talked to the saloon keeper about her plans.

Henry went inside.

The wind coming off the bay whirled snow around the Villiesse sleigh as Pauline waited, working to convince herself Elvira was safe.

Henry returned, his brow furrowed with concern. He told Pauline that he had talked to Anton Dupont. Elvira had not been in the tavern since late December. She had been a steady customer, so her absence had concerned Anton. He knew nothing about Elvira's whereabouts. But Anton had told Henry to talk to the men playing cards at the corner table. Those men had told Henry that once Elvira had initiated the divorce proceedings, J.P. had been very uneasy. He had repeatedly declared: If Elvira ever referenced "those old poisoning matters," she would have to die.

A cold terror struck Pauline. In that mid-December divorce meeting, that was exactly what Elvira had done. Maybe, Pauline fretted, J.P. had followed through on his threat.

For nearly fourteen years, Pauline and her extended Coppersmith family had believed they were protecting Elvira by keeping silent about J.P.'s involvement in his second wife's death. By exposing him, they would draw attention to Elvira's potential involvement in the death of her former husband, too, and this would reignite their family's shame.

Pauline now had a sinking feeling that her family had grievously erred in making that decision.

The sky darkened and stars appeared. Pauline and Henry, chilled to the bone, pulled up to Pauline's childhood home. While Henry led the horse and sleigh around to the barn, Pauline knocked on the front door before stepping into the warmth of her parents' home. They sat by the kitchen hearth, her father drinking beer, her mother coffee. Elvira was nowhere to be seen.

Pauline removed her damp cloak and approached her parents. As she warmed her frozen hands and feet by the fire, she explained the purpose for her unexpected visit. Pauline said she was looking for Elvira and asked whether her sister was living with them.

Pauline's mother seemed surprised by the question. She said she had not seen Elvira since Christmas. In the winter months, Pauline's mother said they were secluded from their children to the south. To travel a dozen miles by sleigh in the freezing cold was too much for her mother's aching bones. But she had heard from Pauline's youngest sister, Flora, that a judge had awarded Elvira her divorce from J.P., although Elvira had not been present in the courtroom.

The weight of the hard day suddenly landed on Pauline. Her knees faltered as her hands trembled. Seeing her struggle, Pauline's parents looked concerned. They both stood, with a little difficulty.

Protecting their family was paramount to her parents. That knowledge crushed Pauline. They had raised seven children to adulthood, and those children had produced more than thirty grandchildren and five great-grandchildren. Pauline's fears about Elvira's safety would devastate them. Although Elvira had been troublesome, she was still their daughter. They had always provided her support, protection, and love. They would have done anything for her.

Henry entered the house and removed his wet coat and hat. He rubbed his hands together to warm them as Mrs. Coppersmith instructed everyone to take seats around the kitchen table. She poured Henry and Pauline a cup of coffee to take the chill off.

After the four were seated, Pauline told her parents everything she knew about Elvira's disappearance. Then she said what she feared most: that Elvira was dead and J.P. was responsible.

Her parents were stunned. They had known there was trouble between their daughter and J.P. for years, which had led to their divorce, but this information from Pauline was devastating. Yet, they believed her.

Tears dribbled down her mother's cheeks as she rocked back and forth in her chair. Pauline's father railed about J.P. Soquet and the criminal way he had treated his wives. How the first two were dead and Elvira, his voice caught, could be as well.

He paused, silent. He now regretted not conveying to the authorities more than a decade ago what J.P. Soquet had told him about the death of his second wife. Perhaps he could fix that mistake now.

Pauline touched her father's arm and agreed: it might not be too late.

At Pauline's words, her father's resolve turned to steel. He said Xavier Martin would be the proper person to talk to. He understood their Belgian language. He would know what to do.

-∞-

In the second week of February 1887, Pauline and Henry watched through the window of her parents' Green Bay township home. Low gray clouds rolled overhead. Pauline's brother-in-law, William Lancelle, was in the house as well. William stepped outside as a coach pulled up and three men climbed out. Pauline knew two of the men, Xavier Martin and Attorney J.J. Tracy.

Pauline's father had sent word to Xavier Martin twice, requesting he come to the Coppersmith home. When Xavier had failed to respond to her father's requests, Pauline had traveled to Xavier's office to speak with him directly. He had promised Pauline he would arrive at her parents' home that afternoon with the proper authorities.

Through the open door, Pauline could hear William instruct the driver to go around back to the barn where he could feed and water his team. Then William told the three men to follow him into the house. After the visitors hung their coats on hooks, they settled down on one side of the rectangular kitchen table.

Pauline's father, Alexis, sat at the head. Pauline and Henry took seats next to William. Pauline's mother provided coffee to everyone except her husband, who wanted beer. She took a seat at the opposite end of the table.

Introductions were made all around. The third man was Sheriff Watermolen, a Flemish Belgian. Alexis said he was prepared to reveal information about J.P. Soquet he had only shared with his family. He asked Xavier to translate his words and write them down in a statement, which Alexis would sign. He was an old man, he said, and he feared he might not live to testify if J.P. Soquet ever went to trial.

As a notary public, Xavier swore Alexis Coppersmith in. Pauline was proud of her father as he revealed the truth about his encounter with J.P. Soquet fourteen years ago. How J.P. had told him that if the authorities exhumed the body of his second wife, Esperance, he would be "in for it," since she and August Minsart had been poisoned with the same kind of poison. Then Pauline's brother-in-law relayed his conversation with J.P. Soquet, who had told William if his second wife was not "unburied," he was "in for it" since "his woman" had been poisoned.

As Xavier had translated, Pauline had watched the eyes of Attorney

J.J. Tracy and Sheriff Watermolen, their attention alert and focused.

Fading afternoon light canted across the table by the time it was Pauline's turn to speak. She had learned some English since moving to Green Bay. But that day she used her native tongue so her parents and brother-in-law could understand. Pauline shared what Elvira had told her on the day of Father Daems' funeral: that in the spring of 1874, Elvira and J.P. had removed his wife's body from her casket. J.P. had carried the body from the grave in a gray blanket and buried it by a grove of plum trees on their neighbor's land. Pauline told Xavier that she believed another man by the name of J.B. Rose had served as a lookout.

After Xavier translated, Attorney Tracy and Sheriff Watermolen talked excitedly between themselves. The sheriff asked Pauline whether the body was still in that grove of plum trees. Pauline said that according to her sister, J.P. had moved the body soon after, likely to some spot on the Soquet farm.

The room was silent except for the crackle of burning logs in the hearth and tree branches lashing against the Coppersmith homestead.

Pauline's father's large shoulders were slumped, his empty beer stein pushed to the side. He said if J.P. had been willing to poison his second wife, a woman who had borne him seven children, he would have had no qualms in killing his third wife. Especially, Alexis added, since Elvira could finally have testified against that devil. Her father's voice echoed with anger and sadness, then sighed. He prayed Elvira was still alive, though she had not been seen for nearly two months. What else could he do?

Pauline placed a hand over her father's.

TROUBLING EVIDENCE

XAVIER

A DRIZZLY SNOW FELL, nasty and cold, as the coach traveled south along the state road. Inside the carriage, the body heat of Xavier Martin, Sheriff Watermolen, and Attorney Tracy kept them all warm on their long ride back to Green Bay. The weather, Xavier knew, would not keep the faithful away from the nearby Robinsonville chapel.

All Wisconsin Belgians knew the story of eighteen-year-old Adele Brice. The Blessed Virgin appeared to her three times in October of 1859 on Adele's way home from early morning Mass at Holy Cross Church. The Blessed Virgin had commanded Adele to "gather the children in this wild country and teach them what they should know for salvation." Adele's father had built a small family chapel in Robinsonville where his daughter had seen the apparitions. Adele had traveled from home-to-home throughout the Door Peninsula, offering to do housework in exchange for the privilege of teaching their children the Roman Catholic catechism. Within three years, the faithful had replaced the small Robinsonville chapel with a larger one and built a school and convent.

Robinsonville Chapel (Photo 284, Belgian-American Research Collection, University of Wisconsin-Green Bay Archives Department)

Xavier knew the Catholic Diocese of Green Bay did not recognize the "so-called miracle." Bishop Krautbauer forbade his Door Peninsula priests from officiating at the chapel near Robinsonville, especially on August 15, when Catholics celebrated the Feast of the Assumption of the Blessed Virgin Mary. In the bishop's eyes, the "pilgrimages" proved to be "scandalous picnics." Nevertheless, the stance of the Catholic Diocese had not stopped the believers. Xavier wondered if the Coppersmith family would make a visit to ask the Virgin for help in locating their missing daughter.

The coach drove past snow covered farmland as Xavier, Attorney Tracy, and Sheriff Watermolen discussed the Coppersmith family's recent revelations. Xavier realized they were dealing with three different situations. First, the poisoning death of August Minsart. That morning, during the coach ride to the Coppersmith home, Xavier had shared the information Elvira had provided him and City Attorney Charles E. Vroman. That J.P. had murdered her husband, August Minsart, by mixing poison into his griddle cakes. Even if Elvira Soquet's information was true, the three men agreed, it was worthless unless she was still alive and could testify under oath. Attorney Tracy recommended they leave August Minsart's death alone for the time being. Xavier and Sheriff Watermolen concurred.

The second situation was the alleged poisoning death of J.P. Soquet's second wife, Esperance. The sheriff now had the sworn testimony of Mr. Coppersmith and the information from Mr. Lancelle and Mrs. Villiesse, which included J.P.'s alleged admission, "his woman" had been poisoned. To prove Esperance's death had been caused by poison rather than childbed fever, Sheriff Watermolen said they would need to disinter Esperance Soquet's grave and perform an autopsy on what might be left of her remains. He glanced beyond the trees toward Old Holy Cross Cemetery. The odds were, based on Pauline Villiesse's information, Esperance's remains had been removed from the grave. Nevertheless, the sheriff continued, that supposition had to be confirmed. District Attorney J.C. Neville would need to request a court order from a judge. But Watermolen added, the D.A could only act if a complainant reported Esperance's potential poisoning murder to law enforcement.

Attorney J.J. Tracy leveled his gaze at Sheriff Watermolen and said he would be the complainant. Although Tracy had lost credibility thirteen years ago by arresting Elvira Soquet for the poisoning death of her husband, Xavier was pleased that Tracy was ready to take on a different Soquet, namely Elvira's husband, J.P.

As the carriage squeaked and groaned, the three men addressed the third, most imminent, situation: the disappearance of Elvira Soquet. Xavier explained the measures Pauline Villiesse had already taken to locate her sister, but Xavier insisted that further investigation was required. Because Elvira Soquet had last been sighted by her neighbor on the Minsart property in the final days of December, Sherrif Watermolen believed there was probable cause to secure a search warrant for the Minsart house. He would complete the paperwork and have it signed by a judge.

Xavier gazed out the coach window. After years, harboring his own suspicions and the Belgian community's broader ones, he felt the right men were finally committed to bringing J.P. Soquet to justice.

Xavier stood beside Sheriff Watermolen the next day outside the Minsart home, a search warrant in hand. They knocked. As expected, no one answered. The sheriff broke a side window and shimmied inside. He opened the front door for Xavier and the two men walked through the first-floor rooms. Packing crates filled with household belongings were in the parlor and first-floor bedroom. Kitchen chairs were knocked over and dishes shattered. The foul smell of rotted food penetrated the air. The two men mounted the stairs to the second-floor bedrooms. Both were musty from disuse but in order.

After returning to the main floor, the sheriff lit a kerosene lantern and descended the wooden stairs to reach the root cellar. Xavier followed. A damp earthy scent blended with aromas of herbs, apples, and yeasty beer. Braided bunches of onions and garlic hung from the ceiling. The walls of uncut stones were sealed with mortar. A stack of wooden crates stood by one wall. Another stack had toppled over and some of the crates were in pieces.

Xavier's breath caught. On the dirt floor, near the toppled crates, he spied "bunches of hair" beside what could be blood. It appeared to Xavier as if a boot had tried to rub the dark reddish-brown substance into the dirt floor to cover up evidence.

Sheriff Watermolen located traces of what could be blood on the stone wall and on broken crates.

Xavier realized he was likely standing in a crime scene.

He and the sheriff collected as much evidence as possible. But Elvira Soquet was definitely not in the home, neither alive nor dead.

The two men located a hammer and nails and used the slats from the broken cellar crates to board up the shattered window. Xavier found a key hanging on a peg and used it to lock up the house.

Xavier planned to tell Pauline Villiesse what they had discovered. It disturbed him. He knew he had gotten in too deep. He wanted to bow out—to simply attend to his real estate business, his job as city assessor, and his wife and children. But Xavier had been involved with J.P. Soquet for too long; it was too late to turn back. It had become increasingly urgent for him to get justice for Esperance and Elvira.

·∞·

On the afternoon of Wednesday, February 16, 1887, Xavier waited beside his friend District Attorney J.C. Neville inside the Brown County Courthouse jail vestibule. Xavier fiddled with his pocket watch attached to a chain.

Over the past few days, local newspapers had printed articles about the mysterious disappearance of Elvira Soquet. That news had brought the Belgian community out of the woodwork with old stories about the Soquet family. Now that Alexis Coppersmith's daughter was missing, his fellow Belgians had decided to speak up, despite their collective fear of J.P. Soquet.

One Belgian neighbor after another had arrived at Xavier Martin's office. He translated while D.A. Neville transcribed the Belgians' allegations concerning J.P. Soquet's crimes and the shared confidences of Elvira Soquet. Whatever sins Elvira had committed in the past, the Belgian community had decided to put them aside to give the Coppersmith family their support.

Xavier shifted on his feet, waiting impatiently for Sheriff Watermolen's arrival.

D.A. Neville had considered the gathered evidence. Although he believed J.P. Soquet could be responsible for multiple crimes, Neville had decided to focus on one: the poisoning death of his second wife. Neville had presented that evidence to Justice V.B. Bromley who had issued a warrant for J.P.'s arrest for the first-degree murder of Esperance Soquet, on the 27th day of June, 1873.

But D.A. Neville had kept the arrest warrant a secret, fearing J.P. would flee.

The door to the jail vestibule opened and Sheriff Watermolen stepped in, a handcuffed J.P. Soquet beside him.

Xavier was relieved.

But when J.P.'s eyes zeroed in on Xavier, he felt a sudden cold dread.

·∞·

The next morning, Xavier walked one block from his office to the foot of Pine Street. The construction of the city's first Toboggan Slide was in progress. It would be forty feet high with three divisions and a stairway on either side. The incline length would be 180 feet long, descending to the frozen Fox River. Xavier knew Rudy and Albert, who were thirteen and eleven, were eager to use the slide. The *Gazette* had run ads which promised to "Prolong your life at least by 10 years by taking 20 rides on the Toboggan Slide."

As Xavier walked to the courthouse, he wondered if maybe he would even take a ride on the slide with his sons. Xavier was fifty-five and Augusta a mere thirty-five. He would not mind extending his life so he could spend more time with his precious family.

Xavier hoped, at least, he had lived long enough to see justice served for J.P. Soquet.

Inside the courtroom of Justice V.B. Bromley, J.P., dressed in his Sunday best to signal his financial stability, shuffled in beside Sheriff Watermolen. One of his attorneys, Mr. John H.M. Wigman, was present, as was District Attorney J.C. Neville. A *Daily Gazette* reporter sat beside Xavier, scratching down J.P.'s physical description: "A Belgian of medium stature, fully fifty years of age, with full, grizzled beard, and appearing to be a farmer in comfortable circumstances."

Justice Bromley turned to District Attorney Neville. The prosecutor said he had not had sufficient time to subpoena the State's witnesses due to the secrecy of J.P.'s arrest.

The justice said he understood. Given that, Bromley announced the prisoner's preliminary examination for the first-degree murder trial of his wife, Esperance Soquet, would be postponed until the following Wednesday.

Attorney John H.M. Wigman asked about his client's bail.

Justice Bromley said, as a justice of the peace, he had no authority to permit bail to a prisoner charged with first-degree murder. That request had to be heard by a Brown County Circuit Court judge.

Xavier was relieved. With any luck, that higher court judge would deny bail, and J.P. would stay locked up until his trial.

The community would feel safer.

So would he.

WISHFUL THOUGHTS

PAULINE

PAULINE AND HENRY used the key Xavier Martin had provided to enter the Minsart house. She was glad that J.P. would not suddenly show up. Pauline was amazed that the information she and her family had given to the authorities had led to J.P.'s arrest for his second wife's murder fourteen years after the fact. Pauline only prayed it was not too late for her sister, and that she might be found alive.

The prior week, Xavier had told Pauline about the disturbing evidence he and Sheriff Watermolen had found in the Minsart cellar. In bed that night, Pauline had lain awake in the darkness, her heart's powerful beat echoing in her ears. Pauline now recognized why her sister had waffled so much about initiating her divorce from J.P. Pauline should have seen it before. Elvira had rightly feared that as soon as she became a free woman, the "old man" would come for her. J.P. would never trust that she would remain silent about his crimes. And he would have done anything to keep her from speaking up.

Even so, Pauline would not give up hope. She could not. Perhaps Elvira had found a way to get away from J.P.

Inside the Minsart kitchen, Pauline gagged from the putrid odor of decaying food. Dishes and chairs were broken. Some sort of violent quarrel had clearly transpired within the house.

Henry carried a kerosene lantern down the stairs into the cellar, and Pauline followed. She closed her eyes as her feet touched the dirt floor. Pauline tried not to imagine what might have occurred inside the cellar's four walls. Xavier Martin had told her he had found hair and blood. Pauline wanted to believe his discoveries had some other explanation, some accident that had occurred, maybe even long before Martin Simonar had seen Elvira for the last time. Pauline could visualize her sister living in the Minsart house, all alone, drinking to drown her sorrows and grief. To refill her pint glass, she would have staggered down the cellar stairs and crossed to the beer keg against the far wall. Perhaps Elvira had tripped on the crates, scattering them across the dirt floor. Maybe she had fallen and cut her head, leaving traces of blood and hair.

Maybe. Pauline's mind grasped. Maybe her sister was still alive.

While she and Henry had lived with Elvira in the Minsart home, Elvira had shown Pauline where she had hidden her jewelry and money. Pauline walked over to the back wall containing a loose rock. She wiggled it out of its spot, and her shaky fingers reached inside. Pauline pulled out a cloth bag secured with a cord and managed to untie it. The bag contained a thick roll of greenbacks and jewelry.

Pauline stifled a sob and looked at Henry. They both understood what this meant: Elvira would not have disappeared without taking the cloth bag to start a new life. Elvira had to be dead.

Yet, until her body was found, Pauline told Henry, she still had to hold onto hope. Even if there had been an altercation between her sister and J.P. in the cellar, Elvira could have escaped. She was twenty years younger than J.P. and could outrun him. If Elvira had escaped, she would not have stayed in Brown County. She would have taken a train to someplace like Milwaukee or Menominee. Elvira would not know of J.P.'s arrest. She would not know she could safely return home.

It was possible, however unlikely, that she was out there, somewhere.

Inside the Brown County Courthouse on February 23, 1887, Ash Wednesday, Pauline and her two younger sisters, Fannie Vandenbusch and Flora Lancelle, sat together for J.P. Soquet's preliminary hearing. All three sisters were Catholic. Their foreheads and those of others in the courtroom were likely marked with a cross of ashes from early morning church services.

Justice Bromley sat behind the bench. He would determine whether there was probable cause to bind J.P. over for trial for the first-degree murder of his second wife, Esperance Soquet.

Pauline gazed over at J.P. Soquet sitting beside his attorneys, Mr. Hudd and Mr. Wigman. If only Pauline's sister, Elvira, could have been seated beside Pauline. Elvira would have been gloating about that devil, J.P., who might finally get his comeuppance. Still, Pauline knew, J.P. could easily weasel out of his first-degree murder charge. To convict him of poisoning his second wife, without any physical evidence to prove Esperance had even been poisoned, seemed extremely difficult to Pauline. J.P. had seasoned attorneys in Hudd and Wigman, both known for keeping their clients out of Waupun State Prison due to lack of evidence. In Elvira's 1874 first-degree murder case, when the State had accused her of poisoning her husband, the same attorneys had done just that.

Justice Bromley's courtroom was packed, mainly with Belgians from the country, including many from the Hannon family. Pauline knew the proceedings would be slow. Most of the witnesses could not understand English. The interpreter for Soquet's preliminary hearing would be Francois Crikelair, taking a break from his work of painting and repairing the Duck Creek Catholic Church and its steeple. Pauline was gratified her children had learned English in school. Since Pauline's arrival in Green Bay five months ago, she had been slowly learning the language, due to her seamstress business.

District Attorney John C. Neville first called Esperance Soquet's eighty-one-year-old father, Jean Joseph Hannon, to the stand. He testified to the June events of 1873 when his daughter had died soon after giving birth to her seventh child, a healthy little girl named Clara. The day after the birth, he said, his daughter had complained of an intense burning in her stomach. The following day, the pain intensified, and Esperance told her father she believed she was dying.

Mr. Hannon stifled sobs as he talked about Friday, June 27. He had held his daughter in his arms as she had taken her last breath at about four in the afternoon, while his wife had held their newborn granddaughter. The next morning Esperance's face and head had turned black and her body had bloated.

D.A. Neville asked Hannon what sort of conversations he had had with his son-in-law, the defendant, following Esperance's death.

"Soquet came and told me that Mrs. Soquet was getting black, and that he wished for $50 that she would not become black." Pauline could see the pain in Mr. Hannon's eyes. He seemed reluctant to continue, but the D.A. waited.

Some months after this, Mr. Hannon said that J.P. had come to his house and asked if he had heard anything about the movement on foot to disinter the remains of his wife, who was also Mr. Hannon's daughter. Hannon had told Soquet, no, but offered to go to the home of his sister, Mrs. Doyne, and ask her. She had been to town and might know something of the matter. "Mrs. Doyen had told me that there was a public rumor that Soquet's wife was going to be unburied. I told Soquet ... [and] he exclaimed, Marie, what shall I do?" Mr. Hannon had told Soquet, "Go with them when they do it." And J.P. had driven away.

Pauline could hear whispers in the courtroom as Esperance's elderly father, with the help of a cane, stepped down from the stand and took a seat beside his younger brother Philippe.

Anne Joseph Edwards, Philippe Hannon, and Son (Photo 268, Belgian-American Research Collection, University of Wisconsin- Green Bay Archives Department)

Pauline felt a pang of disappointment. Mr. Hannon should have told the authorities about his conversations with J.P. fourteen years ago. Although J.P. had not admitted he had poisoned Esperance, his comments and questions had hinted at that fact. But Pauline realized family ties had bound Mr. Hannon. He had already lost his daughter. No matter what J.P. might have done, J.P. was still the father to Mr. Hannon's seven grandchildren. They had already lost their beloved mother. Perhaps Mr. Hannon had not been able to bear the idea they would lose their father as well. Or, perhaps, Mr. Hannon had feared J.P.'s wrath, and who could blame him.

Whatever the case, Esperance's father had kept silent. Pauline knew she and her family had made the same choice. They had all been responsible for allowing J.P. to continue his reign of terror. Pauline regretted that choice more deeply with each passing day.

∞

In the afternoon session, Pauline and her sisters watched as their father Alexis Coppersmith took the stand. At seventy-six, he had feared he might not be alive to testify, but his health had improved. Pauline knew it would be difficult for her father to be on display before his fellow countrymen. The initial affair of Elvira and J.P. Soquet had prodded him with shame and anguish for more than a decade, and he knew his daughter's actions had initiated the devastation of the Hannon family.

Pauline's father testified that his daughter, Elvira, was J.P. Soquet's third wife, and that she had recently disappeared.

D.A. Neville nodded and asked Alexis about a conversation he had had with his former son-in-law, J.P. Soquet, back in the spring of 1874.

As Alexis testified how J.P. had said he would be "in for it," since his wife and August Minsart had been poisoned with the same kind of poison, Pauline listened to the commotion in the gallery.

"Now," her father said, "you've asked me enough questions. I must go and get a glass of beer." He looked up at Justice Bromley and said, "Got any beer, here?"

Everyone laughed, including the justice. Pauline realized her father was trying to hide his emotions. He was trying to suppress his worry about Elvira and what Soquet had done to her.

District Attorney Neville called his next witness, Mr. William Lancelle, and Pauline squeezed her youngest sister's hand. The testimony of Flora's husband mirrored what he had relayed to Xavier, the sheriff, and Mr. Tracy. Fannie's husband Peter Vandenbusch was sworn in next. He testified about the day his brother-in-law, August Minsart, had died, including J.P.'s reaction when a neighbor had sniffed the "medicine" bottle discovered in the kitchen.

The final witness called by District Attorney Neville was Dr. Andrew Munro, who had delivered Esperance Soquet's last child. He testified at length about the three visits he had made to the Soquet home prior to Esperance's death.

Pauline listened intently to his testimony as did the crowd. The physician provided insight into Esperance's symptoms leading up to her death. But Pauline did not know whether his observations pointed only to poisoning or perhaps to a disease like childbed fever.

J.P.'s attorney, Mr. Wigman, cross-examined each witness, aiming to challenge their testimony and to expose inconsistencies. The defense did not call any of their own witnesses.

Pauline wondered at that. But then again, who would they call other than J.P. Soquet? At this point, Pauline believed his attorneys might have felt it was too risky. Instead, their purpose had likely been to glean information from the State's witnesses, which would aid them in preparing for J.P.'s defense, if he was held over for trial.

Justice Bromley would now make his decision. He examined a document on the bench as everyone waited. He gazed out at J.P. Soquet and announced: As a justice of Brown County, he was convinced there was a reasonable basis to believe the defendant was guilty of his accused crime.

Pauline shared a delighted glance with her sisters as Justice Bromley bound J.P. Soquet over for trial. He said J.P.'s first-degree murder case would be placed on the Brown County Circuit Court docket for the spring term where the Honorable Samuel D. Hastings Jr. would preside.

Bromley said Judge Hastings would consider the defendant's application for bail. But that would not occur until Monday, February 28, five days away. Justice Bromley questioned whether offering bail to a prisoner arrested for first-degree murder was even legal.

J.P. slunk down in his chair while Pauline and her sisters lifted their heads in a show of family solidarity.

Their sister, Elvira, was missing. But Pauline vowed she would be present each day at J.P.'s trial. She believed Justice Bromley's decision to bind J.P. over for trial seemed promising. But thirteen years ago, at Elvira's preliminary hearing, the judge had done the same before D.A. Tracy had eventually dropped Elvira's case for lack of evidence.

Pauline realized the evidence at J.P.'s hearing had all been circumstantial. She knew District Attorney Neville had to do better than that to bring J.P. to justice. Pauline desperately hoped he would. For Elvira, for them all.

THE HUNT

XAVIER

ON MARCH 22, 1887, Xavier Martin rattled along in Sheriff Watermolen's open-air rig, warm robes across their laps. A half dozen carriages followed, each filled with deputies and volunteers dressed in warm overcoats, gloves, hats, and boots, ready for the elements. They were all headed toward the Soquet farm in the Preble township. Xavier knew the grave of Esperance Soquet still needed to be disinterred, but that task had been postponed until they searched the Soquet property.

About one month had passed since Justice Bromley had bound J.P. Soquet over for trial. Five days after the preliminary hearing, J.P.'s attorney, John H.M. Wigman, had appealed to Brown County Circuit Court Judge Samuel D. Hastings Jr., asking him to consider bail for his client. But as the weeks had passed, it appeared to Xavier that Judge Hastings had honored Sheriff Watermolen's request to delay the bail hearing until the ground had begun to thaw. This would give the sheriff sufficient time to search the Soquet farm for the remains of J.P.'s second and third wives: Esperance and Elvira.

Elvira had been missing for three months. Xavier, like most everyone, assumed she was dead. But he would not say that. Sheriff Watermolen feared if J.P. was released on bail, he would move his third wife's body, if she was in fact dead, and his second wife's remains from each of their current locations to spots where they would never be discovered. If the search party found Elvira's body, Soquet could be charged with her first-degree murder as well as Esperance's.

The carriage directly behind Xavier carried his fishing partner, Green Bay City Attorney Charles E. Vroman.

D.A. Neville had recognized that J.P. Soquet's case would be difficult to manage alone so he had asked Vroman to be his co-counsel. But so far, Brown County officials controlling the purse strings had not confirmed whether he would be compensated. Xavier knew his friend was not worried. If the county could not pay him, Vroman had told Xavier there were private citizens who would do so. It was imperative to have a powerful prosecution team in place to combat the formidable team of Hudd and Wigman.

All the carriages pulled up in front of the Soquet home. The sheriff and Xavier stepped out, as did Attorney Vroman. The latter carried a search warrant signed by Judge Samuel D. Hastings. The three men walked across the plank sidewalk, and Sheriff Watermolen knocked on the door. Jule Soquet answered it. J.P.'s son was twenty-one years of age, old enough to vote. His eighteen-year-old sister, Rose, was behind him. Jule confirmed they were the only two people living in the house while their father was in the Brown County jail.

Attorney Vroman provided Jule with the search warrant. Xavier, speaking in Walloon, explained its ramifications. He told Jule the men would be conducting a search of the home, the outbuildings, the barn, and the 160 acres of farmland owned by his family.

Walking back to the sheriff's rig, Xavier recalled that J.P. owned an additional forty acres of forested land near the Minsart farm, which Elvira had sold to her husband. Xavier told the sheriff he could locate the deed for that forested land and pinpoint its location. But both men agreed, virgin forested land would be nearly impossible to search. Hopefully, that would not be necessary.

The horses were tethered to the fence, and blankets placed over their backs. As Sheriff Watermolen organized the search party, Attorney Vroman told Xavier he could not stay to assist. Vroman had received information about a potential incident related to Elvira Soquet's disappearance. He said he needed to follow up and determine the validity of that information.

Curious about what Vroman was tracking, Xavier watched his friend depart. But that was not his concern today. He joined the search party in anticipation of finding the remains of J.P.'s second wife and perhaps also the body of his third wife, which could provide a devastating closure for the Coppersmith family.

Near dusk, Xavier returned to Sheriff Watermolen's carriage exhausted. He, the sheriff, his deputies, and volunteers had spent hours searching the home, outbuildings, and the barn, as well as combing the Soquet fields, spreading out in a line and walking every inch of the 160 acres. They had checked beneath fences, looked under bushes, and hefted rocks, all in hopes of finding a disturbed area, somewhere that a body might be buried.

There had been nothing.

Xavier was disappointed. But during the search, Sheriff Watermolen had pointed out a swamp near the residence. Elvira Soquet's body or Esperance Soquet's skeletal remains could be concealed within that murky spot. Watermolen planned to return as soon as the "frost was fairly out of the ground." That would be his next step, rather than tackling the forty acres of Soquet's forested land.

Six days later, Green Bay City Attorney Charles E. Vroman stopped into Xavier's office. Xavier hoped his friend might share the information he had been tracking about Elvira Soquet's disappearance, but Vroman had another matter on his mind. He was enraged. Vroman had just been at the courthouse for J.P.'s bail hearing. His attorney, Mr. Wigman, had argued his client had strong community ties, and, although J.P. had a prior criminal record, those offenses lacked the current offense's severity.

District Attorney Neville had argued J.P. should be denied bail for two reasons: the severity of his charged crime and the good chance he might try to escape. Nevertheless, Judge Hastings allowed J.P. his release on bail given he secured $6,000 in sureties (about $200,000 in current valuation).

Following the hearing, Vroman had listened outside the courthouse as a *State Gazette* reporter interviewed Attorney Wigman. He had told the young man he felt certain his client would be able to get the requisite sureties.

Over the next week, the Belgians who had provided information to the prosecution were "shaking in their boots" to see whether J.P. would raise enough for bail. Xavier feared if J.P. *was* released on bail, he would not only try to escape to avoid prosecution, but also come after those who were speaking up against him.

Xavier knew he was near the top of J.P.'s list. Xavier had been the translator at the Soquets' divorce meeting and trial. And J.P. still owed

Xavier $40 for those services. At the Soquets' last meeting in December of 1886, Xavier believed Elvira had accused J.P. of not only poisoning her former husband, August Minsart, but more importantly, J.P.'s second wife. Xavier would certainly be called to testify about Elvira's accusation at J.P.'s upcoming first-degree murder trial. If J.P. was out on bail, Xavier knew he would not be safe.

A week passed. So far, J.P. had been unsuccessful in securing the sureties of $6,000 for his release. On April 12, Xavier was included in the party that traveled out to Old Holy Cross Cemetery with D.A. Neville and Under-sheriff Gutbier. Since they had not found the remains of Esperance on the Soquet property, maybe the information about J.P. disinterring her body had been incorrect. Maybe Esperance was still in her coffin. The authorities had to disinter her remains—before J.P. could.

At the cemetery, the sexton, John Gonion, told the men he had dug Esperance Soquet's grave, and he could recall the general location where she had been buried. But nine months after her internment, he said he had noticed her grave had been disturbed.

The men walked around in the area Gonion pointed out. Xavier had been present at Esperance's burial, but with no marker he could not pinpoint the spot.

Dr. F.L. Lewis from Fort Howard had accompanied the party. If they located any remains, he was to transport them to Madison for analysis. But Dr. Lewis warned the group, Esperance's corpse would have undergone significant decomposition. In the casket, they would likely find only skeletal remains, clothing fibers, teeth, hair, and perhaps residual tissue. It was the last thing, the tissue, that could be analyzed for any traces of poison.

Gonion and two other men carefully dug in the area and located some remains but not the coffin of Esperance Soquet. An earthy, musty scent hovered in the air. They continued digging until they hit the lid of another coffin. After removing the dirt, Xavier could see the cover had been crushed by an ax or a similar implement and was tipped up at the side. When Gonion lifted the lid, Xavier could see the coffin was "entirely dry and free from any human remains."

They had found Esperance Soquet's coffin, and it had been empty, just as Pauline Villiesse had said it would be. Xavier was disheartened. J.P. was turning out to be just as vile as Xavier had feared.

In the soil around the outside of the coffin, Dr. Lewis discovered some small bones from what he thought would have been a hand. The under-sheriff questioned whether those tiny bones could be analyzed for poison. The doctor said no. If they did belong to Esperance Soquet, he understood she had potentially been poisoned for a span of only three to four days, between her child's birth on a Monday and Esperance's death on a Friday. That limited exposure would be insufficient for depositing poison in the bones. Still, under-sheriff Gutbier collected the bones to be placed into evidence.

A week later, Xavier sat in Judge Samuel D. Hastings courtroom, not as an interpreter, nor as a witness. Today he was simply an observer. The 1887 spring term of circuit court was in session. Judge Hastings' first action would be the formal arraignment of those Brown County jail prisoners held for probable cause. Among them was Jean P. Soquet. Xavier was drawn in by the crimes J.P. had committed, but Xavier also feared for his life. He felt the need to be aware of everything going on related to J.P. Soquet.

Xavier watched J.P. enter the courtroom beside an officer. They were close enough that Xavier could smell the unpleasant jail scent clinging to the man's clothes. Xavier was thankful that J.P. had been unsuccessful in securing the $6,000 in sureties to be released on bail. He walked briskly to one of the chairs reserved for prisoners. That routine seemed second nature to J.P. Over the years, Xavier knew he had repeated it many times.

When the clerk called J.P.'s name, he stood by the desk with Attorney Wigman as the clerk read J.P.'s rights and charges, which were interpreted by John Douville. J.P. was asked whether he understood his rights and the charges levied against him.

J.P. said he did.

Judge Hastings asked J.P. to enter his plea of guilty, not guilty, or no contest.

J.P.'s gruff voice said, "Not guilty," in English.

After so many court appearances, Xavier realized Soquet had mastered those two words, at least. Xavier looked at the man who had been a terror within the Belgian community for decades.

This time he would not be released with a slap on the hand.

This time he would not be released with a simple fine.

This time he would stand trial, and he would be fighting for his life.

Xavier was ready to do his part to fight for justice—for Esperance, for Elvira, for the Belgian community, and for himself.

PART III

THE TURNING POINT

(1887-1888)

CHANCE FOR JUSTICE

PAULINE

PAULINE ENJOYED the mild fifty-degree weather as she walked west on the Main Street plank sidewalk, heading toward the Brown County Courthouse on Friday, April 22, 1887. The air smelled and tasted fishy. Pauline's home was situated in the same block as the J.S. Johnson wholesale company which dealt in oysters and fish, fresh, salted, or smoked. She crossed the East River Bridge. Along the banks, white and yellow wildflowers grew amid the carcasses dumped by nearby butcher shops.

Pauline felt a sense of purpose knowing she was enroute to attend the first-degree murder trial of J.P. Soquet. She had resolved to be present each day to bear witness to the proceedings, speak her piece, and hopefully watch justice upheld. Pauline's married daughter Flora would watch Pauline's five-year-old Frank for the length of the trial while three of her children attended school and the other two worked.

To Pauline's left was the Reis Hotel, situated at 1148 Main Street where the stagecoach from Bay Settlement made a stop. She walked past E. Schilling company, a wholesale dealer in butter, eggs, and produce. The Schillings also ran a retail storefront which carried general merchandise and farm produce. That was where Pauline shopped. She had discovered living in Green Bay was far easier than surviving in the country. Everything was in walking distance or a short buggy ride away. Like their Main Street neighbors, the Villiesse family kept a few chickens, a cow, and a horse, and Pauline and her two daughters, Delia, seven, and Philomine, twelve, maintained a backyard garden. But all the major farming chores had disappeared.

Henry's new profession was broom making. He designed, constructed, and restored various types of brooms for homes and businesses. Their fourteen-year-old son, Jerome, helped his father select the materials, assemble the broom head, and attach its handle. Pauline's eldest son, Anton, was a wheelsman on a ship. With the money Pauline and Henry had made from the sale of their farm, and the steady pay the two of them and their children contributed each week, their family was getting along nicely.

Pauline crossed Clay Street. The rental home her sister, Elvira, had purchased from Xavier Martin years ago was to Pauline's right. Pauline collected the rent each month and put it aside for the home's taxes and for the taxes on Elvira's other properties. She did so each month with hope and trepidation, and occasionally with frustration at her sister for leaving Pauline with this responsibility.

Pauline realized her sister had been a "bad woman." Nevertheless, even with all of Elvira's faults, she had been the sibling Pauline felt closest to, the one Pauline had confided in, the one Pauline had shared her joys and sorrows with. Pauline blinked back tears. She missed her sister.

Wagons and rigs rumbled past as Pauline turned south on Webster Avenue then west on Cherry Street. At the completion of her mile and a half walk, she climbed the flight of two dozen marble courthouse steps. On the landing, she opened the massive wooden door and stepped into the second-floor entrance hall. Pauline had been inside the impressive building numerous times, yet she still felt a sense of awe. Inside the three-story brick structure was where justice was carried out. Pauline continued up another flight of marble stairs. She entered the wood-paneled courtroom of Judge Samuel D. Hastings Jr., where Pauline hoped J.P. Soquet would be convicted of poisoning his second wife.

Judge Samuel D. Hastings Jr. (History of Brown County, Commemorative Biographical Record)

The judge sat behind the bench, dressed in dark robes and wearing wire-framed spectacles. He had practiced law for fifteen years in Madison and Green Bay prior to winning his current judgeship position in 1883. His opponent had been Attorney John C. Neville, now the Brown County District

Attorney, and in fact it was Neville who would represent the State in the Soquet trial along with City Attorney Charles E. Vroman. Hastings was recognized to be a man of ability and "a gentleman of the broadest urbanity and dignity." He had never been "involved in questionable practices either as a lawyer or a citizen."

J.P. Soquet sat beside his attorneys, Mr. Wigman and Mr. Hudd. Pauline knew the grave of J.P.'s second wife had recently been exhumed. As Pauline had expected, the casket had been found empty. To convict J.P. of poisoning Esperance without any physical evidence would be a high hurdle for the prosecution to overcome. She feared Soquet would walk away from this trial a free man. That fear strengthened her resolve to be there, to do what she could, and to hope her sister had not suffered the same fate as Esperance.

Pauline wanted to believe Elvira could still be alive, but she found it difficult to believe it could be true. Pauline prayed each night that her sister would suddenly return and explain her four month absence. Unless Elvira had left Wisconsin, Pauline believed her sister would have heard about J.P.'s arrest and unsuccessful attempt to get bail, and that she would have come home.

Pauline's brother-in-law, John Villiesse, was seated in the courtroom gallery. Hardly a seat was left vacant. She reached his row and squeezed in front of other seated spectators where barnyard scents and industrial fumes were trapped in the fibers of their clothes. Pauline settled on the wooden bench in the tight quarters beside John.

While living in West De Pere for two decades, John had become proficient in English. He said the attorneys had just completed the selection of twelve jurors, which had been going on since noon the previous day. John had witnessed the entire process. Judge Hastings had introduced the lawyers to the first group of sixty potential jurors the prior day. Those men had been randomly called to the courtroom from Brown County's citizens registered to vote.

John said one of J.P.'s lawyers, Mr. Wigman, had immediately given notice that the defense needed thirty additional minutes to complete an affidavit requesting a change of venue. Wigman had told the judge the affidavit would show why the Soquet trial should not take place in Brown County due to the many local newspaper articles which had incited prejudice against the defendant.

Pauline was startled and confused, but John told Pauline not to worry. The entire trial would be held in Green Bay as expected. Yesterday, Judge Hastings had refused to give J.P.'s attorneys the necessary time to submit the affidavit, infuriating Attorney Wigman.

Following that, Judge Hastings had instructed the attorneys to begin the jury selection process. But after five hours, only one juror, deemed to be unprejudiced, had been selected. That morning, sixty additional potential jurors had been called and questioned. The last juror had finally been secured just before Pauline's arrival. The panel consisted of five jurors from the town of Lawrence, three from West De Pere, two from the town of De Pere, and two from the city of De Pere. None of them, John said, were Belgians, and all of them lived in the southern-most section of Brown County, a good distance from the Bay Settlement area.

Pauline gazed at the twelve men sitting in the jury box as John provided Pauline background on three of them. John first pointed out Mr. J.H. LeRoy, who looked to be about thirty-five. He owned a farm near Dickinson Road in the town of De Pere. In addition to general farming, LeRoy raised stock and ran a threshing machine. He had served as city assessor, school director, and school treasurer. John said LeRoy was well thought of and should be an unbiased juror.

John next identified Mr. Orin S. Kittell whom John knew through the blacksmith trade. The selected juror, about fifty years of age, was a prosperous farmer in the De Pere township. His grandfather had fought in the Revolutionary War, and Kittell had served in the Civil War.

Last, John pointed out Mr. William Gow. He looked to be about seventy, and Pauline thought he must be the oldest man on the panel. John said Gow had been born in Scotland and arrived in De Pere nearly thirty years ago. He owned a profitable wagon making business and was well-respected in the community, having served on the De Pere city council.

Pauline believed nobody could claim those three men were not reputable. It made sense to Pauline that the selected jury contained no men from the Belgian farming community. Close familial ties and rumors would have made it difficult for a Belgian juror to be impartial, she knew. The newly selected jurors would all have clean slates in front of them in regard to J.P. Soquet. Without preconceived notions, they would listen to the trial evidence to determine whether Pauline's despicable former brother-in-law was guilty or not. She felt confident the truth would come out.

The courtroom quieted as the bailiff announced: the case of Wisconsin vs. Jean Philippe Soquet would begin.

Pauline noticed that none of J.P.'s children were in the courtroom. She believed Rose and Jule, still living in the Soquet home, had no ill-feelings toward their father. Maybe J.P. had not wanted them to attend the trial so their belief in his innocence would not change.

As Judge Hastings turned to D.A. Neville, and told him to proceed with the prosecution's opening statement, Pauline noticed Xavier Martin seated across the aisle from her. Pauline's eyes caught Xavier's, and he gave her a nod. Then she turned her full attention back to the attorneys at the prosecution table, in anticipation of the State's opening statement.

FIVE CRIMES

XAVIER

XAVIER MARTIN gazed up at Judge Samuel D. Hastings from the gallery. Since Xavier would be a witness, his fifty-seven-year-old brother, Constant Martin, would be serving as translator for the Belgian witnesses. Xavier was surprised and worried when Green Bay City Attorney Charles E. Vroman, Xavier's fishing companion, stood to give the opening statement, rather than his friend D.A. John C. Neville.

In a criminal trial, Xavier knew the District Attorney, elected and paid by Brown County, should be the lead attorney, or the "first chair," responsible for the overall strategy, the opening statement, and closing argument. The attorney in the "second chair" assisted with tasks like examining witnesses, organizing exhibits, or handling the jury selection and had to negotiate funding from Brown County or some other source. The legal team for the State appeared to have flipflopped, and he did not know what that could mean. Mr. Wigman and Mr. Hudd, shaking their heads, were obviously disturbed as well.

Judge Hastings also seemed confused. He asked Attorney Vroman whether Brown County was paying him to assist D.A. Neville in prosecuting the case.

Vroman said, "No sum has been stated, nor do I understand that there is any money raised, as yet ... [But] I expect to be paid something for my time here."

Judge Hastings frowned. "[So], I understand you expect compensation from some source, but you don't know where it is coming from?"

"Yes. That is about it."

The brows of Judge Hastings furrowed. Nevertheless, he told Attorney Vroman to carry on.

Xavier knew the sister of Judge Hastings' wife was married to Charles Vroman's law partner, Mr. George G. Greene. Perhaps that connection provided Xavier's friend some leeway with the judge. Like most of those gathered, Hastings seemed ready to begin the proceedings.

Vroman stood before the jury and launched into the prosecution's opening statement. He said it would be a roadmap to help the jury understand the case's key issues and how each piece of evidence would fit into the larger picture. To do so, Vroman said the prosecution would provide evidence to tie the defendant, J.P. Soquet, to five crimes.

Xavier was shocked by his friend's bold statement. J.P. was charged with the single crime of murdering his second wife, Esperance. Xavier and many others certainly believed J.P. was responsible for other crimes, but even so, the sole purpose of this trial was to secure a guilty verdict for the first-degree murder of Esperance Soquet. Xavier thought the best path was to stay focused. Yet, as Vroman charged the defendant with his first crime—having had an intimate affair with Elvira Minsart—Xavier understood his friend's strategy was to provide motive for Esperance's poisoning death.

When Vroman charged the defendant with his second crime, of poisoning August Minsart, Xavier was dismayed. Fourteen years ago, Attorney J.J. Tracy had tried to tie August's poisoning death to Elvira Soquet and failed. Xavier did not believe the prosecution should be going down that rabbit hole again. Still, he could tell Vroman had the jurors' full attention. His hold on them grew tighter when he charged J.P. with his third crime: "A brutal course of conduct toward his second wife, Esperance Soquet." If Vroman's assertion was true, Xavier realized that upcoming evidence could provide insight into the defendant's troubled relationship with Esperance, another motive for poisoning her.

The fourth crime Attorney Vroman accused the defendant of was poisoning his second wife, Esperance Soquet. Here, Xavier felt Vroman was on solid ground. The entire trial should be focused on that charge—the only one J.P. was on trial for.

Vroman finally charged the defendant of his fifth crime, of killing his third wife, Elvira Soquet. Again, Xavier was dismayed. That charge was especially dangerous for the prosecution to introduce at trial. He hoped the State would not sacrifice justice by refusing to stay single-mindedly focused on the charge at hand.

As Vroman continued in his opening statement, he brought Xavier into the storyline, making Xavier's stomach twist, though Vroman did not mention him by name. Vroman said that Elvira Soquet, during her divorce pendency, had charged the defendant with poisoning their former spouses: August Minsart and Esperance Soquet. Attorney Vroman said Elvira had even described to him personally, through an interpreter, how the defendant had murdered her former husband, August. How the defendant had "mixed poison with some griddle cakes" and fed them to August who had been "sick abed." And who had died two hours later.

Xavier gazed over at the defendant's table. J.P.'s attorneys seemed livid. They knew nothing about this information concerning their client, partly because Xavier had neglected to translate it to Mr. Hudd during that December divorce meeting.

Xavier refocused on Attorney Vroman who said that while Elvira Soquet had been the defendant's third wife, that information could not have been used as evidence. But the defendant had known, when her divorce was granted, she would become a possible witness and with her testimony, the defendant's conviction would be certain. Without hesitation, Vroman asserted, the defendant had murdered his third wife Elvira Soquet on the evening of December 31, 1886, only four months ago.

Xavier's eyes widened at that accusation and his body shot up straight. The crowd hushed, then whispers broke out.

But there was more. Attorney Vroman said: "Elvira was in the house," owned by herself and her former husband. And the defendant came there. "And there was another man there, assisting Elvira to pack up the little things she had there in that house." The defendant then "broke in the door," and he asked, "'Who is here?' and was told by the man, 'Your wife is here.'" And the defendant said, "'My wife, she must die, and you, too.'" Vroman paused for effect before he concluded the dramatic scenario by saying, "The man rushed out of the house, [and] Elvira was heard to scream for help, and Elvira has disappeared from that day to this."

Xavier was stunned. Apparently, that last information had been what Vroman had hinted at on the organized search day for Elvira Soquet's body. Whomever this man was, the one who had assisted Elvira in packing up her belongings, would have to be a trial witness. While

Xavier was keenly interested in this revelation, the trial's focus should not be on Elvira Soquet and her disappearance. Xavier's overzealous friend had strayed from the trial's purpose. And Xavier was terrified that Vroman's decision to do so would hurt the State's case. Xavier wanted J.P. behind bars, even if his crimes were not all accounted for.

Vroman said in closing the evidence the State would provide would establish the defendant's guilt beyond a reasonable doubt. Xavier's friend looked pleased as he took his seat.

After all the prosecution's passion and fanfare, the opening statement by the defense was subdued and brief. Attorney Hudd, attired in a "Prince Albert coat and white cravat with an immaculate shirt front," wanted the jury to remember there were two sides to every story. He and Attorney Wigman were ready to provide the defendant's side, the one that was the truth. He spoke in general terms about the case and sat down.

It appeared to Xavier that J.P.'s attorneys had not deemed it prudent to outline the strategy they would use for their client's defense—probably a wiser strategy than the prosecution's, Xavier feared.

NEIGHBORS' REVELATIONS

PAULINE

ON THE MORNING of Monday April 15, 1887, Pauline sat in the courtroom without her brother-in-law. She felt less settled on her own, and she would miss his translation for unfamiliar English words and his commentary. His work would not permit him to attend the entire trial. Pauline had worked late into the evening to keep up with her seamstress business while Attorney Vroman's opening statement had circled inside her head. She was not sure what to make of it all.

He had mentioned Elvira's revelation about the arsenic tainted griddle cakes that J.P. had fed to August when he was "sick abed." Pauline believed her sister would have told her about that information if it had been true. Mr. Vroman had also mentioned a man who had helped Elvira pack up her belongings at the Minsart home on December 31, 1886, which had astonished Pauline. Maybe that man would be a trial witness and could shed some light on Elvira's disappearance. Pauline could only hope so.

Constant Martin
(Courtesy of John Mertens)

Pauline watched as Esperance Soquet's father, Mr. J.J. Hannon, was sworn in along with Xavier Martin's brother Constant, who was acting as interpreter.

For many years, Constant Martin had lived in the Red River township along with Pauline. He had been the Red River postmaster, town clerk, justice of the peace, and school superintendent for Kewaunee County. In 1870, he had tragically lost his entire family—a wife and two children—likely to an infectious disease. Soon after, he had moved to Green Bay to partner with his brother, Xavier, in his real estate business. Eventually, he remarried and struck out on his own, launching an insurance business. He and Xavier had both achieved the Belgian immigrant's dream of becoming well-respected and financially successful. Pauline admired them.

Now that Pauline knew rudimentary English, she listened patiently to Mr. Hannon's examination by D.A. Neville, translated by Constant Martin into Walloon, and Mr. Hannon's answers translated back into English. He had testified at J.P.'s preliminary hearing, but new details emerged, centering on Esperance's symptoms and appearance leading up to her death. Mr. Hannon testified his daughter had not yet recovered from confinement after the birth of her child when she was seized with sudden pain and intense burning in the stomach. A few days later, she died. Hannon said he had been at the Soquet home on and off during her illness from Tuesday until Friday, but his wife had been present the entire time to help with the cooking and caring for the new baby. Pauline could see the pain in his face, even after all these years.

D.A. Neville asked Mr. Hannon whether he had heard his daughter making "any noise, hawking or otherwise?"

Attorney Hudd objected, saying the question was leading, but Judge Hastings allowed Hannon to answer.

Mr. Hannon said, "I cannot tell." He also testified he had not seen his daughter vomit, which Pauline believed was not the answer D.A. Neville had wanted by the expression on his face.

Then the D.A. elicited the same testimony from Mr. Hannon as he had given at the preliminary hearing about J.P.'s worry when Esperance's face had turned black. Also, J.P.'s agitation in December of 1873 concerning the rumors that August Minsart's remains had contained poison, and that the authorities planned to dig up Esperance's body as well.

Pauline could hear whispers in the courtroom, as she sat in silence.

Attorney Hudd stood for cross-examination for the defense. He first asked Mr. Hannon about his wife, whose name was not on the witness list. Was there a reason Mrs. Hannon would not be testifying at the trial? Afterall, she would have been the most knowledgeable about Esperance's symptoms and everything that had occurred between the child's birth and Esperance's death.

Hannon admitted his wife would have been the best witness to testify about his daughter's agonizing situation. But sadly, during the past few years, Mrs. Hannon had lost her ability to communicate and was deemed an "imbecile."

Pauline listened as Mr. Hannon was subjected to a rigid cross-examination by Mr. Hudd, but Mr. Hannon did not retract anything he had said. He was finally dismissed.

Pauline felt frustration, as she had after his preliminary hearing testimony. Esperance's father should have told the authorities about his conversations with J.P. back in December of 1873. If Mr. Hannon had done so, J.P. would likely have been arrested before he had had the chance to marry Pauline's sister. Given that, Elvira would have been considered a competent witness to testify against that devil, not only for Esperance's poisoning death, but for the poisoning death of Elvira's husband. Justice could have been served years ago, before all that Elvira had suffered.

The second witness called by the prosecution was Joseph Everard. The large, square-shouldered Belgian farmer testified he had been present at the Soquet home shortly before Esperance's death. While he had been there, he said, Esperance had vomited once.

D.A. Neville asked Mr. Everard if he had observed anything regarding the treatment J.P. "had accorded his wife on her death bed?"

Everard recalled one instance when Mrs. Soquet had risen up from her bed and complained of "burning pains in her breast." The defendant had roughly pushed his wife back onto the bed and said, "You must die; all women are dying."

A rumble of voices filled the gallery. Pauline was appalled to hear those words, and yet she could easily imagine J.P. saying them. She looked over at the jurors who were frowning.

D.A. Neville asked Everard about an event which had occurred at the home of Mrs. Henry Villiesse, the sister-in-law of the defendant, when Everard and the defendant had been arrested.

Pauline tensed. Everard's eyes were on her. Pauline would never forget that night when J.P. had assaulted her. After six years, the jagged scar from her elbow to her hand was still clearly visible.

Everard relayed how angry Mrs. Villiesse had been. She had accused the defendant of poisoning his second wife, Esperance Soquet, and August Minsart, the husband of his third wife, Elvira Soquet. Everard said Mrs. Villiesse had also told J.P., "You know you have unburied your wife, rascal that you are." Everard said J.P. had offered to pay Mrs. Villiesse $35 if she would remain silent about the matter.

Pauline was pleased that Everard had told the truth about her frightening incident. Years ago, at J.P.'s preliminary hearing for the charge of assault and battery, Everard had feared J.P.'s retribution and kept quiet, but no longer. Maybe this time J.P. would pay.

Neville sat down and Mr. Hudd stood. Pauline believed J.P.'s attorneys viewed themselves as important men, armed with learning, out to defend their embattled client against the hand of the State. Pauline both respected and resented their entitlement. Attorney Hudd readily seized upon the fact that Everard had once been in a threshing machine partnership with the defendant, which had been dissolved. Mr. Hudd asked Everard for the reason behind that.

Everard acknowledged some trouble had existed between J.P. and him "which had not been harmonized." Mr. Hudd asked whether the two men's trouble had occurred after the defendant and his son, Jule, discovered Everard in a compromising position with the defendant's third wife, Elvira Soquet. Everard indignantly denied the accusation, yet Pauline could not put such an act past her sister. Pauline was glad Everard was unwilling to say more, as it would likely shame both his family and hers.

After Mr. Hudd repeatedly asked Everard about his earlier testimony, that he had actually witnessed Esperance vomit, Everard seemed flustered and admitted, "I will not say she vomited."

J.P.'s neighbor, Christine Simonar, testified she had stopped at the defendant's home on the Thursday before Esperance's death, and Christine had heard J.P. say, "[Esperance] must die." Another witness named Polidore Williams testified he had run into J.P. and his wife three weeks before her death. Polidore had asked the couple where they were headed. When J.P. had told Polidore he would be taking Esperance around for the last time, "as he expected her to die soon," Polidore had been stunned.

Pauline was disturbed by the neighbors' testimony. So many people could have reported their suspicions earlier, but nobody, including Pauline, had done so. The neighbors had been afraid of J.P., and Pauline and her family had believed they were protecting Elvira from her alleged crime and its ramifications. Pauline regretted her choices, and it seemed like the others did, too.

Rosalie Williams, a first cousin to Esperance, did not seem intimidated by J.P. as she testified about the way he had mistreated his second wife. While Esperance had been pregnant with their sixth child, Rosalie said, J.P. had sworn constantly at Esperance. And even when Esperance had been far along, he had driven her out into the field and marked out the work she had to do, and J.P. had told Esperance that if she failed to perform that work, within the specified time, he would "pound her."

Pauline sat back. Rosalie's testimony was the evidence the prosecution had promised to provide to prove J.P. Soquet's third crime of "a brutal course of conduct toward his wife." Pauline realized the Soquets' interaction had occurred about three years before Esperance's death. Eighteen months later, J.P. had started his affair with her sister. Maybe J.P. and Esperance had been on poor terms for a number of years prior to Esperance's death. Maybe J.P. had tired of the woman who had borne him six children. Maybe J.P. had had his eyes set on her sister for many years, the fresh-faced Elvira, only twenty-six, to replace his forty-one-year-old wife. Pauline wondered at it all, but she despaired. What did it matter now that her sister was missing?

D.A. Neville asked whether Rosalie had visited Esperance Soquet during the days leading up to her death?

"I was ... at the house just after the birth of Mrs. Soquet's child, and she said she was well indeed. She had never been better just after a child birth." Rosalie had stopped over again two days later, "and found that lady sick in bed. Her face was very white, and when I expressed wonder at this, Mr. Soquet said she had a fever."

In Mr. Hudd's cross-examination, Rosalie confirmed she had not witnessed Esperance vomiting when she had been at the Soquet home.

But the next witness, Mrs. Mary LeCoque, a first cousin to Esperance Soquet who kept a saloon in Green Bay, said J.P. had told her, "Mrs. LeCoque, my wife has vomited, and I think she is going to die." J.P. had told Mary those words soon after she had arrived on Thursday, one day before Esperance's death. Mary said she had watched J.P. force his wife to eat a kind of "gruel," even when Esperance had complained that swallowing hurt her. J.P. had carried the gruel out of the room that Esperance had not finished. He had also carried away a bowl that

Mary believed to be Esperance's vomit.

Pauline had eyed J.P. Soquet during Mrs. LeCoque's testimony. His chair had tilted forward as he had watched her intently. She had been the only witness who had testified that J.P. had served his wife gruel, which Pauline believed could have been doctored with arsenic.

Pauline walked back to her Main Street home that night. She mulled over the day's events and wondered what would happen as the trial progressed. The neighbors had testified, but they were not experts who knew the symptoms of arsenic poisoning. Would it be enough? Pauline's sister had accused J.P. of poisoning his wife. Yet Pauline believed the defense could provide a believable alternative: that Esperance Soquet had died from childbed fever. Pauline knew of many women the infection had killed. But she doubted, as did so many others, that childbed fever had killed Esperance.

MEDICAL TESTIMONY

XAVIER

ON TUESDAY MORNING, April 26, 1887, Xavier was lucky to find a seat in the crowded spectator section of the Brown County Courthouse. The Soquet trial was drawing attention, not only within Brown County, but across the state and beyond. A lady next to Xavier said there were reporters in the courtroom from Madison, Milwaukee, and even Chicago.

District Attorney John C. Neville called Dr. Andrew Munro to the stand. He was the physician who had attended to J.P.'s wife during the birth of their last child and Esperance's subsequent illness. Xavier knew the Scotsman, born near Glasgow. They were both fifty-five-years-old, but Munro looked a decade older, due to the physician's chronic alcohol abuse. Munro's face was puffy with purplish spider veins around his cheeks and nose.

Dr. Munro testified that he had made three visits to Esperance Soquet before she had died. The first had been on Sunday for the birth of her child. When he had left Esperance in the early hours of Monday morning, she had been "doing nicely."

Munro's second visit had been on the Tuesday following the birth. Dr. Munro had returned to the Soquet home per the defendant's request. The defendant had told Dr. Munro, through an interpreter, that his wife had been complaining of burning pains in her stomach and a burning sensation in her throat and mouth. When Dr. Munro arrived on that Tuesday, he had touched Esperance, and she had shrunk away from him. Her pulse had been weak. Overall, there had been a general irritation of her entire system, especially in her stomach and abdomen. Dr. Munro had checked Esperance's uterus, and it had been normal. He had prescribed powders of bismuth and morphine for Esperance, which he had provided from his medical bag.

Dr. Munro testified that on his third visit, Esperance had been weaker still and was suffering from frequent purging of the bowels. Her face had been red and swollen, her eyes, unnatural, and her demeanor had indicated excruciating pain. Since Esperance could not speak English, Munro said she had pantomimed to him, pointing at Mr. Soquet as he had left the room. Munro said Esperance had looked like she was begging for mercy, taking his hand and kissing it. Dr. Munro had examined Esperance's uterus again, and it had been normal. At that point, Munro had wondered whether the defendant's wife was suffering from some sort of corrosive poisoning. Munro had examined the cooking utensils but found nothing.

D.A. Neville asked Dr. Munro, "What are the symptoms of arsenical poisoning?"

Attorney Wigman objected. He said the witness had not been shown to be an expert.

Judge Hastings agreed, sustaining the objection, until the prosecution could further examine Dr. Munro's qualifications.

D.A. Neville asked Dr. Munro, "Are you a member of any medical society?"

"Yes. Brown County ... for ten or twelve years."

"Graduate of any medical college?"

"No." But Munro said he had studied at Glasgow University and earned a nonmedical degree in Edinburgh. In 1862, he had arrived in Canada and practiced medicine with his brother, John, who had a medical degree. Two years later, Dr. Munro had arrived in Green Bay, and he had practiced medicine ever since.

"Has [your practice] covered cases of poisoning?"

"Not that I remember."

At Dr. Munro's admission, Xavier frowned.

"Have you made a study of that branch of practice, as well as other branches, and in the same way?"

"Just in the same way, yes."

"State whether a knowledge of poisons and their effects is a part of the knowledge of a practicing physician."

"It certainly is."

D.A. Neville turned to Judge Hastings. Evidently, the judge was satisfied with Munro's credentials, because he said, "You may state ... the symptoms of arsenical poisoning."

Mr. Wigman objected again, stating the witness had not shown himself qualified. But Judge Hastings overruled the objection.

Dr. Munro finally testified the symptoms of arsenical poisoning could include abdominal pain, nausea, vomiting, bowel purging, hawking, chest pain, shortness of breath, sore throat, abnormal heart rhythm, and red and swollen skin.

D.A. Neville crossed his arms and nodded. He asked Dr. Munro, after his three visits to the Soquet home, whether the defendant had contacted him again.

Dr. Munro said Mr. Soquet had traveled to Green Bay the next day and located Munro at the Main Street tavern of Peter J. Anhauser. Soquet had asked Munro to accompany him back to his house to see his wife, but Munro had refused to go. "I told Soquet, and the crowd, there was no use of my going."

D.A. Neville asked why Dr. Munro had refused.

"I declined to go under the circumstances. I knew I would be damned if I would go. I said that $5 were very handy, and Soquet paid me each time, but I would not go for $500 now. Because there were more potent agencies seemingly at work than my little powders. And I declined to have anything more to do with Esperance Soquet's situation. I was getting made a fool of, some way or another. That was about the burden of my conversation. I declined to go and gave my reason."

Xavier and the crowd sat there in hushed silence, all straining to hear each syllable of Dr. Munro's accusatory testimony.

"And what did the defendant say or do?"

"Well, he talked Belgian, and that beat me."

"Was there any part of that which you understood?"

"I understood the latter part, that he concluded to go and get another doctor. I think that was the result, only a few minutes of conversation, a minute or two."

"Did you, in any language that you used in that conversation, charge this man with having murdered his wife?"

"Objection!" Mr. Hudd said, the question was leading.

Judge Hastings told the district attorney, "The question is objectionable in that shape."

Neville reworded the question: "What did he say, with reference to that idea, the language as near as you can tell?"

Mr. Hudd objected again, and the judge overruled.

"Well," Munro said, "I can't give the exact words now. But the inference was plain. That I considered he, or somebody else, was prescribing something for his wife. Soquet's reply was in French, so I knew nothing [the defendant] said. There was an interpreter, but he didn't interpret what I said nor the answer back." Neville nodded and took his seat.

J.P.'s defense attorney, Mr. T.R. Hudd, stood to cross-examine Dr. Munro. Hudd first asked Dr. Munro about his frequent visits to local taverns and saloons. Dr. Munro admitted he spent time in local drinking establishments such as Hogan's Saloon and the Main Street tavern of Peter J. Anhauser. Hudd's eyes drifted over toward the jury box, as if to measure the jurors' reaction, then he refocused on Dr. Munro. "Have you had a case of arsenical poisoning to treat yourself, individually, as a physician?"

"No."

"Have you ever been present at a person's death when you knew he had died from the effects of irritant poisoning?"

"No."

"Then all you know about the symptoms of arsenical or irritant poisoning ... is from theory, from your knowledge as a student of medicine?"

"And from books and from reading scientific works upon that question."

"Not from any practical observation of your own?"

"No."

Attorney Hudd paused, letting Munro's testimony sink in. Then he asked the doctor about his second visit to Esperance, when she had complained of burning in her throat and stomach.

Munro confirmed he had given her powders of bismuth for her stomach issues and morphine for her pain.

Attorney Hudd said he understood arsenic was commonly found in bismuth powders.

Munro confirmed that was true if the powders were not pure. The elements of arsenic and bismuth were often found together within the ore deposits mined for bismuth.

Attorney Hudd nodded, giving Dr. Munro a knowing smile and asked whether the symptoms, he had observed in Esperance, could also occur in cholera? Dr. Munro confirmed some of Esperance's symptoms could occur in cholera such as an upset stomach and vomiting, dehydration, purging of the bowels, irritable behavior, and an irregular heartbeat.

Mr. Hudd asked about puerperal fever, or childbed fever, and whether its symptoms were also similar to arsenic poisoning?

Dr. Munro said, "No," the symptoms were not similar. In puerperal fever, Munro said the symptoms typically included a high fever, chills, lower abdominal pain, difficulty urinating, and the possibility of foul-smelling vaginal discharge.

Before assisting Esperance Soquet with the birth of her child, Mr. Hudd asked whether Dr. Munro had been involved with any recent cases of puerperal fever.

Dr. Munro said he might have had one or two cases within ten or twelve hours before assisting Esperance Soquet with her birth. But, Dr. Munro interjected, that fact would have no bearing on Esperance's case. He had already stated her symptoms were not similar to those seen in puerperal fever.

Mr. Hudd still charged ahead. "As a physician ... don't you know there is a possibility of carrying [puerperal fever] from one sick body to another?"

D.A. Neville objected to relevance, and Judge Hastings sustained. But Xavier could see the damage had been done.

At being forced to change his line of questioning, Mr. Hudd's mouth formed a tight line. He said that other witnesses had stated that Esperance's face had turned black soon after her death. Hudd asked Dr. Munro whether he had observed that condition in other deaths.

Munro testified a darkened face on a deceased individual was primarily due to livor mortis, the pooling of blood due to gravity after circulation stopped. That process would begin within an hour of death and become well-defined in a few hours. Blood settled in the lowest part of the body, causing a discoloration which could appear as dark purplish or blackish areas, particularly on the face, if it was facing down. Dr. Munro confirmed a discolored or black face would be no particular evidence of poison.

Hudd firmly nodded before he sat down.

D.A. Neville asked Dr. Munro a final question: In his expert opinion, as a physician, what did he believe caused Esperance Soquet's death.

Dr. Munro said he believed the defendant's wife had been poisoned with arsenic. Munro added that he had announced that loudly to a number of people at the tavern when J.P. had come for Dr. Munro the last time. The doctor said he had even told the tavern owner, Peter Anhauser, to notify the District Attorney.

As Dr. Munro was excused from the witness stand, Xavier struggled to piece it all together. He wondered whether Dr. Munro had actually told the tavern owner to notify Mr. J.J. Tracy, the Brown County District Attorney at that time. Peter Anhauser had passed away so it was conveniently too late to ask him. Maybe Dr. Munro had simply been trying to cover his tracks on the stand, for not reporting his poisoning suspicions to the authorities himself, as any responsible doctor should have done.

Xavier worried that Dr. Andrew Munro had not come across as a trustworthy witness due to his drinking issues and lack of experience with poison. Yet, over the years, Xavier knew the Scotsman had demonstrated many fine qualities of "perception, good judgment, and positive conviction." He was known to have a "gentle spirit" and provided kindness to Brown County's "poor and afflicted"—admirable traits. Dr. Munro had also accumulated many loyal friends among his medical brethren.

However, Xavier would never have engaged Dr. Munro, because of his drinking, for the delivery of his first six children, nor his upcoming seventh, who was due within the month.

Xavier recalled Esperance Soquet's funeral in June of 1873. At that time, the Belgian community had generally assumed Esperance had died from childbed fever, since other neighborhood women had recently died from that infection. On the stand, Dr. Munro had confirmed he had had one or two cases of childbed fever within 10 to 12 hours of assisting Esperance with her birth. Xavier now speculated whether J.P. had perhaps engaged Dr. Munro back in 1873 hoping the physician would infect his wife, too. But when Esperance had displayed no symptoms of ill health, in the hours following the birth, maybe J.P. had realized he had needed to take matters into his own hands. It was a chilling possibility.

Three additional doctors followed Dr. Munro. The first was Dr. Austin F. Olmsted who had earned a medical degree at the Cleveland Homeopathic Hospital College and had practiced for thirteen years.

Xavier was distressed when Dr. Olmsted, like Dr. Munro, testified he had never treated a case of poisoning. D.A. Neville still posed a hypothetical question to the physician: "If you were called to a patient who had been in childbirth ... the uterus in normal condition, healthy ... childbirth normal, the patient normal, and on the second or third day, ... this patient was suffering from these symptoms: constant hawking, ... burning pains in the throat and stomach, vomiting and purging, inability to retain food, ... sensitiveness of stomach to pressure, ... pulse low, weak, quick ..." Neville's gaze met Dr. Olmsted's before he asked, "What would your diagnosis be?"

Attorney Wigman objected adamantly to the question's foundation. J.P.'s attorney said Dr. Olmsted had not been shown to be a qualified witness.

Judge Hastings overruled.

J.P.'s attorneys seemed furious, not only about the judge's decision, but about Judge Hastings overall treatment of the two defense attorneys. Xavier thought he recognized some bias from Hastings toward the State. The judge seemed to be looking out for his fellow First Presbyterian parishioners: Dr. Olmsted, Attorney Vroman, and D.A. Neville. Xavier belonged to that same congregation. When he testified, he wondered whether he would receive the same sort of preferential treatment from Judge Samuel D. Hastings.

D.A. Neville smiled at the judge's ruling and asked Dr. Olmsted, once again: Based on Esperance Soquet's symptoms, observed by Dr. Munro and the other witnesses, "what would you say was the matter with the patient?"

"I should suspect an irritant poison had been administered ... arsenic."

Neville gave Olmsted an affirming nod and asked, from those same symptoms, as compared with cholera or puerperal fever, "which would you say the patient was suffering from?"

"I should say she was suffering from arsenical poisoning."

The second of the three additional physicians was Dr. Benjamin C. Brett, who had graduated from Dartmouth's medical department. For twenty-six years, Brett had been a practicing physician including his service in the Civil War. When Dr. Brett testified, he had treated one person who had been poisoned, Xavier brightened. At last, there was a physician with first-hand experience rather than simply book-learning.

Dr. Brett confirmed he had listened to the testimony of Dr. Munro and the other witnesses. Based on that testimony, Dr. Brett believed there were "strong grounds" for suspecting Mrs. Soquet's death had been due to poison and not cholera or puerperal fever.

Dr. Benjamin C. Brett (Men Who are Making Green Bay 1897)

Xavier noted the prosecution team looked pleased as D.A. Neville sat down.

In Attorney Hudd's cross-examination, he asked Dr. Brett whether he had ever witnessed the face of a deceased person turning black.

Brett reiterated what Dr. Munro had said, that livor mortis usually caused that condition. A black or discolored face would provide no particular evidence of poison.

Attorney Hudd nodded, and said he had no further questions for the witness.

The fourth and final medical witness was Dr. F.L. Lewis, a graduate of Chicago's Rush Medical College. Dr. Lewis testified he had seen "one case" of arsenical poisoning during his years of practicing medicine. From the evidence provided by Dr. Munro and the other witnesses, Dr. Lewis believed there were strong reasons to suspect arsenical poisoning in Mrs. Soquet's case rather than cholera or puerperal fever.

The medical testimony was unanimous, which buoyed Xavier's hopes.

Judge Hastings called for a noon recess and Xavier left the courtroom. He descended the stairs and stepped out into the brilliant sunlight. Xavier watched Dr. Munro head down the street, no doubt in search of a tavern. He had been Esperance Soquet's attending physician, the only doctor, other than the late Father Daems, who had actually observed Esperance's symptoms. Xavier knew the medical testimony all depended on Dr. Munro's accurate diagnosis.

Xavier wondered once again whether Dr. Munro had been looking out for himself on the stand. Could he have lied about Esperance's uterus being normal to protect himself? Dr. Munro had admitted he had treated one or two cases of puerperal fever within ten or twelve hours before the delivery of Esperance's baby.

But Xavier had to remember the symptoms the neighbors had observed in Esperance Soquet had seemed to match poisoning better than childbed fever. Only Rosalie Williams's testimony had mentioned Esperance had had a fever, a symptom of childbed fever, and that had been solely based on what J.P. had told Rosalie.

Xavier could see how difficult this case was going to be for the jurors. Arsenic poisoning was rare in Brown County. Of the four doctors who had testified, with their combined medical experience of about one hundred years, only two had dealt directly with a confirmed poisoning case. Still, the four doctors' expert medical opinions had been unanimous: Esperance Soquet's symptoms indicated poisoning.

Xavier surveyed the jurors as they filed out of the courthouse and headed toward a nearby restaurant for their mid-day meal. The doctors had spoken, but Xavier had no idea what the jurors might decide. There had been no autopsy or analysis of Esperance's remains to provide absolute proof she had died from arsenical poisoning. Xavier hoped the physicians' medical conjectures would be enough.

MOTIVE AND REGRET

PAULINE

THE APRIL 26, 1887 afternoon session of State vs. J.P. Soquet began at one o'clock. The jurors were seated in their box, their bellies full. So was Pauline's. She had packed a mid-day meal of bread, cheese, and a small jug of cider. Although the weather was chilly, she had taken a walk to Washington Park and found a bench near the Stars' baseball diamond. She had needed to go outside and focus on something other than the trial. The stress was wearing on her, and her mind was constantly running through testimony, thinking of options and outcomes, and worrying desperately about her sister. Lunch in the park had given her the refreshment she needed to continue.

Martin Simonar would testify next, and then his wife would be recalled to the stand. Pauline was certain the couple, who still lived next door to the Minsart house, would relish sharing their stories about her sister and J.P. Soquet. The idea made Pauline squirm. They would provide evidence of what the prosecution had called J.P.'s first crime of having had criminal intimacy with Elvira Minsart.

When Attorney Vroman asked Martin Simonar whether he knew the defendant, J.P. Soquet, the witness answered: "You bet I do." Simonar said he had often seen J.P. sneaking across the field to the Minsart house. In fact, so many times that a path had been beaten between the two homes. J.P. had also attempted to hide by crawling on all fours behind Mrs. Minsart's fence. While testifying to that point, the thin, agile man sprung from the witness chair and got down on all fours, just as Pauline had observed him doing fourteen years ago. Amid hoots and hollers, Simonar ran across the courtroom, impersonating J.P. Soquet.

Judge Hastings banged his gavel, calling the courtroom to order.

Pauline tempered her anger.

The crowd finally quieted as Judge Hastings remonstrated Attorney Vroman for not controlling his witness, and Simonar returned to the witness box. He continued his testimony, unperturbed, even proud, Pauline thought.

Simonar described how he had watched J.P. sneaking into the Minsart house to see Elvira when August was working in the fields. He said J.P.'s stealthy trips had continued for nearly two years before August Minsart's death. Simonar had also seen Esperance Soquet and their children barge into the Minsart house to bring J.P. home. One night, when Minsart was out of town, Simonar had seen J.P. leave the Minsart house at four in the morning as Elvira Minsart had opened the gate to let J.P. out. Simonar said he had scolded J.P. and told him, "No good" would come from him going there. J.P. had told Simonar, if he ever came into the Minsart house while J.P. was in the company of Mrs. Minsart, "either [Simonar's] bones or [Soquet's] would stay there."

The testimony of Simonar's wife, Christine, matched her husband's. Over an eighteen-month span, prior to August Minsart's death, she had watched J.P. go over to the Minsart farm two or three times a week. She had also seen Elvira's husband, August, and his brother, Ignace, throw J.P. from the Minsart house.

Another Belgian, Clement Williams, testified that he had told the defendant, he was "a foolish man" to keep company with Elvira Minsart.

D.A. Neville asked Clement whether he could recall J.P.'s response.

Clement's cheeks colored above his thick mustache as he repeated J.P.'s words. That if Clement knew "what pleasure Mrs. Minsart could give a man, he would never go anywhere else."

The crowd gave hushed whispers. Pauline wanted to bow her head, but she lifted it to survey the jurors' reactions. She was ashamed to see their lips curled in disgust. Pauline remembered all this talk from fourteen years ago. For that reason, Pauline herself had traveled to her sister's home to talk with Elvira only a few weeks before August's death. If only Elvira had been willing to break off her relationship with J.P. Soquet, Pauline knew, none of these past years of misery would have happened.

·∞·

Pauline reached the three-story white-brick courthouse on Thursday April 28, 1887. A full week had passed since the Soquet trial had begun. Pauline climbed the marble steps outside, the wind whipping at her bonnet. She had spent extra time getting ready that morning. Attorney Vroman had told her she would likely be taking the stand before the close of court that day. She wanted to feel confident and ready. Pauline wanted to set shame aside so she could pursue a guilty verdict for J.P. Soquet—to honor all that her family and her sister had suffered.

Pauline entered the courtroom and the bailiff directed her to sit in the first two rows behind the prosecution table, which were reserved for witnesses. The prior day, the prosecution had focused on what Attorney Vroman had deemed to be J.P.'s first crime, being criminally intimate with her sister. Now Pauline assumed the prosecution would focus on his second crime, poisoning her sister's former husband, August Minsart. Pauline knew it would not be any easier to prove now than it was fourteen years ago.

Martin Simonar was recalled to the stand and testified he had been inside the Minsart house on the day of August's death. Simonar said he had found August lying on his face with his work clothes on, "matter running from his mouth." J.P. had arrived, and Simonar had heard him say that Elvira Minsart would make a good wife.

Joseph Williams, the brother to Polidore and Clement, testified he had gone into the Minsart kitchen and discovered a medicine bottle. When he had sniffed it, J.P. had told him to be careful, that he would not take any of it for "fifty dollars." At that time, Joseph had speculated whether August Minsart's death could have been caused by poison, either by August's hand or someone else's.

D.A. Neville asked Joseph Williams whether August Minsart's face had appeared discolored

Attorney Hudd objected. He argued that two of the physicians, Dr. Munro and Dr. Brett, had testified, a discolored face was no indication that the subject had been poisoned.

Judge Hastings said he did not recall either doctor having testified to those facts, and the judge told the witness he could answer.

Attorney Hudd fumed in his seat.

Pauline could understand his frustration. Judge Hastings had obviously not been listening to the four doctors' entire testimony. She listened as Williams testified that August Minsart's face had turned black. He said he had told J.P. that Elvira Minsart was a "bad woman" for not taking better care of her dead husband. J.P. had responded: "She could be made a good woman. If Soquet had her, he would make a good wife of her."

Williams's words about J.P. disgusted Pauline, but his testimony about her sister made Pauline feel sad. Elvira should not be defined by that single word: "bad." Yet Pauline had used that same word to describe Elvira countless times. Pauline recognized not everything about Elvira was bad. Her sister had generous and kind qualities as well. She had given Pauline and her family a place to live twice. Elvira had tried to help her stepdaughter, Mary, before J.P. managed to have his eldest child committed to a hospital for the insane.

Pauline thought of the grief her sister had carried. Pauline knew Elvira had experienced little happiness in her two marriages. The only joy she had seemed to have had in her miserable life was with little Henry and her visits with Pauline's family and their parents. When Henry had died, likely at the hand of J.P., Elvira had been devastated. At that point, Pauline realized Elvira had made a final turn for the worse. Who could blame her? And it shamed Pauline to remember that her sister had purposely begun abusing J.P.'s youngest daughter to exact revenge.

Pauline's relationship with Elvira had been complicated. But they had each supported each other through heartbreaking times. Pauline closed her eyes, she realized she had been thinking about her sister in the past tense. But how could she not? Elvira had been missing for more than four months.

The next witnesses would be Pauline's family members. Her younger sister, Fannie, and Fannie's husband, Peter Vandenbusch, testified about the day of August's death, both indicating that their brother-in-law's face had turned black and blue. "I had seen a great many people who had died in the old country," Peter testified. "But I had never seen a corpse looking so bad as that one did."

J.P.'s attorney, Mr. Hudd, made a motion to have Peter's answer struck as improper and incompetent.

Judge Hastings denied the motion, and D.A. Neville continued. He asked Peter, and then the next witness, Pauline's brother, Isadore Coppersmith, whether they had seen J.P. shortly after August Minsart's burial in June of 1873.

Both Peter and Isadore testified that they had seen J.P. several times at the Coppersmith home talking to August's recent widow, Elvira. Pauline's eldest brother, Desire, also testified to some information that Pauline and her family had not known until recently. He said he had taken supper with J.P. in late December of 1873, soon after August Minsart's body had been disinterred. J.P. had told Desire that Green Bay attorneys, whom he had consulted, had told J.P. that there would be no hope for him unless he disinterred the body of his wife and concealed it.

Isadore Coppersmith (Pauline's brother) (Courtesy of Brian Schultz on Ancestry.com)

Pauline watched the jurors' eyes land on the defendant's table where J.P. sat beside Hudd and Wigman. But even as the crowd responded, it seemed that nothing could shock Pauline anymore. The jurors had to be speculating whether J.P.'s current attorneys were the ones J.P. had received such sinister advice from.

Pauline realized her brother's testimony was a key piece of evidence. As was the testimony of her father, Alexis Coppersmith, and her brother-in-law, William Lancelle, who spoke next about J.P.'s admission: that he would be "in for it" if they would not help him unbury his wife, since Esperance had been poisoned with the same kind of poison found in August Minsart.

D.A. Neville finally called Pauline's name. Her stomach filled with dread, but she was resolved to tell the truth—to do whatever she could to send J.P. away. Once seated in the witness box, her eyes zoomed in on J.P. She refused shame. She would finally get her chance to reveal all she had witnessed between her sister and J.P., as well as the confidences Elvira had shared with her. That afternoon in the courtroom, J.P. would finally get a piece of Pauline's mind.

Attorney Vroman asked Pauline whether she had known about Elvira's involvement with J.P. Soquet prior to August Minsart's death.

Pauline testified she had discovered her sister and J.P. together inside the Minsart home three times prior to August's death. While August had been working in the fields, just weeks before his death, Elvira had asked Pauline for advice. She had wanted to know whether she should run away with J.P., who had saved $5,000 for their escape. At that time, Pauline said, her sister believed J.P. was a "good man," unlike her husband, August Minsart, who had been nothing to her "but a dog."

Pauline glanced at the jurors. She could not read their faces. Most were farmers, and she wondered whether their relationships with their wives had ever reached a similar point. Pauline wanted to explain why Elvira had said those words. That her sister had felt as if August had treated her more like a servant than a wife. But Attorney Vroman moved on. He asked Pauline about any specific conversations she had shared with her sister and the defendant following the deaths of their spouses.

One time, Pauline said, when she was with J.P. and Elvira, her sister had accused J.P. of poisoning his wife and Elvira's husband, August Minsart. J.P. had responded by attacking Elvira with his fists. Pauline's steady voice continued as she testified to the time she and J.P. had been "taking the coffee together and they were talking, and Soquet, here," Pauline pointed at J.P., "was complaining that his wife, [Elvira], ... was not doing any work. Mr. Soquet was then telling that during the time of his previous wife, that she was a good worker; and I replied to Soquet, he had a good chance to keep her; he had better have kept her."

Pauline gazed at the jury. She could see that some of them looked pleased by her boldness. But the jurors did not know her. She was a tough woman, finally ready to speak the truth, shameful though it was, to send J.P. to jail. Her resolve had continued to grow since her sister's disappearance. But Pauline feared that justice would come too late for Elvira.

Pauline talked about J.P.'s many arrests over the years. How he had paid the same attorneys, which were currently representing him, about $1,400 to defend him (about $50,000 in current valuation).

Attorney Hudd lunged to his feet and said Pauline's statement was not true. He had a right to contradict her, but Judge Hastings said that sounded about right for "forty lawsuits" and told Attorney Vroman to continue.

Pauline could see that J.P.'s attorneys were incensed. But they would be angrier still after her next words. Pauline reiterated her conversation with Elvira, when the two of them were driving back from Father Daems's funeral. That Elvira had admitted she had helped J.P. exhume the body of his second wife. Through back-and-forth questioning, Pauline testified that according to her sister, John B. Rose had stood watch as the defendant had carried Esperance's corpse away in a gray blanket. Soquet had then buried the body under some plum trees on their neighbor's land.

While Pauline testified, the courtroom had stilled. Once she finished speaking, an undercurrent of voices filled the space.

Attorney Vroman asked whether Pauline knew the burial location of Esperance's body.

Pauline said, "No." Her sister had believed J.P. had likely moved his second wife's remains from their original location to somewhere on the Soquet property.

Attorney Vroman asked Pauline whether J.P. had ever threatened her own life.

Pauline's eyes pierced J.P.'s as she gave her account about the Minsart house break-in, corroborating Joseph Everard's testimony. Pauline said she had accused J.P. of poisoning his wife and her sister's husband, and disinterring Esperance's body. J.P. had reacted by trying to kill Pauline with a broken whiskey bottle.

Pauline stepped down from the witness stand. She was exhausted, but confident she had told the truth and done what she could do. Would it be enough to convince the jury that J.P. had poisoned Esperance? She thought of Elvira. Her sister's first-hand knowledge about J.P.'s poisoning deeds would have put him away for good.

Of course, J.P. had known that.

Pauline shuddered and swallowed her grief.

THE TRANSLATOR

XAVIER

XAVIER HAD LISTENED to the testimony of Pauline Villiesse. She was the strongest and most dependable member of the extended Coppersmith family. She was the eldest sister, the one who had tried to create a better life for Elvira by encouraging her to divorce J.P. But by doing so, Xavier feared that he and Pauline had tragically assisted Elvira in sealing her fate. Xavier believed Elvira was dead. If Elvira had remained separated from J.P., rather than seeking a divorce, she may have had a future—a miserable future—but a future. This strengthened Xavier's determination to see J.P. behind bars.

Xavier refocused on the trial as D.A. Neville called Victoria Von Jenck to the stand. She testified to a quarrel she had witnessed in a tavern some years back between J.P. Soquet and his third wife, Elvira Soquet. "Mrs. Soquet threatened to tell all she knew," Victoria stated, "and Soquet said he did not care, as the authorities could prove nothing against him."

The next two witnesses testified about the tissue samples Dr. Ayers had cut from August Minsart's stomach. The doctor said he had sealed them in a jar, and he had personally driven them to Professor Daniels at the State University in Madison. Professor Daniels testified, from the analysis of those tissue samples, he had discovered eight grams of arsenic, "sufficient to kill about ten men."

The next testimony centered on the disappearance of Esperance Soquet's body from her gravesite at Old Holy Cross Cemetery. John B. Gonion testified he had dug the grave where Mrs. Soquet had been buried, and he had been present when the authorities had recently dug up the coffin and discovered it had been empty. Dr. Lewis of Fort

Howard testified about the small bones he had located in the dirt around Esperance's coffin.

Soquet's attorney, Mr. Hudd, asked Dr. Lewis: "Was it not a common thing to find a grave without a skeleton in it?"

"That might be the case in some localities," Dr. Lewis admitted.

"It is common in localities where a number of doctors live, is it not?" Mr. Hudd was insinuating that Esperance's grave had been robbed for medical use. The press had enlightened Xavier and other readers about the demand for cadavers, which were utilized by medical colleges. Grave robbing was a commonplace, though of course highly illegal activity. The corpses were often those of the poor or criminals, to avoid outcry.

In the courtroom, as the "back-and-forth sally" between Attorney Hudd and Dr. Lewis continued, on the subject of grave robbing, Xavier realized the defense had provided an alternate scenario for the missing remains of Esperance Soquet. But he could not dwell on that; he needed to keep his wits about him.

The time had arrived for Xavier's testimony. He was ready to share what he knew, ready for it to be all over. D.A. Neville asked Xavier to walk through his credentials. He mentioned his real estate business, which he had owned and operated for twenty-five years, and his elected role as Green Bay city tax assessor. He mentioned his prior jobs as teacher, postmaster, town clerk, justice of the peace, register of deeds, alderman, court translator, and founding member of the Wisconsin Society for the Prevention of Cruelty to Animals.

Xavier looked over at J.P. Soquet, and he testified about the will he had authored for the Soquets in May of 1873, which had favored the survivor. A month later, Xavier said, Esperance had died. He testified he had been present for her burial and for her grave's recent exhumation at Old Holy Cross Cemetery where the coffin had been empty.

D.A. Neville asked Xavier about the third Mrs. Soquet, Elvira. Could he recall a meeting held in Xavier's office where the defendant and Elvira had both been present?

Xavier watched J.P.'s eyes turn flinty and sharp as Xavier testified about that meeting, five months ago, during the Soquets' divorce pendency. Xavier told D.A. Neville that Elvira had stated, "She wanted to be boss in her own property and live by herself ... In their dispute, she said she didn't want to sign [the divorce] paper. [If she did], she was afraid that Soquet would kill her or poison her, the same as he had done formerly."

Xavier was not surprised when Attorney Wigman leaped to his feet and objected on three grounds: Mr. Martin's words "were first, hearsay; second, spoken between man and wife; third, were immaterial, only intended to prejudice the jury."

Judge Hastings overruled Attorney Wigman's objection, on each and every ground.

Xavier realized J.P.'s defense attorneys considered him to be a major threat to their case. Unlike the testimony from the Belgian witnesses, recalled from fourteen years ago, Xavier's testimony about the Soquets was recent, and he was not prejudiced by family or neighborly ties.

Given the judge's permission to continue, D.A. Neville asked Xavier what he believed Elvira Soquet had meant when she had said, "She was afraid that Soquet would kill her or poison her, the same as he had done formerly."

Xavier said he believed Elvira had been "referring to the deaths of Esperance Soquet and [August] Minsart."

Xavier saw Attorney Wigman scowl while D.A. Neville looked pleased.

The D.A. asked Xavier whether any other exchange had occurred in that same meeting between Elvira Soquet and the defendant.

Xavier said Elvira had told J.P. that "She could send him to the state prison for the rest of his days, and he replied that when he would go, she would go too."

Xavier's eyes darted toward the jurors. They were listening intently. They had seemed to respect his position and credentials in the community. He hoped they would trust his testimony.

Neville asked Xavier whether he had attended another meeting with Elvira in late December when the defendant had not been present.

Xavier said he had acted as interpreter between City Attorney Charles E. Vroman and Elvira Soquet.

D.A. Neville asked Xavier what had been covered at that meeting.

Xavier said Elvira Soquet had discussed the defendant's involvement in the 1873 death of her former husband, August Minsart. But before Xavier could continue his testimony and mention the poisoned griddle cakes, Attorney Wigman objected. He said the information was immaterial to the case, only intended to prejudice the jury.

Judge Hastings hesitated. He sustained the objection, finally giving the defense a win, and instructed D.A. Neville to move on.

Neville pursed his lips but did as he had been told. He asked Xavier, "Have you seen or heard of Elvira Soquet since?"

"No," Xavier said, but he added that about two months ago, he and Sheriff Watermolen had visited the Minsart home in Humbolt, where Elvira had been living.

"Did you find anything there that ... could inform you where [Elvira Soquet] was?"

Attorney Wigman objected, claiming Xavier was "incompetent." Judge Hastings overruled.

Xavier said, "Yes ... I found some bunches of hair in the cellar. Some traces of blood, and some attempt to conceal blood. I saw indications of a struggle."

The courtroom filled with whispers, and Judge Hastings used his gavel to quiet the crowd.

D.A. Neville sat down and Attorney Wigman stood. He crossed his arms, leaning back on one heel, and asked Xavier how he had become so involved in the case being tried.

Xavier relayed that after J.P.'s third wife, Elvira, had gone missing, her father, Alexis Coppersmith, had asked Xavier to come to his home. Xavier testified that Mr. Coppersmith had wanted to provide a sworn statement about the defendant, which their family had kept secret for fourteen years. This was the same information Mr. Coppersmith had testified to in court that day. Xavier said he, Sherriff Watermolen, and Attorney J.J. Tracy had taken down Mr. Coppersmith's statement. Attorney Tracy had then filed a complaint against the defendant which had led to his arrest.

Attorney Wigman said condescendingly, he understood all that. Wigman asked whether or not it was true that the only reason Mr. Coppersmith had sought Xavier out in the first place was because Xavier had been spreading rumors? And those rumors had concerned Mr. Coppersmith's daughter, and what she had allegedly said at the Soquets' divorce pendency meeting? The same meeting where Xavier had charged the defendant $40 for his services for acting as "wet nurse" between the Soquets and their attorneys? The same $40 which the defendant had failed to pay Xavier?

Xavier was taken aback. That simply was not true. Xavier adamantly denied his accusations. But before Xavier could elaborate, Wigman said he had no further questions. Xavier stepped down from the stand, distressed at the way his testimony had ended. Yet he believed he had done his job to help secure justice, not only for Esperance Soquet, but also for the sister of Pauline Villiesse.

D.A. Neville announced the State rested its case.

Xavier glanced over at Pauline. He was not surprised to see the devastated look on her face. She had patiently waited to hear the testimony about the man who had allegedly been inside the Minsart house with her sister on December 31, 1886.

No records provide the identity of the "anonymous man." Attorney Vroman likely never knew the man's identity himself. It's possible Vroman wove the rumored "anonymous man" into his opening statement, hoping the man would come forward to testify. But like so many others in the Belgian community, the man had likely feared retribution if J.P. was acquitted at trial.

In the courtroom, Xavier knew, as much as he had wanted to hear the "anonymous man's" testimony, even if he had come forward, the focus of the current trial was to prove J.P. murdered his second wife, Esperance, not his third wife, Elvira. There was a good chance the defense would have objected, and Judge Hastings may have even been inclined to disallow the man's testimony.

Xavier gave Pauline a compassionate smile. At least Judge Hastings had allowed Xavier's testimony about the blood and hair evidence he and Sheriff Watermolen had located in the Minsart house. Xavier hoped his testimony would aid the jurors in reaching a guilty verdict and provide some solace for Pauline and the extended Coppersmith family.

Judge Hastings told the defense attorneys to call their first witness.

Attorney Hudd called Mr. E.A. Phillips.

Seven years earlier, when D.A. Neville had been the Green Bay mayor, Neville had fired three policemen for "failure to perform their duties" and appointed three men to take their place. One of those hired was Mr. E.A. Phillips. Before Phillips was allowed to testify, D.A. Neville called for a sidebar with Judge Hastings and Attorney Hudd. At the judge's request, the bailiff removed the jury from the courtroom.

While Phillips sat inside the witness box, and everyone in the spectator section looked on, a heated discussion commenced between the attorneys and Judge Hastings. The judge ruled that Phillips testimony would not be allowed, and the witness was excused. Xavier noticed that Attorney Hudd's cheeks had turned a purplish red, angered by this perceived injustice and the power it would rob from his defense.

The jurors returned to the courtroom, and Attorney Hudd called the defense's next witness, Mr. Gotlieb Erdman. Xavier recalled what the Belgian farmer had said on the day of Esperance Soquet's funeral. Dr. Munro had delivered Erdman's child shortly before J.P. and Esperance's. Erdman had believed his wife's symptoms, prior to her death, had been similar to Esperance Soquet's, and that both women had died from puerperal fever.

D.A. Neville immediately requested another sidebar, and the bailiff ushered the jurors out of the courtroom for a second time.

Another heated discussion occured between the attorneys and Judge Hastings. The latter finally ruled that Gotlieb Erdman could not testify. Xavier figured Judge Hastings had likely deemed Erdman's testimony to be irrelevant since Dr. Munro and the three other physicians had all ruled out puerperal fever as the cause of Esperance Soquet's death.

Xavier watched J.P.'s attorneys seethe at the defendant's table as the jurors took their seats in the jury box. Hudd and Wigman were getting no breaks from Judge Samuel D. Hastings.

A dozen additional defense witnesses were examined, each for about ten minutes. Nothing of importance came out of their testimony, as far as Xavier could tell. The only witness left to testify would be Jean Philippe Soquet—if he chose to speak for himself.

Xavier knew J.P. had the constitutional right to remain silent, and that the burden of proof was on the prosecution's shoulders. The State had to convince the jury, beyond a reasonable doubt, that the defendant, J.P. Soquet, with premeditated intent, was guilty of poisoning his second wife. Xavier wondered whether J.P. would be bold or fool-hardy enough to take the stand.

Attorney Charles E. Vroman had once told Xavier that he never put a client inside the witness box unless he or she had insisted. It was too risky. Lay people could not imagine what a skillful prosecutor could do.

If J.P. decided to take the stand when court resumed the next morning, Xavier believed his defense attorneys' goal would be to show J.P. in the most favorable light. They hoped the jurors would gain sympathy for the man who had lost his wife and the mother to his seven children.

But if D.A. Neville and Attorney Vroman got their crack, Xavier knew they would relentlessly challenge J.P.'s credibility. To make him appear untruthful and enraged. Knowing J.P. Soquet, Xavier believed this would not be too difficult for the State to accomplish.

PERPETRATOR OR VICTIM

PAULINE

PAULINE HEADED toward the courthouse on May 3, 1887, speculating about whether J.P. Soquet would dare to testify on his own behalf. She did not want to hear a word he might say, yet she believed his vile character would reveal itself on the stand.

She had prayed her sister would miraculously arrive at the courthouse to testify against J.P. before the trial's end. Or, more likely, that Elvira's body would have been found in the swamp near the Soquet farm, adding to the trouble J.P. was facing.

Pauline had heard that Sheriff Watermolen and his deputies had planned to return to the Soquet farm to hunt through the adjacent swamp. She hated to imagine her sister dead, but to find Elvira's body in the swamp now would likely be too late to make a difference in this trial. In the Door Peninsula, snapping turtles were prolific. They scavenged for both plants and animals in swamps and marshes, ambushing their prey with their powerful jaws. Pauline would have been contacted if her sister's body had been discovered by the authorities. But maybe the snapping turtles had located Elvira before the authorities had.

The thought sickened her.

The trial was taking a toll on Pauline's mental health.

She steeled herself as she entered the courtroom. Many Belgians from the country were present, anticipating J.P.'s testimony. And they would not be disappointed.

When Judge Hastings called court to order, he asked whether the defense had any further witnesses. Mr. Hudd announced the defendant, Jean P. Soquet, would testify, and excited murmurs reverberated throughout the packed courtroom.

Pauline eyed Soquet as he was sworn in. Although he was a prosperous farmer, he wore the same attire as most tillers of the Belgian fields: a sack suit over a cotton shirt. His beard had been trimmed, but his brutish face could not be altered. Pauline waited impatiently, stomach knotted, for J.P.'s testimony. With each passing second, she loathed him more.

Attorney Hudd asked J.P. where he lived as Constant Martin translated.

"In Jail," Soquet gruffly said, causing laughter in the courtroom.

Attorney Hudd asked J.P. to step through the days leading up to his former wife's death on Friday, June 27, 1873.

J.P. testified that he had engaged Dr. Andrew Munro about nine or ten days prior to the birth to attend to Mrs. Soquet.

Pauline was surprised. She figured J.P. had contacted the doctor only a few days before Esperance's delivery. Yet Pauline knew there had been an epidemic of childbed fever, and Dr. Munro had been connected to many of those cases. Had J.P. engaged Dr. Munro hoping to infect Esperance during her delivery? Perhaps that was why J.P. had told Polidore Williams he was taking Esperance around for the last time. This scheme would be alarming, even for J.P.

J.P. testified Dr. Munro had only made two visits to the Soquet home, not three, as the doctor had testified. The first time was on Sunday night when Esperance went into labor. J.P. had fetched Dr. Munro at his house in Green Bay while J.P.'s neighbor, Mrs. Malfroid, had tended to Esperance. The two men arrived back at the Soquet home a few hours before the child's birth, and Dr. Munro stayed for a few more hours following the birth. J.P. said he drove the doctor back to Green Bay in the early hours of Monday morning. Dr. Munro asked J.P. to drop him off at Hogan's Saloon. J.P. said he then traveled back toward his home and continued to drive ten miles north to the Green Bay township to pick up Esperance's mother.

Pauline hunched forward, listening intently. This was the first time she had heard J.P. recount those days.

J.P. said that the day following his child's birth, Esperance was not feeling well, and that he had driven to Green Bay for the doctor again. Dr. Munro returned and provided Esperance with some powders of bismuth and morphine. When J.P. drove the doctor back to Green Bay, Dr. Munro, once again, "insisted on stopping at Hogan's saloon ... and he drank there."

Pauline cringed to hear J.P. undercut the doctor's credibility, even though his drinking was no secret to anyone.

On Wednesday, June 25, two days after his child's birth, Esperance's condition had worsened. J.P. testified that he drove to Green Bay after Dr. Munro again and found him drunk at Peter Anhauser's Main Street saloon. The doctor refused to return with J.P. Instead, Munro told J.P. to give his wife some of the powders which he had left on the previous visit.

After returning home, J.P. said his wife and mother-in-law had suggested he go for Father Daems, the Bay Settlement Catholic priest, also known to be a skillful healer. J.P. testified he drove to the Holy Cross Church rectory and returned with Father Daems. Over the next two days, the priest treated Esperance with medicine until she died on Friday night.

Attorney Hudd asked J.P. whether Father Daems had pronounced his wife's cause of death.

J.P. testified that according to the priest, his wife's sickness was "incident to childbirth."

Attorney Vroman objected to relevance. He stated that Dr. Munro and the three other doctors who had testified had all stated that, in their expert opinion, Esperance Soquet's symptoms had not indicated childbed fever.

The judge sustained the objection and told Attorney Hudd to move on.

Father Daems had passed away nearly a decade ago, so Pauline knew he could not refute nor substantiate J.P.'s claim anyway. Pauline wondered what Father Daems would have testified to on the stand. He had been a very honorable and upstanding man, beloved by all. Father Daems was familiar with many medical remedies and had acted as the Belgian settlements only doctor for many years. If Father Daems had suspected that Esperance had been poisoned, Pauline believed he would have reported his suspicions to the authorities. But he had not.

Attorney Hudd asked J.P. whether he had ever been alone with his wife during the time between the birth of their child and her death.

Esperance's mother had been present at all times, J.P. testified, and she had remained until after the funeral. J.P. also said he had given Esperance whatever food she had wanted, which had been prepared by her mother.

Attorney Hudd asked whether he had given Esperance any poison.

J.P. said he had not. He had never had any poison in his possession.

The attorney asked whether J.P. had pushed his wife down onto the bed during her illness.

J.P. said he had not, and he "wouldn't dare to do it either." He also said he had never told Esperance that she must die, nor said those words about his wife to anyone else. J.P. teared up when he said Esperance had died at his side. Her death had devastated him and their seven children. To this day, they felt her loss.

His display of emotion rattled Pauline. She could sense J.P.'s regret for having poisoned Esperance, and he had said as much over the years. Pauline was glad that the need for translation had dampened the emotional impact of his words for those who could not understand Walloon.

J.P. said he and Esperance had been married for eighteen years, and he had never struck her, although they had engaged in little quarrels. "We lived in peace and on good terms because she was a good woman." Pauline thought that this was the version of events J.P. had come to accept as true, a better version of life to save his own hide.

Attorney Hudd asked J.P. his final question. After his wife had been laid to rest in Holy Cross Cemetery, had he secretly exhumed her body from its coffin.

J.P. swore he had not and seemed unnerved by the accusation.

Mr. Hudd said he had no more questions.

Pauline thought his lawyers had coached him well. He seemed more sympathetic than she and many in the crowd knew him to be.

D.A. Neville stood and approached J.P. Pauline hoped he could undo any damage that J.P.'s testimony had caused.

Pauline listened as J.P. made stout denials of D.A. Neville's allegations, those which discredited or implicated him. J.P. denied his children had ever found Mrs. Minsart and him alone in her house. J.P. denied he had ever told anyone the authorities would find the same kind of poison in his wife's body as had been found in August Minsart's. J.P. denied he had ever paid or offered to pay anyone to aid him in exhuming his wife's body or to silence them from telling others he had.

Pauline shook her head at J.P.'s last denial. Ever since she had taken his $35 bribe to remain silent, after he had broken into the Minsart home, she had regretted her decision. She had enabled him to continue his terrible deeds for six more years. If she had told the authorities about J.P. disinterring his wife's grave back then, or the poisoning murders,

Elvira might still be in Pauline's life. J.P. was standing on his word now, and Pauline had waited to use hers until it had likely been too late. She put those thoughts out of her mind and focused on the trial.

The D.A. stood squarely in front of J.P. and said, "Did you and your last wife, in company with Jean B. Rose, go to the cemetery in ... 1874, and with Rose keeping watch, did you and Mrs. Elvira Soquet take up the body of Esperance Soquet and carry it away in a gray blanket and bury it near some plum trees. And after that, did you alone [take] the body from that place and [bury] it in another spot on the farm?"

J.P. listened to Constant Martin's lengthy translation, his agitation growing, before he answered, "No Sir!"

D.A. Neville said he would not accept that answer. He asked whether it was not true that J.P.'s eldest son, Fred, had uncovered his mother's remains in the family fields after J.P. had moved her body there.

While Constant translated for J.P., those who understood English, including Pauline, shifted in their seats at that disturbing question.

Again, J.P. denied the D.A.'s accusation vehemently.

Pauline looked at the jurors and was pleased to see their faces had settled into a look of distrust. Pauline knew rumors had spread about the final resting spot of Esperance's body. That it was buried under the foundation of the Soquet home or that J.P.'s eldest son, Fred, had found his mother's remains while plowing the fields. Some people claimed J.P. had killed Fred to keep him from contacting the authorities. Perhaps that was why Fred had not been heard from in so long.

Pauline knew the community loved to discuss those grisly rumors, but she also knew there was no evidence the stories were true, even though she had a mind to believe them. The prosecution had not called anyone to testify to any of those rumors, to turn them into factual evidence. Yet, when D.A. Neville asked J.P. the next question, Pauline knew he was trying to do just that: "When your [eldest] boy [Fred] was on the farm, what did he do?"

Attorney Hudd objected.

Judge Hastings peered down from the bench and said, "I don't see any objection."

"[My question]," D.A. Neville said, "has a direct connection with this offense."

Hastings' brow wrinkled. "Well go on."

Neville turned to Constant Martin. "Does [the defendant] know the immediate cause of the boy leaving the farm?"

"Objection." Attorney Hudd shouted. "Immaterial and incompetent."

Judge Hastings overruled.

Constant Martin translated for J.P. "Yes," Constant said, "he knows [why the boy left the farm]. After [his son] got through the work on the farm in the field, his son asked the defendant [if he could leave] ... and [his son] went and worked at Smith's mill in Michigan."

"What did his son do on the farm?" Neville asked. Did he "plough and drag"?

Neville and the courtroom attendees patiently waited as Constant translated for J.P.

"His son," Constant said, "was the one that was doing all the farm work at that time."

"[So, the defendant] says that his son did not take up the body of his wife?" D.A. Neville waited again while Constant translated.

"Yes, [his son did not]," Constant said, "and he repeats it now."

Neville's lips compressed, but he moved on. "Does [the defendant] know Vandenack's boys?"

Constant conferred with J.P. and said the defendant knew both boys, Clement and Gustave. "The whole family worked the farm on their own account. Soquet had rented the farm to Vandenack."

"Did [the defendant] at one time go to De Pere for one of these boys?"

Constant translated and J.P. said, "No."

"Didn't he go after one of those boys to get him to testify in a case ... when he was arrested one time for whipping his daughter?" Neville waited as Constant talked to J.P.

"He never whipped his daughter," Constant recounted J.P.'s words. "He never was arrested for whipping his daughter."

For once, Pauline believed J.P. was speaking the truth. He had never been arrested for whipping his daughters, as far as she knew. But she remembered something just as chilling: J.P. had been arrested for whipping his little son. Poor little Henry. The loss that had finally broken Elvira.

"Didn't the defendant go to De Pere after either Clement or Gustave, and on the way from De Pere to Green Bay, tell this boy what he wanted him to testify to? And did the boy say that he could not do that. That he would not swear false. And then didn't [the defendant] say to him that a false oath was nothing; that [he] had made hundreds of false oaths and was ready to make some more?"

Attorney Hudd objected loudly stating the questions were "wholly immaterial, incompetent, and improper."

"The only objection," Judge Hastings told D.A. Neville, "is that you didn't fix a time. The rule is, you must call the witness's attention particularly to the time and place."

"This conversation took place on the road between Green Bay and De Pere," Neville clarified, "about two years ago."

Based on that clarification, Judge Hastings told Neville to repeat his questions so Constant could translate. Pauline felt the delays draining the urgency of the question.

J.P.'s answer was brief. "No, he denies it," Constant said. "He says he hasn't even been in De Pere."

Pauline watched her former brother-in-law, J.P. Soquet, step down from the stand. She wondered if he was walking to freedom. Throughout the prosecution's cross-examination, J.P. had maintained a surprisingly unruffled demeanor. He had known the high stakes he was dealing with. How could he not? He had put on an unsettlingly good display of reserved composure for the twelve jurors who would decide his fate. He could not fool Pauline, but she was not so sure about the men in the jury box.

The final witness called to testify for the defense was Jean B. Rose. According to Pauline's sister, Rose had stood watch when J.P. and Elvira had removed Esperance's body from the grave. On the stand, Rose denied participating in the disinterment of Esperance Soquet's body. After J.P. had paid Rose for his lookout assistance, Pauline assumed, J.P. had likely held that threat of Rose's potential arrest over Rose's head. And with that final witness, Pauline watched the defense rest their case.

Pauline was mentally exhausted and emotionally drained. The courtroom clock neared 3:30 on Tuesday, May 3, 1887. Between the State and the defense, forty-eight witnesses had been examined, most of them requiring an interpreter. Pauline knew without a shadow of a doubt that J.P. was guilty. She had always known it. But she worried that the evidence presented at trial might not be strong enough to finally send J.P. to the Wisconsin State Prison.

CLOSING ARGUMENTS

XAVIER

XAVIER LOOKED AROUND the gallery where "a number of ladies were listening," including Pauline Villiesse. He had watched her reaction during J.P.'s testimony. Xavier could tell she had been angered as much as he by the man's blatant lies, but neither of them had been surprised. Xavier hoped the Vandenack boys' testimony, though it had gone nowhere, had at least established J.P.'s prior behavior related to the court system—that "a false oath was nothing." If it had, how could the jurors believe anything that had come out of J.P.'s mouth?

Xavier believed Judge Hastings would call it a day, but no. The judge announced the final arguments in the case of the State vs. J.P. Soquet would commence. The judge apparently was the only one not worn out by the trial. Perhaps, like Xavier, he just wanted to get it over with. The trial had run for twelve days. Now finally, an end was in sight.

First up would be Attorney Charles E. Vroman for the State. Xavier watched as his friend took a wide stance in front of the jury panel. Xavier listened as Vroman carefully reviewed the case, presenting it "concisely and clearly." Vroman told the jury, in closing, that the evidence provided by the State had established the defendant's guilt beyond a reasonable doubt.

As Vroman sat down Xavier worried that his friend had not fulfilled his promise to the jury—to prove J.P. was guilty of five crimes. The State had certainly tied J.P. to two crimes: his criminal affair with Elvira Minsart and the most important crime, the poisoning of his second wife, Esperance Soquet. Xavier only hoped the prosecution's chain of circumstantial evidence for those two crimes had been enough for the jurors to conclude J.P. Soquet was guilty of murder in the first degree. Hopefully the jury could see what Xavier had been sure of for so long.

-∞-

Court resumed at 9 A.M. on Wednesday, May 4, 1887. The defense would have their last chance to advocate for their client's innocence in the death of his wife, Esperance Soquet.

Attorney John H.M. Wigman stood before the jury, a serious expression on his face. Xavier still believed he was one of the best attorneys in Brown County and "a devoted worker for the underdog." Wigman and his partner, Mr. T.R. Hudd, had certainly fought for their client. The two defense attorneys' next goal would be to convince the jury there was reasonable doubt that J.P. Soquet had poisoned his wife.

When Mr. Wigman began, he announced the only reason the defendant was even on trial was because of Xavier Martin.

Xavier was stunned.

Mr. Wigman claimed Xavier had initiated the defendant's prosecution because J.P. had failed to pay Xavier the $40 J.P. owed him for translation services.

Xavier's mouth dropped. Unthinkable. He knew no one in the spectator section would believe that. But what about the jury?

Xavier was boiling inside. J.P. had been good at stirring up trouble for his entire life. With his freedom on the line, he had done so again. Xavier and Wigman had been on good terms for nearly two decades. Xavier hoped the Soquet matter would not injure their future relationship.

"That Esperance Soquet is dead—is not denied," Wigman continued, crossing his hands behind his back. "But did she die from the effects of poison? The prosecution failed to show what she died of, but it claimed that it had some proof from Dr. Munro. He testified that he called on Esperance Soquet thrice; defendant swore he called only twice, the Sunday night and the Tuesday following. Dr. Munro did not see Esperance, according to his testimony, since Wednesday, according to Soquet, not since Tuesday. She died on Friday night. How could Munro or any doctor testify what she died of, not having seen her for three days before her death, nor since her death, without any autopsy. But [Dr. Munro] said he had some suspicions of some irritant poison. He admitted that he left her [with] powders [of] bismuth and morphine. It is well known that arsenic is commonly found in bismuth. [Dr. Munro] admitted that at the time, he generally had more than his share of beer.

"It was fourteen years before the trial." Attorney Wigman's eyes zeroed in on the jurors. "The doctor claims he had suspicions that some other agencies were at work. Yet he took not the least measure to verify any suspicion he claimed to have entertained, did not even administer an antidote. There is no proof that he, at any time, examined the vomit, if there was any, ... or that he took any measure of caution or detection. It was his duty, as a physician, to save the life of Esperance Soquet, and it was his duty, as a citizen, to expose a crime. Yet he does neither," Attorney Wigman huffed.

"[Dr. Munro] keeps this to himself for fourteen years, waits until Father Daems, who attended [Esperance] after him, is dead. Until [Esperance's] mother, who was alongside her daughter from Monday until Friday, becomes an imbecile. And then, after a lapse of fourteen years, for the first time, [Dr. Munro] tells his story in court." Wigman shook his head in disbelief.

"Is it not reasonable to presume that his [testimony] was only imaginations, produced by the inebriating cup? And that we are bound to suppose that he entertained no suspicion that Esperance [had] suffered from any ... consequent of child birth? And that if any suspicion of irritants was entertained [by Dr. Munro], he [did not consider] her symptoms to be the result of the powders of bismuth and morphine he prescribed? An overdose perhaps?"

Wigman paused and surveyed the jurors.

Xavier had watched the jury panel throughout Wigman's closing argument, and Xavier was worried. The jurors were totally riveted on Wigman's words. Xavier feared they were buying into his arguments, seeding dangerous doubt about J.P.'s guilt.

"Take away Dr. Munro's testimony," Wigman said, "and nothing is left. The other experts base their opinion primarily on Munro's testimony. There is no proof that any poison was administered by the defendant. Mrs. LeCoque testified that he gave her gruel. Soquet admits that he gave [Esperance] whatever was prepared for her by her mother, whenever she called for it, and whatever she called for, same as any faithful husband would do. But not a syllable of proof that he gave her poison; that he ever bought or ever had poison."

Wigman said the jury might question why Esperance's body had no longer been in its grave. The attorney reminded them about the very feasible alternative: that her corpse had been stolen by grave robbers who supplied cadavers to medical colleges for a very handsome fee. The prosecution provided no proof that the defendant had removed his wife's body from her grave. So, Wigman said, the jurors simply could not presume he had done it.

"The prosecution claimed that long before [Esperance's] death, Jean P. Soquet had premeditated her death." But Wigman said Esperance's death could just as likely have been from childbirth consequences, as the defendant testified, and as Father Daems had stated at the time of her death. "It was a fact, which the defense attempted to establish on the trial, but which the court refused us to permit to prove, that at about the same time, in the same neighborhood, women were dying of puerperal fever."

At that last comment, directed at the judge, Xavier watched Hastings frown.

"Soquet had lived with his wife for eighteen years," Attorney Wigman continued, "'in peace and on good terms,' as the defendant testified, 'because she was a good woman.' Not a single witness was produced to show that at any time during their married life they had any dispute or dissension, not even [Esperance's] father, except this witness Rose Williams, who testified to a matter three or four years prior to Esperance's death."

Wigman shook his head. "It would be difficult to find, in the annals of crime, one more revolting than this alleged murder the prosecution attempts to charge the defendant.

"The solicitude [the defendant] showed the deceased during her sickness, the constant attendance of her mother, and his willingness to have a physician attend her on Tuesday, and subsequently, when she was feeling worse; the fact that for fourteen years, not even suspicion was thought of by either her father or mother or anyone else; and the fact that this prosecution was instigated by this man, Xavier Martin. Because his $40 fees, as wet nurse between Elvira and the attorneys, were not paid, all point to a different and more reasonable theory upon which to account for [the defendant's arrest and prosecution] for [his wife's] death."

Xavier took a calming breath as Wigman sat down. Now that the defense's comments were getting ugly, Xavier was prepared

Attorney Hudd stood. He would have his say, and Xavier anticipated more accusations aimed his way. Attorney Hudd placed his hands on the rail before the jury and stated that D.A. Neville had had no authority to appoint an assistant in Mr. Charles E. Vroman, whom the jury had heard from extensively throughout the trial. As of today, the jurors should know the State had not agreed to pay Mr. Vroman, so who would be paying him? Well, Mr. Hudd said, of course those in the community out to get the defendant's conviction. Mr. Vroman had a financial interest in the case, and he had offered evidence in the trial with no basis to prejudice the defendant.

Attorney Hudd compared J.P. Soquet to Jesus Christ, who had been put to death on circumstantial evidence, as Hudd said the prosecution was employing to convict J.P.

Xavier was floored. To say something like that to such deeply religious people was unthinkable.

The attorney spoke of the press and reporters, who he claimed had been informed by Xavier Martin. The press, Mr. Hudd said, broadcasted Xavier's statements far and wide concerning the domestic troubles of the Soquets, which were not true. And Xavier Martin's only purpose had been to create prejudice against the defendant for a nonpayment of $40 in translation costs from the Soquets' divorce action. If not for Xavier Martin, Hudd alleged, the misinformation on which J.P. was now being tried would never have surfaced, and the thousands of dollars of expense to the county would have been saved.

Xavier smoldered in his seat, worrying what the jury would believe about him.

When court recessed for the day, Xavier's friend, Mr. Charles E. Vroman, found Xavier. Vroman said the defense had attempted to crucify them both. J.P.'s attorneys needed scapegoats for the case to deflect the blame from J.P.

Xavier knew Hudd and Wigman had represented J.P. for two decades and had repeatedly gotten him off with minor fines and hardly any jail time. They knew how to finagle the outcome their client wanted—at all costs.

Hopefully this time would be different.

·ꝏ·

On the morning of Thursday, May 5, 1887, D.A. Neville would have the last word. The prosecution had the burden of proof. Xavier watched as Neville took the floor in front of the jury to deliver the State's rebuttal argument, to address any points raised by the defense, and to reinforce their case.

In opening, D.A. Neville replied at length to Mr. Hudd's comparison of the defendant, J.P. Soquet, to Jesus Christ. Mr. Neville regarded Mr. Hudd's words as blasphemy and alleged that Mr. Hudd had manifested great ignorance in making such a comparison.

The D.A. said there was no doubt Attorney Charles E. Vroman would be paid by the court for his assistance in trying the State's case. The jury should know Mr. Vroman had pledged not to take any pay from the private sector. Instead, he had assisted throughout the trial on a pro bono basis, a generous gesture and a very honorable action.

D.A. Neville next attacked the theory of the defense: that if not for Xavier Martin, J.P. Soquet would never have been arrested and put on trial. Neville turned toward Xavier and thanked him for assisting the Coppersmith family after their daughter, Elvira Soquet, the defendant's third wife, disappeared.

Xavier's shoulders relaxed. He hoped the jury believed D.A. Neville's character endorsement: that Xavier was upstanding and honest. Xavier also appreciated Neville's reminder of Elvira's fate which hopefully had refocused the jurors on J.P.'s undeniable guilt.

Neville's gaze returned to the jury as he reviewed the prosecution's theory in a concise manner. Neville implored the jury to bring in a guilty verdict for the defendant, Jean Philippe Soquet. The jury owed that to his second wife, Esperance Soquet, murdered at the age of forty-two. She had left seven children behind, who had dearly loved their mother. Neville said Esperance would still be alive, enjoying her children and grandchildren, if not for her husband, J.P. Soquet, who, with malicious intent, had murdered his kind and caring wife for his own selfish desires. He paused and let the emotional weight of his words sink in.

Xavier was moved. The trial was not all about J.P. Soquet. Esperance Soquet deserved justice, even if it was too late to save her life.

Xavier glanced over at Pauline Villiesse.

Elvira Soquet deserved justice as well, wherever she might be.

JUDGMENT

PAULINE

THE TRIAL'S CLOSING ARGUMENTS ended at about 3:00 p.m. on May 5, 1887. Pauline sat beside her brother-in-law, John Villiesse. Only the judge's charge remained before the jury would begin deliberation. John had listened to the closing arguments with Pauline, and his whispered translation had helped Pauline understand the confusing parts. He would be there for the judge's charge as well.

Pauline stared over at J.P. He had sat patiently at the defense table throughout the closing arguments, hardly able to understand a word that had been said since they had been delivered in English. J.P. had to depend on his attorneys to do the right job for him. Pauline did not understand why the defense had targeted Xavier Martin in their closing arguments. She admired the man and all he had done for her family, and she hoped the jurors would believe the prosecution's defense of his character.

Judge Hastings instructed the jury that the burden of proof was upon the State to establish the existence of every material fact, beyond a reasonable doubt. The jurors were to reach a unanimous decision on whether the defendant, Jean Philippe Soquet, with malicious intent, caused the death of his wife, Esperance Soquet, on Friday, June 27, 1873. Murder was the only offense charged and the only offence that the evidence tended to prove. "That while the fact that Esperance Soquet died from the effects of poison cannot be proved ... the prisoner's admission ... out of court ... may be considered by the jury in connection with the other testimony."

At about 4 o'clock, Judge Hastings gave the case to the jury.

Pauline watched the twelve men file out, heading into the little ante room off the courtroom. The bailiff stationed himself outside the door. Pauline and her brother-in-law decided to wait for a few hours in case a verdict came in. They were not alone. Many of the Belgian witnesses remained, including Xavier Martin. Pauline doubted their wait would be rewarded that day, but she could not leave. She was desperate to know if there would be justice for Esperance, for Elvira.

The attorneys left the courthouse. Judge Hastings retired to his chambers. The clerk still lingered at his desk. Pauline and John talked. Xavier Martin joined them as the courtroom clock ticked. Forty-five minutes passed.

Pauline heard the bailiff open the jury room door and enter. Moments later he returned to the courtroom and announced: The jurors had reached a verdict.

Excitement and fear rippled through Pauline. The jurors had deliberated for less than one hour. After two weeks, Pauline could not fathom how they had reached a clear consensus so rapidly. She knew J.P. was guilty, but the jury had to wade through confusing evidence about a man they did not know.

Xavier told Pauline a quick verdict often meant the evidence presented had been convincing. But in J.P.'s trial, she knew the State's evidence had all been inferred with no solid evidence. Could that fact have convinced the jury there was reasonable doubt?

Pauline's deepest fear was that J.P. Soquet would walk away as a free man. That he would not pay for all the harm he had caused. That all her sister had suffered would be meaningless.

The clerk of courts dispatched messengers for the attorneys. An officer departed to fetch the defendant from his jail cell. Soon they were back. Pauline thought J.P. looked nervous.

The bailiff called court to order.

Judge Hastings entered and took his seat behind the bench.

The jury filed in and settled onto their chairs. The elected foreman was Jonas LeRoy, who had served as city assessor, school director, and school treasurer. The clerk of courts asked the foreman if a verdict had been reached.

Jonas LeRoy rose and answered. "It has."

"Do you find the defendant, Jean P. Soquet, guilty or not guilty according to the information?"

In a firm voice, Mr. LeRoy said, "Guilty of murder in the first degree."

Flooded with relief, Pauline fell back in her seat as the Belgian witnesses who understood English cheered and shared the verdict with their neighbors. Esperance's father, Mr. Hannon, had remained in the courtroom with some of his family. Pauline watched tears run down the old man's wrinkled cheeks. After fourteen years, J.P. Soquet had been found guilty of murdering his daughter.

Pauline's gaze landed on that devil of a man. Although J.P. knew little English, his face had turned white. He had understood the jurors' verdict.

Pauline glanced over at Xavier Martin who was grinning. Both believed J.P. deserved to be put away for good, for Esperance and for Elvira.

Mr. Wigman stood and gave notice to Judge Hastings the defense would apply for a new trial. An officer approached J.P. and pulled him to his feet. Until sentencing, J.P. would be locked up inside the Brown County jail.

Pauline listened as Judge Hastings thanked the jury for their attention during the trial. Hastings said he had no doubt the verdict was "the sincere conviction of each of them" and discharged them from further duty.

Pauline and John, among the other spectators, followed the twelve jurors down the stairs. Pauline's brother-in-law approached the fellow blacksmith, Orin S. Kittell. He told John only three ballots had been taken during deliberations. The first ballot was informal: ten votes for conviction and two for acquittal. On the first formal ballot, the vote stood eleven to one. The one juror who stood for acquittal could give no reason for his decision. After a short discussion, he added his vote to the other eleven.

Another juror told a *State Gazette* reporter, "The decisions of many of us were formed before we reached the jury room. The lawyers might have argued till doomsday, but it had gotten to be such a recital of what we already knew from the evidence, that it had but little weight with the jury. The facts presented on the stand were considered by us. I think everyone of the jurors has a perfectly clear conscience in the matter."

Pauline left the courthouse, her shoulders lifted. She could feel how much the trial had weighed on her. She was relieved that justice had been served for Esperance Soquet, and that J.P. would remain behind bars.

But Pauline longed for Elvira. Her sister was still missing. After J.P.'s first-degree murder conviction, the authorities would believe they had no reason to look for Elvira. The man likely responsible for her disappearance and potential murder was already behind bars. To find her sister would be solely up to Pauline and her family. Yet what could they do except to wait, pray, and hope that someone, anyone, would come forward with information?

TRAGEDY AND TRIAL ERRORS

XAVIER

ON MAY 29, 1887, two weeks after the Soquet verdict, Dr. Palmer delivered Xavier and his wife's seventh child. Augusta was thirty-five and had not given birth for nearly four years. Unlike the first six births, she had a rough delivery due to the infant's size.

On the third day of Augusta's confinement, she complained of headaches and nausea. Xavier and their servant woman took turns staying at Augusta's side as she vomited into a bowl or used the chamber pot for her bowels. Xavier sent for the doctor. "Cold fits" overtook his wife's body, followed by extreme heat, perspiration, and thirst.

Fear unspooled inside Xavier's chest.

He gazed down at his kind and compassionate wife, the devoted mother to his children, and the love of Xavier's life. They had gone through so much just to be together, and they had built a beautiful life and family he was proud of. He felt truly blessed to have a large family while his brothers, Constant and Elie, had just one surviving child each.

But now Xavier feared the life he and Augusta had built together could end tragically.

The doctor arrived. Augusta's weak voice told Dr. Palmer about her abdominal pain, initially mild but now severe. Urinating was extremely painful and her milk production had stopped. The doctor checked Augusta's uterus. There was a strong odor and discharge.

Xavier's panic rose when the physician asked him to step out of the room to talk. In the hallway, Dr. Palmer said that Augusta's symptoms indicated puerperal fever.

For nearly two weeks, Xavier had been immersed in the Soquet trial, with its testimony about that same childbirth infection. He had never imagined that this dreaded disease would enter his own home.

Dr. Palmer told Xavier to hold onto hope. About 20 percent of those infected survived.

Xavier returned to Augusta's bedside and held her hand. He prayed she would be one of those women who survived. He could not lose her. Neither could their children. Rudy was thirteen and Albert eleven. Next came Pauline, nine, followed by eight-year-old Freddie. The youngsters, Evelyn and Richard, were six and four, with the new baby rounding out their number.

Over the next week, Dr. Palmer provided the best treatments available to him. Some doctors applied leeches to the abdomen for bloodletting or provided various herbal concoctions and purgatives. Some disinfected the birth canal by irrigating it with a 2 percent solution of carbolic acid. Due to the severe pain of the infection, treatments often focused on managing the symptoms with morphine powders rather than curing the root cause.

At that time, no doctor knew the best course of action.

Day after day, Augusta lay on her back, listless and weak. Xavier feared the worst. His wife's pulse raced and her breathing was difficult, due to her swollen abdomen pressing against her lungs. In the face of her impending death, Augusta told Xavier their children must be baptized.

Although the First Presbyterian Church practiced infant baptism, Augusta's church from the old country had practiced believer's baptism, waiting for the child to be old enough to make their own decision. Augusta had asked Xavier to follow that practice, but now she wanted to make certain, before she passed, that all of their children "received Christ's covenant sign."

Xavier's eyes brimmed with tears as Reverand L.J. White of the First Presbyterian Church carried out Augusta's wishes with their seven children. The last words Augusta spoke were: "Oh, Jesus! Let these little children come to you, please!"

Augusta died at sunrise on Friday, June 11, 1887, surrounded by Xavier and their children. Xavier felt profound shock and numbness. He had never considered he would outlive his spirited young wife. He looked around at their children, all overwhelmed by their tremendous loss.

A few days later, Xavier's grief expanded when his newborn child died and was buried at Woodlawn Cemetery next to its mother. High on the bluff overlooking the Fox River, Xavier and his children stood by the two gravesites. How could he raise his children on his own while providing his family a livelihood?

Xavier felt helpless and alone.

·∞·

About a month later, on July 16, 1887, Xavier left his office to walk to the Brown County Courthouse for J.P. Soquet's sentencing hearing. The days since Augusta's death had been full of pain for his entire family. But he knew he and his children would find some way through.

They were a prosperous family, living in a flourishing city. Green Bay had nearly doubled in size to about 8,000 citizens since Xavier had moved into the city in 1862. Its streets were crowded with industrious people. In some areas, electric lights had been installed. Churches were numerous, the public school where his children attended had few to equal it, and the teachers were first-class. Green Bay's future prosperity was certain, and Xavier had to believe his future without Augusta would also be secure, even if the days were difficult now.

Xavier arrived at the courthouse and climbed the stairs to reach the third-floor hallway outside the Brown County Circuit Court of Judge Samuel D. Hastings. Pauline Villiesse stood among her family members who had testified at the trial. She approached Xavier. He knew his eyes reflected the muddle of loss as he accepted her condolences. They both entered the courtroom and took seats in different rows of the spectator section. In front, beside the clerk of courts, sat Xavier's brother, Constant Martin, who would act as interpreter.

Court was called to order and Judge Hastings took his seat behind the bench. He began proceedings by denying the defense's motion for a new trial for the defendant.

Mr. Wigman took exception to the judgment of the court and gave notion that he would take a bill of exceptions to the Wisconsin Supreme Court.

Xavier had expected that Hudd and Wigman would fight for another trial. The defense only had to find one mistake in the proceedings, which the Supreme Court would agree with, to overturn the trial and order a new one.

In the meantime, however, J.P. was called for sentence.

He stood, as did Mr. Wigman and Mr. Hudd.

Judge Hastings asked J.P., through Constant Martin's translation, whether the defendant "had any reason why his sentence should not be passed upon him."

J.P. said he did not.

"As I cannot talk to this man so that he can understand me," Hastings continued, "I see no useful purpose in passing any comments upon this case, or talking to him in reference to the crime of which he is convicted. The prisoner has been tried and convicted of the crime of murder in the first degree, and it becomes the duty of the court to pass such sentence as the law provides in such cases. The judgment and sentence of the court is that he be punished by confinement at hard labor in the Wisconsin state prison at Waupun, Wisconsin, during his life and that the first two days of said confinement be solitary."

When the sentence was interpreted, J.P. began to sob.

Outbursts of cheering and audible gasps resounded through the courtroom.

Judge Hastings silenced the crowd.

J.P. vowed he was an innocent man. He had never killed anybody either in this country or in Europe. He said the testimony against him had been false.

Xavier was gratified by J.P.'s sentence. But he was also intrigued by his vow that he had not killed anyone in America *or Europe*. Had J.P. left Belgium on the run because he had murdered someone in his homeland? If so, that inflammatory information could have forewarned the authorities decades ago about the type of man they were dealing with.

Xavier watched as an officer led J.P. out of the courtroom in handcuffs. His attorneys would be submitting briefs to the Wisconsin Supreme Court requesting a new trial for J.P. Soquet. But that would take years. In the meantime, the Brown County community would sleep better knowing this man was locked up in the Waupun State Prison, eighty miles south

Waupun State Prison 1893
(Wikimedia Commons)

of Green Bay.

Xavier felt a sense of calm come over him as he looked at Esperance's father and at Pauline Villiesse. The man who had murdered Esperance would no longer be walking free. The man who had abused and likely murdered Elvira would be behind bars. But, Xavier frowned, J.P.'s secrets would be locked up with him.

·∞·

On June 16, 1888, about a year after Xavier lost his wife to puerperal fever, he had a "genuine surprise in store for his friends." Each received an invitation to attend an 8 p.m. ice cream social at Xavier's Crooks Street residence. An hour before, Court Commissioner Bromley quietly married Xavier to Amelia Dendooven of Kewaunee County. Xavier's fishing friend, Attorney Charles E. Vroman, stood as witness.

Xavier, at fifty-six, had never believed he could replace Augusta, his wife of nine years. But through friends, he was introduced to forty-two-year-old Amelia, a fine and intelligent woman. Her husband, Edward, had passed away four years earlier. Unlike Xavier's first two wives, Amelia came into the marriage with money of her own and four children, two boys and two girls, ages ten to eighteen. Until recently, Amelia had been the senior member of the Luxemburg firm of Dendooven, Filz & Ley, general merchants and manufacturers, of Kewaunee County.

Amelia Dendooven Martin (Courtesy Blodgett, Fay Willis via John Mertens)

After their quiet marriage ceremony, Xavier's guests arrived at his Crooks Street home. Charles Vroman greeted them one-by-one and walked them up to the new bride and groom. Xavier smiled over at his new wife with affection, if not love. He was grateful to have Amelia in his life to help care for his children, and he for hers.

·∞·

Six months later, Xavier and Amelia accepted a supper invitation from Charles and Emma Vroman. That night, the Martins' coachman drove them to their friends' 619 S. Quincy Street home. Xavier was proud of his new wife and proud of his family as they recovered from grief. Amelia was quite the businesswoman. She had recently purchased eighteen residential lots "in the suburban portion of Green Bay" and two lots from Mr. Rufus B. Kellogg in blocks 35 and 45 of the Astor neighborhood, where she planned "to erect two cottages for rent."

The Martins' coach pulled up to the enormous hipped-roof Vroman home. Inside, the two couples talked while enjoying a delicious meal. Amelia and Emma discussed the winter apples available at John Beth & Sons and the special bargains in cloaks and shawls being offered at Jorgensen, Blesch and Company.

Charles finally brought up his trip to Madison, which he had just returned from. He and Assistant Attorney General L.K. Luse had given oral arguments in the case of Jean P. Soquet, Plaintiff in error, vs. The State of Wisconsin, Defendant in error. Vroman said Attorney Wigman had made the oral arguments for Soquet, requesting a new trial.

Wigman had argued that Vroman had appeared on behalf of the State without being appointed. But, as everyone at the dining table knew, after the former trial, Charles had been retroactively appointed by the court for his prior assistance to D.A. Neville in the prosecution. Brown County had been ordered to pay Charles for his work on the trial and any further work connected to the trial. Charles said Wigman had also argued that in Vroman's opening address to the jury, instead of focusing solely on Soquet's charged crime of murdering Esperance, Vroman had introduced other alleged crimes attributed to J.P. "to prejudice the jury and to arouse their passions against the defendant."

Charles then talked about the errors Attorney Wigman believed Judge Hastings had made in allowing certain State testimony into evidence including Xavier's testimony about the discussion he had witnessed between J.P. and Elvira during the couples' divorce, and the testimony Xavier had given concerning the hair and blood evidence he had discovered in the Minsart house.

However, the primary errors delivered by the defense to the Supreme Court justices concerned the qualifications of Dr. Andrew Munro and Dr. Austin F. Olmsted. Charles said he and Assistant Attorney General Luse had contended, "That an expert may be competent, although his knowledge is derived from study, without experience or observation." Attorney Wigman, on the other hand, had argued, "The opinion of an expert witness must be founded upon personal experience and not upon what he has read."

Xavier worried about this expert witness argument.

Charles said that they would have to wait for the Wisconsin Supreme Court's decision about whether to allow another trial, this one likely not in Brown County.

·∞·

Two days later, on November 8, 1888, Vroman entered Xavier's office with a disturbed countenance. Vroman said the Wisconsin Supreme Court had rendered its decision in the Soquet case. The Court had reversed judgment and ordered a new trial. He said the justices believed there were numerous trial errors, but the major one listed was that two State witnesses, Dr. Munro and Dr. Olmsted, "were not qualified to testify as medical experts, as they had only book knowledge and no experimental knowledge of arsenical poisoning." Vroman said their evidence had been ruled as "incompetent."

This was just what Xavier had feared.

Vroman said the State would be trying the case all over again, and Brown County had appointed him to try the new case. This time, Vroman said, he would have razor-sharp focus on *only* proving the single charge: that with premeditation, J.P. Soquet had poisoned his second wife, Esperance Soquet.

While that seemed wise, Xavier wondered about J.P.'s other crimes. The testimony about J.P. poisoning August Minsart and his abuse of Elvira Soquet had helped the jury see just what kind of man they were dealing with. Without those troubling details, Xavier feared a new jury might not have enough evidence to convict J.P. again.

And if that was the case, Xavier further worried what J.P. would do once he was freed.

PART IV

THE INEXPLICABLE

(1890-1944)

NEW VENUE

PAULINE

PAULINE'S SISTER, Elvira, had been missing for three and a half years. On May 7, 1890, a loneliness for her sister still pooled inside Pauline as she sat inside the Winnebago County Courthouse in Oshkosh, Wisconsin. She hated to imagine what J.P. Soquet had done to Elvira in late December of 1886, whether Elvira had suffered, whether she had cried out for their mother or Pauline, whether her sister had gazed into J.P.'s evil eyes as her life had come to an end.

Judge George W. Burnell would preside at the second trial of State vs. Jean P. Soquet. J.P.'s attorneys, Wigman and Hudd, had filed an affidavit for a change of venue on the grounds of prejudice of Brown County judge, Samuel D. Hastings. Another Brown County judge had granted the application.

Judge G.W. Burnell (findagrave.com contributed by Bill Hart)

The city of Oshkosh, with a population of about 22,000, was located fifty-five miles south of Green Bay. Its growth had been fueled by the lumber and paper industries which employed primarily German immigrants. Also known for its entertainment and nightlife, Oshkosh had earned the nickname of "Sin City" among locals.

The *Daily Northwestern* newspaper mocked the Belgian witnesses scheduled to testify at the Soquet trial. The article stated:

> *Perhaps no more heterogeneous collection of people [was] ever seen in Winnebago Court House than the witnesses who are here attending the Soquet trial. Nearly all of them are Belgians. The garments that some of them wear would form a splendid study for an artist who Loves to paint in bright colors. There is a pretty Lass of nineteen who wears a dress, which may have done service at her mother's wedding. Beside her stands a tall giant figure of a man who has some facial disease, which prompts him to partially conceal his countenance with a napkin. In fact, all the witnesses in dress, personal appearance and peculiarities are strikingly grotesque. Few of them understand a word of the English Language and nearly all the testimony will have to be given to the jury through the aid of an interpreter.*

Forty-five-year-old Pauline was one of those Belgians in the courtroom who could have taken offense to the newspaper article or conversely, died from laughter, as the Door Peninsula Belgians were said to do. She had arrived that morning on the Chicago & Northwestern passenger train which operated a line connecting the cities of Green Bay and Fort Howard to Milwaukee with a stop in Oshkosh.

The attorneys had selected nine jurors from Winnebago County, none of Belgian descent. Four of them were of note: William James Fleming, born in Milwaukee, who worked for the Post Office and was "one of the most popular and influential citizens of Oshkosh"; Captain Henry C. Johnson, a former Norwegian seaman who had operated a freight and passenger schooner on Lake Winnebago and currently owned a well-cultivated farm of 160 acres; Joseph H. Staudenraus, a German immigrant and Civil War veteran, who owned the Tremont House and served as a city building inspector; and F.M. Stowe, a veterinary surgeon of English descent.

William J. Fleming (Commemorative Biographical Record of the Fox River Valley counties of Brown, Outagamie and Winnebago)

Pauline eyed J.P. Soquet, his thick-set frame leaning back in a chair at the defendant's table. She had not seen him since his sentencing hearing three years ago. He turned his head slightly. At the age of sixty-three, J.P.'s beard was full and his hair partially gray. He was dressed in a dark sack suit over a white cotton shirt, which the press described as "of such poor quality that it must be that of a farmer." J.P.'s attire was certainly nothing like the dapper suits of his attorneys, Mr. Hudd and Mr. Wigman.

Attorney Charles E. Vroman sat at the prosecution table in the capacity of District Attorney. Attorney A.W. Weisbrod of Oshkosh would assist him. Attorney Vroman had talked to Pauline a number of weeks ago, informing her she would not be called to testify in the second trial. She had been disappointed. She had wanted to tell the jury everything her sister had relayed to her about that devil J.P. Soquet. But Mr. Vroman had said, in the Wisconsin Supreme Court brief, submitted by J.P.'s attorneys, most of Pauline's testimony had been considered hearsay, even though Judge Hastings had allowed it.

Mr. Vroman had told Pauline he could not afford to make those same mistakes again. He had assured her his decision would be for the best. He wanted to put J.P. away for life as much as Pauline did. But in order to accomplish that he had to base the second trial's testimony solely on proving J.P. had murdered his second wife, Esperance.

While it made Pauline uneasy, she had no choice but to trust Vroman. Since Pauline would no longer be a witness, she could attend as much of the trial as she chose. The court had ruled witnesses could only be present in the courtroom when they testified and for closing arguments. Xavier Martin was not testifying either. Pauline took comfort in his presence alongside her in the courtroom.

Pauline planned to stay in Oshkosh until Friday evening, two and a half days away, when she would catch the 5 p.m. train back to Green Bay. Then, she planned to return on the 5:55 a.m. train on Monday. Henry and their children, now ranging in age from eight to twenty, could manage without her for the span of the trial.

Seated in the row behind the defendant's table were two of J.P. Soquet's children: Rose, age twenty-one, and her brother Jule, twenty-four. None of the Soquet children had attended their father's first trial. Perhaps his attorneys had realized their mistake in not revealing that J.P.'s children supported their father, though Jule and Rose would not be testifying on his behalf.

The bailiff announced, "All rise! This Honorable Court is now in session. Judge George W. Burnell presiding." The fifty-one-year-old judge entered and took his seat behind the bench. He had served in the Civil War and helped found the Oshkosh Yacht Club. Prior to his election to Circuit Court Judge, six years ago, he had served as the Winnebago County District Attorney.

Once the bailiff brought in the newly selected jury, who took seats in the box, the judge told Attorney Vroman to proceed. Pauline listened to his opening statement and was pleased to hear that it did not stray from the pertinent storyline. Vroman said in 1872 Jean P. Soquet, his wife, Esperance, and their children lived on a farm about eight miles east of Green Bay. About two miles from their home lived August Minsart and his wife, Elvira. Between the fall of 1872 and the spring of 1873, a criminal intimacy existed between Jean P. Soquet and Mrs. Elvira Minsart. August Minsart suddenly died and an autopsy proved he had been poisoned by eight grams of arsenic, enough to kill ten men.

Attorney Vroman paused to let that sink in.

Pauline heard rustling inside the courtroom. Many spectators knew the entire Minsart-Soquet saga. Others, like the jurors, did not. Attorney Vroman continued. Two weeks after August Minsart's sudden demise, he said, Mrs. Esperance Soquet also died with identical symptoms. Many years passed before her grave was opened to analyze the stomach contents. But instead of finding Esperance's corpse in her coffin, the authorities discovered her remains had disappeared.

Pauline checked the jurors' reaction. Many seemed horrified.

In the meantime, Vroman said, Mr. Soquet and Mrs. Minsart married. But their wedded life was not "the dream of felicity" they had expected, for they had since divorced.

Pauline noticed that Attorney Vroman had not even mentioned her sister's disappearance as he drew his opening statement to a close. She understood why, but it still hurt to hear her sister overlooked.

He said the State would provide evidence to prove the defendant, Jean P. Soquet, with premeditated intent, murdered his wife, Esperance Soquet, so he could marry his lover, Mrs. Elvira Minsart.

A woman beside Pauline expressed her disappointment at not hearing about J.P.'s other purported murders.

Pauline had to agree yet understood why. She knew the Belgian community had charged J.P. with at least five murders, those of his three wives, his little boy, and August Minsart, while the authorities had only charged him with Esperance's death. Attorney Vroman had indeed been cautious in his opening statement to ensure he made no errors which could keep J.P. from being convicted of murdering his second wife.

Attorney John H.M. Wigman (History of Brown County, Commemorative Biographical Record)

From the defendant's table, Mr. Wigman rose and positioned himself in front of the jury to present the defendant's case. The substance of his speech was that for fourteen years no one had heard anything about the case until the prisoner's third wife, Elvira Soquet, asked for a divorce from her husband, Jean P. Soquet. Wigman said it had been obtained and that the costs had amounted to $80. The defendant had paid $40 of that amount and was unable to raise the remaining $40, which had been claimed by a man named Xavier Martin for his translation assistance. On account of that trouble with Mr. Martin, Attorney Wigman said, J.P.'s criminal prosecution had been initiated.

Pauline glanced over at Xavier as Attorney Wigman continued. He asserted the only point on which there would be any direct evidence in the case would be that August Minsart, the former husband of Soquet's third wife, had been poisoned. Anything else the State would claim would not only be circumstantial evidence and irrelevant, but so highly colored by prejudice as to be valueless. And if that evidence had been ruled out at the former trial, Wigman said in closing, this man, J.P. Soquet, would not have been convicted of poisoning his wife.

Three major witnesses for the State had passed away since the first trial: Pauline's father, Alexis Coppersmith, Esperance Soquet's father, Mr. J.J. Hannon, and Dr. Andrew Munro, who had attended to Esperance Soquet in the last week of her life.

Attorney Vroman offered into evidence the official stenographer's report of Dr. Munro's testimony from the first trial. Attorney Hudd immediately objected. He claimed the defendant had the constitutional right to see an opposing witness face to face. Attorney Vroman countered saying the defendant had watched Dr. Munro testify at the former trial, which should be sufficient. The objection of the defense was finally overruled by Judge Burnell. However, he stated, he would adjourn court for the day so he could read through Dr. Munro's prior testimony and determine what portions would be allowed into evidence.

Pauline stood to leave the courtroom. She was exhausted from her early morning travels and the day's proceedings. She lugged her heavy carpet bag to the Oshkosh House. The hotel contained a dining room and beer hall and was located two blocks from the courthouse. Pauline sat at one of the communal dining tables for supper. Everyone there, it seemed, was connected to the trial in some way: those who had attended the prior trial, like Pauline, and were interested in the outcome of the current one; out-of-town newspaper reporters; and some of the State witnesses testifying the next day.

Oshkosh House (Courtesy Lee Reiherzer)

As the local fare of roast pork, root vegetables, and homemade bread was served, conversation centered on the latest article from the *Oshkosh Times* newspaper titled "The Blood-Stained Career of Soquet Now on Trial in Circuit Court for Murder." A gentleman said the paper claimed that everything printed had been testified to at the prior trial, which he knew was not true. He believed the newspapers had turned Soquet's macabre saga into a scandalous dime novel where everybody in Wisconsin, and perhaps across the country, was on the edge of their seats, anticipating the next installment.

Many guests mumbled their agreement while eyeing the reporters at the end of the table, scribbling notes. One Belgian diner asked the man to read the article. He said he could speak and understand English, but he never learned to read or write it. Pauline fit into that category, too, and she was pleased when the gentleman agreed to read the article aloud.

As the gentleman opened the paper and began to read, Pauline listened to the guests dissecting the article. Most of the information Pauline had heard before. She waited patiently until the gentleman reached the section about her sister: "On the evening of Dec. 31, 1886, Soquet, revolver in hand, entered the Minsart house, to which Mrs. Minsart-Soquet had removed on separating from Soquet ... He was met at the door by a man, and Soquet demanded, 'Who is here?' The man responded, 'I am here and your wife is here.' ... 'She must die,' the blood thirsty scoundrel exclaimed ... and he strode into the house."

The gentleman looked up from the paper as the supper guests talked excitedly.

Pauline frowned. The article's version of the drama troubled her. Still, she had heard it before. Other than the revolver, Attorney Vroman had relayed most of those words in the prosecution's opening statement at J.P.'s first trial.

The diners quieted as the gentleman cleared his throat and continued to read about the man whom J.P. addressed at the Minsart home, who was "so frightened that he fled and never stopped until he reached Red River, twelve miles away. From that hour to this, not a trace of the unfortunate woman has been discovered ... Neighbors testify to hearing a woman's shrieks from the house."

Pauline recognized that the statement about the unknown man had some basis in truth, but not the one about her sister's shrieks. The Simonars were Elvira's closest neighbors. If they had heard shrieks coming from the house, they would have testified to that at the first trial.

The waitress came around to pour coffee for each guest as the gentleman continued to read about Xavier Martin, who had aided the sheriff in searching the Minsart house, and how the two men had located blood and hair evidence.

That information was painful for Pauline to hear, although she had reconciled herself with those facts. But she had not heard the next words the man read that "tracks of a hand-sled were also discovered leading to Soquet's house."

Pauline listened as the dining guests speculated. One person said, if this man Soquet had killed his third wife in the Minsart home, he could have pulled her body away on a hand-sled through neighbors' fields to avoid discovery. Another guest pointed out, as far as he knew, nobody had reported seeing sled tracks.

Pauline agreed. She believed that information about seeing sled tracks was a fabrication. But the next words the gentleman read were the most sensational and also the most disturbing to Pauline: "The testimony of Soquet's grandchildren furnishes the key to the mystery. 'Grandpa baked two whole nights in the oven,' said the little ones, 'but he didn't bake any bread.' Soquet had killed the woman who had been first his mistress, then his wife, and who had shared his crime and guilty secrets, then cremated her body in a large oven."

Pauline shivered and stood. Of course, no one had testified to that gruesome scenario at the prior trial. It probably wasn't true, she reasoned. But even so, that rumor could explain why her sister's body had not been found.

Pauline was desperate to make sense of what had happened to her sister. No matter how unlikely, this assertion and its implications gnawed at her.

Example of Summer Kitchen (George Waulet Farm - Outdoor Kitchen, Photo 569, Belgian-American Research Collection, University of Wisconsin-Green Bay Archives Department)

She left the dining room chatter and walked toward her room. Pauline knew the brick oven in the Soquet summer kitchen was large enough to bake a dozen loaves of bread at one time. J.P. also had young grandchildren who visited from Coleman, Wisconsin, with J.P.'s daughter, Elisabeth, and her husband, Sam Bebeau. In the middle of the night, while everyone was perhaps sleeping inside the house, J.P. could have built a wood fire in the oven chamber of the summer kitchen a few steps from the house. Once the interior walls were coated with white ash, he could have inserted Elvira's body and closed the oven's iron door. After a few days, nothing would have remained of her sister's body but ashes. It was far-fetched. It was unsettling. Yet, it could have happened.

Pauline held back tears as she entered her stuffy room. She opened the window and listened to the melancholy cries of night birds passing.

Pauline believed her sister was dead. For that reason, about a month ago, Pauline had talked to Attorney F.C. Cady to determine how she should handle Elvira's Main Street rental house. Since Elvira's disappearance, the Villiesse family had maintained the home, collected the rent, and paid the property taxes. Pauline and Henry did not want to keep doing this forever. Attorney Cady had filed a complaint in essence stating: If Elvira Soquet did not appear in court within a three-month period, Pauline would be awarded the title to Elvira's rental property. The court summons had first been printed in the *State Gazette* on April 8, 1890, and each week since. The summons would run for two more months.

Pauline hoped her sister would appear to claim her property, to show she was alive. But the odds were slim. Everyone thought she was dead. And even if she were alive, Pauline knew Elvira would never be safe with J.P. alive.

TRUE EXPERTS

XAVIER

XAVIER CLIMBED the flight of steps to enter the Winnebago County courthouse on the morning of Thursday, May 8, 1890. He understood the prosecution's strategy: to only introduce evidence related to the charge of J.P. poisoning his second wife. The reason Xavier would not be called as a witness was that his prior trial testimony focused on J.P.'s third wife, Elvira.

Winnebago County Courthouse (Wikimedia Commons)

It pained Xavier to hear Attorney Wigman mention him in his opening statement, claiming that J.P.'s criminal prosecution had only been initiated because of Xavier Martin's petty vendetta against the man for his nonpayment of $40. Xavier wanted to deny that accusation to the jury from the witness box. But Attorney Vroman told him that Mr. Coppersmith's testimony, to be read into the record from the former trial, would cover some of that ground and would carry more weight with the jury than Xavier's denial.

Xavier hoped that was true.

Xavier entered the main pavilion on the second floor with its soaring tower and limestone accents. The sheriff's residence had recently been constructed on the first floor adjacent to the new jail cells where J.P. Soquet was housed.

Xavier reached the third-floor courtroom and found a seat. The bailiff called court to order and Judge Burnell entered. Once the jurymen were in their box, the trial of State vs. J.P. Soquet proceeded.

The court reporter read into the record the sections of Dr. Munro's prior testimony allowed by Judge Burnell. Xavier noticed a key question had been omitted. In the former trial, District Attorney Neville had asked Dr. Munro, "What are the symptoms of arsenical poisoning?" After many objections by J.P.'s attorneys, Judge Hastings had allowed Dr. Munro to give his "expert opinion." Xavier now knew Dr. Munro could not be considered an expert since he had no first-hand experience with any arsenical poisoning cases. In the current trial, there was no mention about Dr. Munro's "expert opinion," however the testimony Judge Burnell allowed still provided Esperance Soquet's symptoms, as witnessed by Dr. Munro. The physician's prior testimony—that a blackened or discolored face was no indication of poisoning—was also included.

Three doctors followed who all had first-hand experience with arsenical poisoning: Dr. Brett and Dr. Lewis, from the former trial, and Dr. R.H. Bingham of Oshkosh. All testified that Esperance Soquet's symptoms, witnessed by Dr. Munro, indicated arsenical poisoning. Dr. Brett also testified to the nature of puerperal fever. As Xavier listened, he experienced his dear wife Augusta's suffering all over again. He recognized each of the puerperal fever symptoms intimately. The notable difference between childbed fever and arsenical poisoning, Dr. Brett testified, was an abnormal uterus, accompanied by a putrid discharge and high fever.

Xavier's grief threatened to overwhelm him, but he forced himself to stay focused.

Dr. Brett firmly stated Esperance Soquet's symptoms would not indicate puerperal fever, as did Dr. Lewis and Dr. Bingham.

Xavier knew the physician testimony was crucial for Vroman's case. Three doctors, deemed experts due to their first-hand experience with poisoning cases, had stated Esperance Soquet's symptoms indicated arsenical poisoning. But none of them had attended to Esperance Soquet during her illness. The three doctors' testimony had all been based on the symptoms provided by Dr. Munro. In cross-examination, Dr. Brett admitted that Dr. Munro had frequently been under the influence of liquor, although, when sober, he had been a "most excellent physician."

·∞·

Over the ensuing days of the trial, Xavier listened to the neighbors' testimony, as in the first trial, about the criminal intimacy between the defendant and Mrs. August Minsart, and the neighbors' visits to the deathbed of Esperance Soquet.

A few witnesses provided new information. Joseph Everard stated, "I found Soquet's wife sick on the bed. She stuck her finger in her mouth and vomited." Afterward, J.P. "worked his finger around in Mrs. Soquet's vomit, divided it up in little piles, and seemed to be examining it closely." Mrs. Rosalie Williams testified that Esperance Soquet had complained about something in her throat and how she wished she could pull it out.

During the cross-examination of Everard and Rosalie, Attorney Hudd read both witnesses their former trial testimony and asked why their current testimony included new revelations. Both Everard and Rosalie wiggled uncomfortably on the stand, attempting to explain. Eighteen years had passed since Esperance Soquet's death. The testimony of those two witnesses, who suddenly remembered a circumstance more accurately in the current trial than the former one, seemed far-fetched to Xavier. The jurors would likely feel the same.

The next testimony focused on Esperance Soquet's remains, including J.P.'s requests to unbury his wife's body, the means by which it was allegedly done, and the body's conjectured final location. That evidence included Joseph Everard's testimony about J.P.'s assault on Mrs. Pauline Villiesse.

Everard said Mrs. Villiesse had "scored Soquet roundly." She had told the defendant, "He was a scoundrel and had poisoned his wife and afterwards unburied her body, placing it in a gray blanket and reinterred it on his farm." J.P. had begged Mrs. Villiesse to cease and told her, "If she would only be quiet, he would pay her $35." Later, Everard said, J.P. had told him the woman's talk about "those old poisoning matters" had given him concern, and he had insisted that Mrs. Villiesse "must be silenced in that regard."

Xavier glanced over at Pauline Villiesse. He could see she was pleased by Everard's testimony. He had provided the same information she would have given if she had testified.

The court reporter next read into the record the former trial testimony of Mr. Alexis Coppersmith that the judge had allowed into evidence. Mr. Coppersmith had testified he had sent word to Mr. Xavier Martin three times to come to his Green Bay township home. Based on the Coppersmith family's urgent third request, Mr. Martin had arrived at the Coppersmith home with Sheriff Watermolen and Attorney Tracy. Mr. Coppersmith had testified that he was the defendant's former father-in-law. His daughter, Elvira, had been J.P.'s third wife, who had since divorced him. Xavier noticed that Mr. Coppersmith's mention of Elvira's disappearance had been omitted from the testimony.

The recounted testimony stated Xavier Martin had sworn Mr. Coppersmith in and had translated his testimony into a statement, which Mr. Coppersmith had signed. That information had included Soquet's admission to Coppersmith that he would be "in for it" if his wife's body was not unburied, since she had been poisoned.

Xavier sat back against the hard wooden spectator bench. Hopefully Mr. Coppersmith's testimony had provided the jury some insight into Xavier's connection to the case to quash the defense's claims about his vendetta against Soquet. But Mr. Coppersmith's testimony had not included the information about Xavier's translation assistance during the Soquets' divorce. Xavier wondered whether Mr. Coppersmith's testimony would be enough.

·∞·

By late afternoon on Wednesday, May 14, 1890, on the sixth day of the trial, thirty prosecution witnesses had testified. Court was about to adjourn when Xavier's friend, Attorney Vroman, announced he had one final prosecution witness and asked the deputy sheriff to summon Joseph Willett to the courtroom.

Xavier was curious about this man, since he had not appeared at the first trial. So was the rest of the courtroom who scrutinized the man as he walked down the aisle.

Joseph Willett was sworn in and testified he had been released from the Wisconsin State Prison in Waupun two years ago after spending sixteen months inside. He was French Canadian and had frequently conversed with the defendant, Jean P. Soquet, who had been a Waupun inmate during those same sixteen months. Since J.P. did not know English, the chaplain had arranged for the two men to spend considerable time in each other's company. Willett had brought J.P. a French Bible upon his request. J.P. had told Willett his attorneys had been trying to get him a new trial, but he had little hope they would succeed.

Attorney Vroman asked Willet whether the defendant had shared any personal confidences with him.

Willet said J.P. had shared many, since J.P. had figured he was in prison for life and had nothing to lose. He had told Willett that he had been very much in love with Elvira Minsart. Because of that, he had killed his wife, Esperance, so he could marry Elvira. But it had taken J.P. twice as much poison to kill Esperance as it had to kill August Minsart.

Willett's last testimony provoked a substantial reaction within the entire courtroom. The jurors sat forward in their seats, anxious to hear more. Xavier glanced at the defendant's table. Mr. Wigman, whose mouth hung slack, had not expected Willett's revelations and his testimony had "nearly made Mr. Hudd's curly hair straighten." J.P. had covered his face with his hands. Although he could not understand a word of the testimony, J.P. "evidently knew the nature of it." Even Judge Burnell seemed dazed. He had removed his glasses and was fiercely polishing them as Willett, prompted by Attorney Vroman, continued.

Willett said J.P. had described his fear after the authorities had dug up August Minsart's remains. Due to that, J.P. had dug up his murdered wife's body one night and carried her remains in a shawl to the woods to conceal them. While crossing his fields, J.P. had told Willett, an arm of the corpse had dropped off. Later, one of J.P.'s sons had plowed up the arm. His son had recognized his mother's wedding ring on the finger. According to J.P., his son had not been seen again.

Everyone in the courtroom sat still, frozen to their spot, breathless with astonishment. Yet that chilling story about J.P.'s son plowing up his mother's arm seemed familiar to Xavier. Had it been printed in the press? Xavier had ripped out numerous articles from local papers since the trial had begun and filed them in his briefcase. At the next recess, Xavier would check.

He refocused as Willett's testimony continued. The ex-convict said after he had been released from prison, J.P.'s son-in-law Mr. Fred Beno, married to the defendant's daughter Josephine, had contacted Willett. Beno had offered Willett money to write a letter to J.P.'s Green

Bay attorneys from a northern Michigan town. Willett was to state that J.P.'s third wife, Elvira Soquet, whose fate was still involved in mystery, was alive.

Xavier's eyes widened. Willett's alleged information could prove J.P. was involved in Elvira Soquet's disappearance and likely her death. Xavier checked the jurors. They seemed confused. No witness testimony had been offered to reveal that Elvira Soquet's fate was involved in mystery.

Xavier had expected that J.P.'s attorneys would have objected to the relevance of that last portion of testimony. But the attorneys had remained silent. Perhaps they had not wanted to spend any more time than necessary on Willett's revelations. It would be their turn next, anyway.

The defense stood to take their crack at Willett. But, even under Mr. Hudd's rigid cross-examination, Willett maintained his statements. Judge Burnell called for a short recess before the defense would take center stage.

During the recess, Xavier opened his briefcase and ruffled through the newspaper articles he had kept. He located the one he was interested in from the *Oshkosh Times*, published on the second day of the trial, which stated:

> *These facts were all brought out during the last trial ... that Soquet robbed his second wife's grave and reburied her on his farm ... One of his sons, while plowing, turned up a woman's arm. Recovering from the shock, he examined it, and on the finger, he was horrified to discover a gold band that he recognized as his dead mother's wedding ring. This was more than he could bear. He fled precipitately and has never been seen since by the inhabitants of Brown County. His death, too, is attributed to Soquet; but this cannot be substantiated, though a witness did testify that Soquet hunted for his son with an axe through the streets of Green Bay one night, and that the weapon was taken away by the witness.*

When Xavier had read those words, he had been amazed by the newspaper's audacity to print such sensational news and claim those "facts" had been brought out during the prior trial. Attorney Vroman had questioned J.P. about his son's unexpected departure in the first trial. Vroman had also attempted to tie his son's departure to the rumor that he had uncovered his mother's remains while plowing. But J.P. had denied those rumors not once but twice.

In the former trial's testimony, Vroman had not specifically mentioned that J.P.'s son had found his mother's arm with a ring on the finger of the hand. Had Joseph Willett read the *Oshkosh Times* article and simply regurgitated what had been printed? Or perhaps Willett had been the source of the article.

How was Xavier to know? More importantly, how was the jury to know? They had been instructed by the judge not to read any articles about the trial nor discuss the trial with anyone. They would not have seen the article which had been printed after the trial had begun.

The first defense witness called was J.P.'s son-in-law, Mr. Fred Beno. He refuted Willett's testimony. Beno said he had never asked Willett to write a letter to attorneys Hudd and Wigman stating the defendant's third wife, Mrs. Elvira Soquet, was alive.

Xavier was surprised that the defense had even placed Beno on the stand. J.P.'s attorneys had drawn further attention to the fact that their client could have been involved in some sort of mystery surrounding his third wife's whereabouts. Xavier thought Fred Beno was lying. How would Willett have known the name of Soquet's son-in-law if Fred Beno had not asked the ex-convict to write that letter to Soquet's attorneys?

Attorney Wigman now called the defendant, Jean P. Soquet, to the stand. As in the prior trial, he stepped through all the circumstances and events surrounding his wife's confinement. He testified that he believed his wife had contracted childbed fever like so many other women in the neighborhood. From that point until her death, J.P. said he had done everything in his power to secure the best treatment for his wife by soliciting the help of Dr. Munro and Father Daems.

J.P.'s attorney asked him questions about his divorce from his third wife, Elvira Soquet.

J.P. confirmed his wife, Elvira, had been awarded a divorce, and the judge had ordered J.P. to pay his wife's attorney costs of $40 and the $40 owed to Xavier Martin for his translation services. J.P. admitted he had failed to pay Mr. Martin. Because of that, J.P. believed Xavier Martin had decided to get even with him by spreading old rumors. Mr.

Martin's false claims were the only reason his third wife's father, Mr. Coppersmith, had called Martin to his home, which had led to J.P.'s arrest and prosecution.

Xavier scowled listening to J.P.'s misdirection of blame.

When Attorney Wigman put his final question to his client: "Mr. Soquet, did you poison your wife?" all eyes were glued to the defendant. After considerable sniveling, J.P. answered, "No," he had "never seen any poison." He had always lived happily with his wife. That no one could have trouble with "so good a woman."

A physician and a druggist followed. Both testified about the drug, bismuth, which was often adulterated with arsenic.

Xavier knew the jurors had to prove J.P. Soquet was guilty beyond a reasonable doubt. The defense was attempting to provide that doubt. Dr. Munro had prescribed bismuth to Esperance Soquet. But this was only after Esperance had complained of burning in her throat and stomach. Xavier feared the jurors might not recall that testimony's specific timeline which had been read into the record from the prior trial.

Xavier watched as Mrs. Jennie Jesmer took the stand on her father's behalf. She was the firstborn daughter of Esperance and J.P. Soquet and "a fine-looking woman". Xavier recalled that Jennie had left home to join a convent soon after her father married Elvira Minsart. Jennie had evidently left the nunnery.

She testified she had been fourteen years old when her mother Esperance Soquet had called Jennie to her bedside, just before her death. She had told Jennie to "help her father take care of the children." At that time, Jennie said her mother had complained of terrible pains in her side. Jennie said her grandmother had prepared all the food her mother had eaten. When Jennie swore there had never been any trouble between her mother and father, she broke down, "choking back sobs".

At the defense table, J.P. sobbed as well. It seemed remarkable to Xavier that J.P.'s children appeared to have remained close to their father.

When the name of Frank Hannon was called, Xavier was surprised. He had no idea what his brother-in-law, married to Xavier's youngest sibling, Celina, would testify to.

Frank said he was the first cousin to the late Esperance Soquet. A few weeks prior to her death, she had told Frank that she was afraid she would die at the birth of her child. Hannon also swore that the testimony of the deceased witness, Alexis Coppersmith, was incorrect. In the spring of 1874, Hannon testified, J.P. and Mr. Coppersmith had not made the trip from the Green Bay township to the city of Green Bay. J.P.'s then wife Elvira had accompanied her father instead. Because of that, Hannon said J.P. could not have asked Mr. Coppersmith to help him "unbury" his wife.

Xavier frowned. His brother-in-law's testimony made no sense. Mr. Coppersmith and his son-in-law William Lancelle had both told Xavier their discussions with J.P. occurred when Elvira Soquet was locked up in jail awaiting her trial for her husband's poisoning death. The trip Mr. Coppersmith had taken with J.P. had been to provide the $2,000 surety to release Elvira on bail.

The next witness was Miss Marie Hannon, one of Esperance Soquet's sisters. Marie testified that Esperance had called at Marie's house on her way home from church the Sunday before Esperance's death. Esperance had told Marie that so many women had recently died soon after childbirth. Esperance was afraid she might die too. Marie also swore her sister had never owned a ring.

The defense rested their case and Attorney Vroman called one rebuttal witness, Mrs. Forsythe, a next-door neighbor to the Soquets. She testified that she had laid out Esperance's body the day following her death. Mrs. Forsythe swore a wedding ring *had* been on Esperance Soquet's finger.

Xavier gazed over at the jury. The last few witnesses' testimony had been contradictory and confusing. He could not tell who the jurors believed. But he knew that what they believed mattered gravely.

FINAL VERDICT

PAULINE

PAULINE SAT in the crowded Winnebago County courtroom on May 16, 1890. Only the closing arguments and the charge to the jury remained in the Soquet murder trial before the jurors would be released to deliberate. Pauline was ready for the trial to be over, ready for what little closure it might bring her. She knew justice would not be enough, but she was ready to see it served nonetheless.

Pauline had heard Willett's claim that Fred Beno asked Willett to mail a letter to J.P.'s attorneys from Michigan and state that Pauline's sister, Elvira, was alive. This news had sent a stir through the spectator section.

While Willett's testimony may have been titillating for the rest of the crowd, its effect on Pauline was just the opposite: It merely cemented her belief that her sister was dead.

Pauline continued to parse the truth from his testimony. Willett's story about J.P.'s eldest son Fred finding his mother's arm in the field was sickening, but Pauline believed there could be some truth to it. Fred Soquet had left home and had never been heard from again. The three Soquet children in the courtroom, Jennie, Rose, and Jule, had hated Elvira and had always loved their father. Those three children had likely never believed that J.P. had poisoned their mother. Fred may have been the lone sibling who had realized his father had been involved in his mother's death.

Attorney Vroman stood to present the State's closing argument. His voice was quiet yet forceful as he pieced together the State's evidence to reach the logical conclusion that J.P. had murdered his wife.

Vroman discussed motive. "It may be robbery or it may be love, and in this case, it was love." He described the clandestine relationship between Mrs. Elvira Minsart and J.P. Soquet. Because their two spouses had discovered their secret meetings and had objected to them, Attorney Vroman said, August Minsart and Esperance Soquet had become obstacles. "They must be removed!" He pounded his fist on the jury rail. "And they are removed! Removed, to make a way so that a brutal man and woman can carry out their plans."

Mr. Vroman touched upon the testimony of Mrs. LeCoque who swore that J.P. fed his wife some gruel, and that J.P. took the bowl away to clean it. "Is it like a man," said Mr. Vroman, "to wash a bowl? No, there is not another man that would do it. Most of us would leave it for the women folks to do. But Soquet is more careful and why? Because he knew there was arsenical poisoning in that bowl."

Vroman addressed Willett's testimony, in which he had sworn that J.P. had confessed to him while the two men had served time in prison. That witness's evidence, Vroman said, had corroborated the testimony from other witnesses, and the defendant had lied on the stand to protect himself. Based on all the evidence, Vroman said in closing, the jury had to convict J.P. Soquet of murder in the first degree.

Pauline sat in silence with the rest of the courtroom. She did not have the energy to think whether his arguments would convince the jury. She just sat and waited for the defense.

Attorney Wigman stood before the jurors and laid the groundwork for the defense's closing argument. First, that in order for the jury to find Soquet guilty they had to find Mrs. Soquet had died; second, that she had died of poison; and third, that the defendant had poisoned her. Mr. Wigman argued that Dr. Munro could not have known whether Mrs. Soquet had died of poison unless he had seen her just before her death, which he had not. Moreover, the last time Dr. Munro had attended Esperance Soquet, he had likely been under the influence of liquor.

Mr. T.R. Hudd continued for the defense. In order for the jury to find J.P. Soquet guilty, Hudd said they had to conclude that Dr. Munro had been sober and had known exactly what he had been doing when he had examined Mrs. Soquet during her sickness. The jury also had to assume the bismuth powders the doctor had provided to Mrs. Soquet had been perfectly pure. Hudd reviewed the testimony of the defense witnesses who had sworn that bismuth was often adulterated with arsenic. Mr. Hudd claimed that even if the jury believed Mrs. Soquet had been poisoned, the bismuth powders could have been the source.

Hudd addressed the empty coffin of Esperance Soquet. He stated that no direct evidence had been offered to prove the defendant had removed his wife's remains, so the feasible alternative of grave robbers had to be considered as the reason her coffin was empty.

Hudd closed with attacks. Joseph Willett was "a liar and a perjurer". What more could they expect from an ex-convict? Hudd ended with his same old charge against Xavier Martin: the case would never have come to trial if not for him.

Pauline was disturbed that the defense had once again made Xavier Martin their scapegoat while portraying J.P. as a victim. It was too much to believe. Yet the defense had planted some reasonable doubt for the jurors, like Dr. Munro's drinking problems and the bismuth powders.

As the closing arguments ended, Pauline stood to take her leave. She felt numb.

On the morning of May 17, 1890, court convened. Pauline glanced over at J.P. He looked nervous. By sundown, there was a good chance he would know whether he was a free man or whether he would be sent back to the Wisconsin State Prison in Waupun. Pauline was ready to know as well.

J.P.'s daughters, Rose and Jennie, were seated behind the defendant's table with their brother Jule and brother-in-law, Fred Beno. All four sensed the gravity of the situation as Attorney Vroman provided the State's rebuttal. His voice rose at times when "stirred by his own deep convictions" that the defendant, J.P. Soquet, was guilty of murder in the first degree.

Mr. Vroman's passion throughout the trial had also stirred Pauline. He never wavered. For the second time, the attorney had given his all to get justice for Esperance Soquet. And Pauline knew that this was the best chance at justice for her sister.

Pauline gazed up at Judge Burnell. After ten long days, the time had come for him to provide his charge to the jury. The prosecution, Burnell said, had claimed Esperance Soquet had died of arsenic poison. The main point for the jury to determine would be whether Esperance Soquet had died of poison. If she had not died of poison, the jury had to acquit the prisoner. But if the jury found that Esperance Soquet had died of poison, they had to determine whether the poison had been administered by the defendant, J.P. Soquet.

The judge touched upon the expert medical witnesses called by the State to help the jury understand the complex evidence and relevant issues. Burnell said those doctors' opinions had been provided to aid the jury in reaching their conclusion. But the jurors should not confuse opinion with fact. Burnell explained what circumstantial evidence meant. It was a chain of events or circumstances, when considered together, which could lead a person to a reasonable conclusion about what had occurred.

Judge Burnell also addressed the testimony of Joseph Willett. The judge said admissions of that kind were usually called weak evidence, as the person to whom the confession had been made might not have heard all the statement, or he could have mistaken a word in the statement, which would materially change the evidence. But Judge Burnell also said that if Willett's admissions had corroborated other testimony in the trial, his admissions could become very strong evidence.

In regard to J.P.'s own testimony, the judge said the jury might take into consideration the fact that the defendant had a powerful motive to color his testimony to suit himself. But on the other hand, the jury might find that if the defendant's evidence had been corroborated, it would be strong evidence.

The judge closed by explaining to the jury the importance of reasonable doubt in a criminal trial. It meant the prosecution's evidence had been so convincing that no reasonable person would question the defendant's guilt. The jurors would not have to be absolutely certain, but based on the evidence, they would have to be firmly convinced.

If there was any reasonable doubt regarding J.P. Soquet's guilt, Judge Burnell said, the jury had to find the defendant not guilty.

Pauline and the rest of the crowd had followed Burnell's explanation of the legal process. It gave Pauline no pause in believing J.P.'s guilt, but now she had to wait to see what the jurors thought.

Court adjourned at 2 p.m. and the jurors filed out of the courtroom to decide J.P.'s fate. For the second time, Pauline waited in the courtroom, hoping for a quick verdict. Some of the Belgian witnesses also remained, as did Xavier Martin. Pauline and the others kept their voices low, as they speculated. Soquet's family members had remained in the courtroom.

The clock ticked. Pauline settled into silence.

One hour passed. A restlessness began to set in. In the first trial, the jurors had reached a guilty verdict in less than one hour.

Judge Burnell's charge to the jury occupied Pauline's mind, and the time passed slowly. If the jury determined Esperance had not died from poison, they had to acquit Soquet. Pauline now dreaded he would walk away a free man, just as he had so many times before.

Fifteen more minutes passed. The crowd lulled.

The spectators began to chatter again, and Pauline's heart ratcheted up.

Another fifteen minutes ticked by. It was now 3:30.

Pauline could only stay for another hour before she had to leave to catch the train back to Green Bay. She felt tension throughout her body. She stood to stretch her legs, but just then, the bailiff entered the courtroom and announced: The jurors had a verdict.

She gazed over at Xavier Martin. Pauline recalled what he had told her at the former trial: A quick verdict often meant the evidence had been convincing. But was this jury persuaded of J.P.'s innocence or guilt?

She would have to suffer that uncertainty for at least thirty more minutes, while the court reconvened. Xavier Martin joined her. Like Pauline, he said he planned to catch the 5 p.m. train back to Green Bay. They felt the preciousness of time.

The attorneys and J.P. Soquet were in their places by 4:00 p.m. J.P.'s three children and son-in-law, Fred Beno, were seated directly behind J.P. Newspaper reporters lined the back wall, prepared to dash out to be the first in line to telegraph or telephone the verdict to their offices.

The bailiff called the court to order.

Judge Burnell entered and took his seat behind the bench.

The jury filed in.

Pauline stared at their faces.

The clerk of courts asked the foreman if a verdict had been reached.

He stood and answered. "It has."

Pauline clutched her hands together.

The clerk asked, "Do you find the defendant, Jean P. Soquet, guilty or not guilty according to the information?"

The foreman said, "Guilty of murder in the first degree."

Pauline released her breath, not realizing she had been holding it, and her hands began to shake.

J.P. Soquet was guilty of first-degree murder for the second time.

Pauline watched J.P.'s head drop into his hands. His two daughters sobbed. Their emotions were so removed from hers.

Pauline smiled with relief, her gaze meeting Xavier Martin's. The same emotion was playing on his face. Both had been resolved to see this through, to see J.P. Soquet meet justice. And now it was happening, again, finally. Now Pauline hoped she could feel released from the trial's hold, the hold J.P. had exerted in her life these past decades. But could she ever be released from the hope of seeing her sister?

SENTENCE AND AFTERMATH

XAVIER

THE CHICAGO & NORTHWESTERN passenger train neared Oshkosh on May 31, 1890. Ten days had passed since J.P. Soquet had been convicted of his wife's murder. Xavier was attending the sentencing hearing and conducting some real estate business in the city. He nodded at Pauline Villiesse and some of her family members who were seated on the train as well.

Xavier recalled how he had frequently taken this trip thirteen years ago to secretly visit Augusta and their two oldest sons. Xavier's heart ached for Augusta. He would never forget the passion and mutual respect he and his second wife had experienced throughout their love affair and marriage.

Amid the clickety-clack of the passenger car's wheels traveling over rail section gaps, Xavier read an article in the *State Gazette*. J.P. Soquet had earned a new title of "a modern Bluebeard" of three wives who had all died or disappeared under suspicious circumstances. He was also called the "Bender of Wisconsin" and the "Fiendish Bay Settlement Farmer". J.P. Soquet's decades of wrongdoings were deemed "unparalleled in Wisconsin, the blackest series of crimes ever engrossed in the annals of its criminal history." It was sensational, but in his opinion, not unwarranted.

Xavier noted that the current article mentioned him, but at least it was complimentary. "A marked feature in the case," the paper stated, "was the unforeseen manner in which some of the particulars were revealed to Xavier Martin of this city ... To Mr. Martin, therefore, is asserted great credit for the successful termination of the trial ..."

Xavier had heard the testimony of Joseph Willett at the trial, but now the newspaper had embellished that testimony. It stated that

J.P. had confessed to committing three additional murders to Willett: Ignace Minsart's drowning death, the murder of J.P.'s young son by "deliberately throwing [him] head foremost down the stairs," and the murder of J.P.'s third wife. According to the paper, J.P. had told Willett he had "choked Elvira Minsart-Soquet to death, and he had baked her body to ashes in a brick oven." Xavier wondered if these claims were fabrications by the newspaper. Or had Willett talked to the press to provide details that had not been revealed in his testimony.

Xavier realized everything printed in the article would be difficult to prove, other than perhaps Elvira Soquet's final resting place. If J.P. had not cremated his wife, perhaps he had buried her on the forty acres of wooded land he had bought from her. The authorities were no longer interested in searching for Elvira Soquet's remains, but maybe someone might stumble upon her bones while hunting.

Inside the Winnebago County courtroom, Xavier listened as Judge Burnell ordered J.P. Soquet to stand, which he did with some effort. The judge asked whether he had anything to say.

Through the help of a translator, J.P. said he forgave all the witnesses who had "perjured themselves" and thereby succeeded in securing his conviction.

Xavier huffed quietly. He heard the sarcastic intonation in J.P.'s actual words spoken in Walloon. J.P. Soquet was not forgiving anyone. Xavier knew if J.P. was not behind bars, he would seek revenge on every State witness who had testified against him. He had earned the title of the Bay Settlement Bruiser for a reason.

Judge Burnell then said, "Jean Philippe Soquet, the sentence of the court is that you shall be punished by confinement at hard labor in the state prison of the State of Wisconsin at Waupun for a term of your natural life. And that one day in each year of such imprisonment to be spent in solitary confinement."

After the sentence was translated, the courtroom reacted. Some spectators sat in tense silence; others cheered. J.P.'s daughter Rose sobbed quietly. Xavier felt an immense sense of relief at this official conclusion to the trial. Those who had testified against J.P. would sleep better knowing he would be locked up for the rest of his life.

Xavier's eyes focused on J.P. He had initially maintained the same stoic indifference he had portrayed during much of the trial. But finally, he collapsed, burying his face in his hands and sobbed.

Across the aisle from Xavier, he noticed that Pauline and her family wore relieved smiles.

J.P. was escorted out of the courtroom and into the small room where the jurors had been sequestered during deliberations. Xavier was surprised that he was allowed to chat with his friends and family for half an hour including his son, Jule, and his son-in-law, Fred Beno. Then circuit court was reconvened. Attorney Wigman made a motion for a new trial in the Soquet case.

Judge Burnell denied the motion.

Xavier hoped the case would not be taken to the Wisconsin Supreme Court again. Enough was enough. Justice had been served, and the community had been through so much for so long because of this man.

As J.P. was led out of the courtroom, Xavier could picture the life he would live at the Wisconsin State Prison in Waupun. It had opened forty years prior and housed around 350 inmates, primarily adult males. About fifty were serving life sentences. J.P. would be awakened at six each morning and a guard would pass him breakfast to eat in his cell. At seven, he would be marched out in lockstep, the prisoners maintaining total silence. Each convict was expected to work ten hours a day. The prison had established a wagon factory and cabinet, shoe, and tailor shops. The sales of the manufactured goods produced enough revenue to run the prison. During J.P.'s first term, he had been assigned to work on the prison's 112-acre farm. He would likely be assigned the same work when he was transferred back to Waupun in a few days.

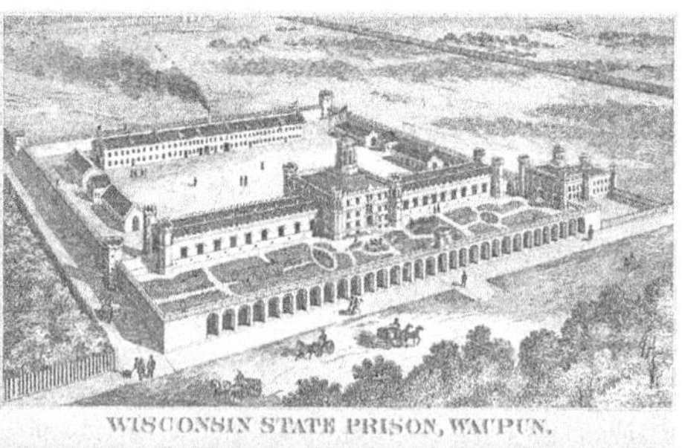

Waupun State Prison (Wikidata)

-∞-

About six weeks later, on July 11, 1890, Xavier opened the *State Gazette* in his office. He was shocked to read that two convicts had escaped from the Wisconsin State Prison in Waupun. Both had worked on the prison farm. He was relieved when neither escapee was J.P. Soquet.

The two men and another prisoner had been given orders to go to the prison farm. Instead of being transported by a guard, the three had been told to walk the mile and a half alone. On the way, the two escapees stopped and told the other prisoner they would follow him in a few minutes. They never did. The two men were traced to a location about two miles south of the prison before the trail ran cold. No other reports had come in.

It seemed amazing to Xavier that the correctional institution had allowed the three prisoners to walk between the prison and its farm unattended. Had their escape given J.P. any ideas?

Xavier shuddered at the thought.

-ooo-

About two months later, on Tuesday, September 20, 1890, Attorney C.E. Vroman, burst into Xavier's office, his cheek color high, his eyes flashing. Vroman said the unthinkable had happened. J.P. Soquet had escaped from the Wisconsin State Prison in Waupun—three days ago—and the local authorities had not been notified until today.

Staggered by the news, Xavier batted around frustrated words with his friend. How could J.P. have escaped? And why had that information not been released earlier? Had the prison suppressed that news in hopes that J.P. would be recaptured quickly to avoid negative publicity?

Both Xavier and Vroman agreed since J.P. was an escaped murderer, the public deserved the right to know immediately.

Still fuming, Vroman left as Xavier closed his eyes and shook his head. What a disaster. J.P. had been incarcerated in Waupun for only four months. After all the drama and expense of two trials, after all the time the witnesses had given up to testify against him, the idea that he had escaped from prison authorities seemed, well, criminal.

Vroman had said a resident of Brandon, Wisconsin, ten miles north of the prison, had reportedly seen J.P. on the night of his escape. Rumor had it that J.P. would return to the Bay Settlement area to visit vengeance on some of his old neighbors—those who had testified against him.

J.P.'s escape terrified many in the community. Xavier tried not to think about J.P.'s vendetta against him. But he did not believe J.P. was stupid enough to come after those who had testified against him. He would not risk being caught and returned to prison.

J.P.'s escape was the talk of Brown County. In the post office, at the theater, at church socials, and in restaurants and taverns, people speculated and feared the Bay Settlement convicted murderer.

Xavier attended a Navarino Lodge No. 1384 Knights of Honor meeting with his friend, Charles Vroman. Xavier told him he had dropped off a letter at the *State Gazette* office, to be published in that evening's editorial section, and titled: "Not Afraid of Soquet". Xavier showed Vroman a copy which said:

> *Concerning the sensational telegrams published in the newspapers of Chicago, Milwaukee and other cities, about the witnesses who have testified in the Soquet trial, on the part of the State, being terrified by the escape of Soquet from the State prison, etc., I desire to say, that so far as I am concerned, I have no fear of the threats made by Soquet against my life. I am not armed and have no one to guard me or my house. I am not hiding, but I am quietly attending to my business every day in the office or on the streets and at home in the evening with my family. Though I am first on the list of those who are to be killed by this professional murderer, I respectfully request my friends to feel about this matter as I do—perfectly easy and unconcerned.*
> *Respectfully yours,*
> *Xavier Martin*

Vroman complimented his friend on his cool head and his decision to allay the fears of others in the community. Both Xavier and Vroman could have reason to fear J.P., but knowing all that was at stake for him, they did not fear his retribution.

Vroman had talked to Honorable Andrew E. Elmore, after he had returned from Waupun to investigate J.P.'s escape. According to Elmore, when J.P. first served eighteen months in Waupun, he had received no "mark" against him. After J.P.'s second trial, Sheriff Barges had delivered him back to Waupun, where he had spent one day in solitary confinement before being placed into his old quarters. The prison authorities had considered J.P. to be quite feeble, "a somewhat broken-down old man," and quite lame, due to rheumatism. Over the past four months, J.P. had been a "good prisoner" and had not evinced any disposition to escape.

Vroman said the warden had been away from the prison on the day of J.P.'s escape. While working at the Waupun prison farm, two guards had been in charge of about a half dozen prisoners. One of the guards was seasoned, the other had just been hired. There was a great deal of work to be done, which included digging potatoes and husking corn. J.P. was assigned to husk corn with the newly hired guard. J.P. worked on one side of a stack of corn while the new guard worked on the other side. Engrossed in the work, the new guard gave little thought to his prisoner. When J.P.'s absence was discovered near dusk, the new guard judged that J.P. had been gone for about an hour and a quarter. Prison guards had hunted for J.P. without success. The guard watching J.P. had since been discharged.

In the early hours following the escape, Xavier assumed, since the prisoners wore striped suits, J.P. would have been easily identified.

Vroman said Xavier's assumption was wrong. The prisoners working on the Waupun state prison farm were clothed in gray suits. Just their shirts were striped. Vroman added that the authorities believed J.P. only had twenty-nine cents to his name. The papers published J.P. Soquet's description, inaccurately stating he was a Frenchman rather than a Belgian of sixty-five years and five-feet, five-and-a-half inches tall, who hardly spoke any English. Of note, the papers stated, was his most distinguishable feature: his cross-eyes. A $100 reward was offered for his arrest and return to prison.

The amount of reward being offered for J.P.'s capture upset Xavier. $100 seemed very little incentive for someone to actively search for J.P., especially considering how violent he was. Xavier vowed he would work to increase the reward for J.P.'s arrest and return to prison.

Xavier sent a telegram to Governor Hoard of Wisconsin. On October 6, 1890, nine days after J.P.'s escape, the governor issued a proclamation, offering a reward of $500 (about $18,000 in current valuation) for "the apprehension and return to prison of the wife murderer, Jean Soquet."

Still, nothing happened. J.P. Soquet was gone.

FEAR, LOSS, AND STRENGTH

PAULINE

PAULINE ENTERED the recently opened New York Mercantile Store on the corner of Washington and Pine on October 10, 1890. It was three weeks since J.P. Soquet had escaped from prison. The anger she had worked so hard to keep at bay during the trial had boiled over.

When Pauline had heard that news from Henry, rage had welled up inside her, so raw, so intense, she could not hold it back. She had run out the door into the backyard, wailing at the top of her lungs. The man who had caused such unbearable grief and havoc in her family was once again a free man. Pauline thought she had finally received justice for her sister. J.P. Soquet should be rotting in jail for disposing of his three wives. She could not fathom how a convicted murderer had simply walked away from the Waupun prison farm and disappeared without a trace. She wept for Elvira and felt the loss and grief their family had suffered anew.

Pauline wandered down the store aisles, her thoughts focused on her sister. Pauline's attempt to locate Elvira by summoning her to court had failed. Elvira's Main Street rental property had been seized by the county three months ago and its title had passed to Pauline. She had sold the property on August, 9, 1890, at a public auction held inside Sheriff Barges' office.

Pauline had lost all hope of ever locating her sister, either dead or alive. Now the man who had abused her, and who had undoubtedly murdered her and then disposed of her by burning or burying her body, had been free as a bird for the past three weeks.

Pauline held out a slim hope that J.P. would be caught. The governor's reward of $500 was a fortune, about the same amount Pauline's entire family lived on each year. If someone in the community was hiding

J.P., that reward money could motivate them to turn him into the authorities. She feared J.P. had outsmarted them all somehow. Like her sister, he was nowhere to be found.

Pauline passed departments such as dress goods, domestic goods, cloaks, and sacques. As she stopped to peruse a display of gloves, she overheard two lady shoppers in fashionable cloaks discussing J.P.'s escape. Pauline inched closer to listen, and one of the women shot her a look of suspicion. Pauline's clothes, clean and respectable as they were, paled in comparison to the two women's attire. What would they think if they knew J.P. was her former brother-in-law? Pauline listened as the two women talked about the Belgian murderer who was believed to be lurking in the Brown County woods, waiting to inflict revenge upon the witnesses who had testified against him. One of the women said J.P. had been spotted in the Bay Settlement neighborhood.

Pauline had talked to her sister, Fannie, and Fannie's husband, Peter. Both had testified at the first and second trials. She knew they were worried. They lived near the Soquet farm. They believed his children Rose and Jule, who had supported their father during the trial, might be hiding J.P. on the farm or near it. He could be hidden deep in those thickets, in a room off a cellar, or in an old armoire stored in an attic. There were so many places to hide. Unlike the bodies he had disposed of, Pauline hoped he would be found.

Pauline selected a pair of gloves. The department clerk wrote up a sales receipt and placed it and Pauline's money into an overhead carriage. Pauline watched in amazement as the clerk pulled a handle to release a catapult spring, launching the carriage across a network of overhead wires to reach the rear cashier station. Moments later, Pauline's change was sent back. The store was indeed new and modern.

Pauline stepped out onto Washington Street and headed for home. She passed a group of men congregated on a street corner attired in three-piece suits, bow ties, and bowler hats, discussing J.P. Soquet. One was claiming money was behind J.P.'s escape. The man was indignant over the Waupun guard, who he guessed had been bribed to look the other way.

Pauline was worried, but she lived in Green Bay. She knew the utmost alarm was being felt by the Belgian families near Bay Settlement. The longstanding fear of J.P. Soquet had reached a new level of terror.

Mid-January of 1891 arrived. Icemen were busy harvesting ice from the Fox River, the quality deemed to be the best in several years. Horsemen had also marked a speeding course on the frozen waterway. Pauline and her two youngest children, George and Frank, now twelve and nine, joined other spectators to watch the horsedrawn sleighs race around. Pauline rubbed her gloved hands together to keep warm while eavesdropping on the conversation of two men bundled up in wool coats. One said that Warden Weeks of the Wisconsin State Prison in Waupun had recently been in Green Bay for a few days. The man understood that the warden had been negotiating with someone who claimed to know the whereabouts of the escaped murderer, J.P. Soquet.

Pauline's heart began to race.

The man said J.P. had been hiding in that area for three months, ever since his escape from Waupun. But J.P. was tired of confinement and desired to return to the penitentiary on two conditions: first, the $500 reward would not be paid, and second, he would not be placed in solitary confinement as was standard for prisoners who were captured after making their escape.

Pauline walked home with her sons feeling hopeful. That news sounded authentic. But did that reason sound like the brutal J.P. she knew too well?

The next day, the *State Gazette* reported that Warden Weeks of the State Penitentiary had denied that J.P. Soquet had been negotiating his return. The escapee's whereabouts were still unknown. The warden said a prison officer had been looking for J.P. Soquet in Bay Settlement, thinking it likely he had returned to the vicinity of his old home. But no trace of the fugitive had been found.

Pauline's mother passed away in July of 1891. Both of Pauline's parents had gone to their graves not knowing the fate of their daughter, Elvira.

The one-year anniversary of J.P.'s escape arrived, and the press reported another sighting. "Soquet has a bad habit of appearing on earth several times each month ... Various rumors, however, have been afloat in regard to [Soquet's] whereabouts. By some it has been said that [he] was back on his native Belgium heath. Others, however, stated Soquet had gone back to his adopted home in the vicinity of Green Bay." The *State Gazette* promised if J.P. voluntarily surrendered himself to the proper authorities, he would not receive any additional punishment.

Pauline did not think J.P. would fall for that, but maybe the mental strain of avoiding capture was wearing on him. Maybe he would decide that prison would be a better option than life on the run.

About a month later, another sensational escape occurred from the Wisconsin State Prison in Waupun. Three murderers serving life sentences were at liberty. They had been employed in the prison wash house where they performed the daily operations of the prison laundry. The prisoners had managed to extract bricks from a wall and fastened the bricks to a board to form a door, which was not noticeable when in place. From behind that brick door, they had dug an underground passageway from the laundry and out beyond the prison wall that surrounded the grounds. A reward of $300 was offered for their return. The next morning all three were captured. And still, J.P. was on the loose.

Two more years passed. On February 1, 1893, Green Bay authorities received a letter from Champion, Wisconsin, located seven miles north of Bay Settlement. An old tramp had been seen around the neighborhood. Everybody believed he was J.P. Soquet. The old man had been begging for money and appeared to be deaf and mute. He made his request for money by writing the words on a slate which he carried with him. He wore blue goggles but only put them on when someone approached. The letter's author stated, "Everybody is afraid of the old tramp." The Brown County sheriff traveled to Champion only to learn that the man was not J.P. Soquet.

Three months later, what would be called the Panic of 1893 swept the country, and any speculation about J.P. Soquet's whereabouts evaporated. The severe U.S. financial crisis and depression, triggered by railroad overexpansion, falling silver prices, and depleted gold reserves, led to bank failures, business bankruptcies, and record unemployment. Tens of thousands of ordinary people, including Wisconsin farmers, lost their homes and savings. After a few hard years, by 1897, the Panic had run its course.

That same year, Pauline was deeply saddened to learn that Xavier Martin had passed away at the age of sixty-six. According to the press, for the past 15 months he had been ill, but he had appeared to be getting better when "a sinking spell" hit from which he had not recovered. His wife and children had been at his side. Xavier had been one of Brown County's longest standing and most respected residents. Pauline knew he had done all he could to seek justice for her sister, although it had ended in disappointment.

Left: Rudoph Martin (Xavier's eldest son), Right: Albert Martin (Xavier's second born son) (Courtesy Blodgett, Fay Willis via John Mertens)

Seven years had passed since J.P.'s escape, and most of the community had forgotten about him. Nothing had been published in the press during the past four years. All of his children had left the area other than his daughter, Josephine, the one married to Fred Beno. The couple now lived in the old Soquet home.

On August 10, 1898, at age fifty-three, Pauline suffered a debilitating accident. She stepped through a hole in a plank sidewalk and she fell backwards, breaking her back. Eight months later, her family secured the firm of Wigman and Martin to represent Pauline in a civil action. Thirty-six-year-old Attorney Patrick H. Martin had gone into practice with his father-in-law, Mr. John H.M. Wigman, after Thomas J. Hudd had retired. It was said that Patrick Martin had "broken more

Attorney Patrick H. Martin (Men Who are Making Green Bay 1897)

dishonest witnesses on the stand than any lawyer of his time." On May 6, 1899, Attorney Martin submitted the paperwork for Pauline to sue the city for $5,000 in damages for her "injuries sustained by a fall on a defective city sidewalk."

Attorney Solomon P. Huntington (Men Who are Making Green Bay 1897)

Seven months later, on November 23, 1899, Pauline provided her sworn deposition in the courthouse office of Brown County Judge H.J. Huntington. She sat beside her attorney, Mr. P.H. Martin. Solomon P. Huntington, the recently elected city attorney, sat across from them. He was thirty-three and the judge's half-brother.

"You claim that you had some fall, do you?" City Attorney Huntington asked Pauline.

"Yes sir. It was a year ago last 10th August. I hurt myself so bad that I will remember it as long as I live. It was about 8 or half past 8. It was dusk."

"How far could you see at that time?"

"I didn't measure."

"Could you see a block?"

"No; I haven't got cats' eyes."

"Were the electric lights lit at that time?"

"I don't know."

"Well ... what occurred."

Pauline said she and her seven-year-old granddaughter were walking home from her son's house when Pauline's right foot fell into a hole in the plank sidewalk that was about a foot and a half off the ground. "My foot went down as far as a little below the knee. I fell backward, but more on my left side, and my left leg was twisted under me. My head [hit] the sidewalk." She said her granddaughter had alerted Pete Bursch who lived nearby. He "hollered to his wife to bring the axe." Pauline said someone also ran to get her son, Jerome. "My son had me in his arms while Mr. Bursch was releasing my foot ... chopped my foot out ... My son took me under my arms from behind, and lifted me up. Pete Bursch helped."

Pauline's son went into the office of Rahr Brewery and "borrowed a rocking chair from Rahr's foreman." Her son and Pete Bursch carried Pauline in the chair to her home, about a block away at 1288 Main Street. She lost consciousness and when she came to, Pauline said she was on the bed. Soon after Dr. Rhode arrived and used a four-to-five-inch instrument to measure her hip injury.

Rahr's East River Brewing Company on Main Street (Souvenir of Green Bay 1903)

"Before he came did you take anything?"

"No medicine at all, except George Grunert put some whiskey in my mouth, and I let it run out on my breast. I didn't know what it was. None of it went down my throat."

"Had you been drinking anything that day?"

"No, I never drank whiskey ... No beer. Nothing at all."

"Were you complaining of your hip?"

"No. It was my whole body; I couldn't move; I couldn't raise my head." Pauline said Dr. Brett arrived and the East River Priest, Father Anderegg, who Pauline had sent for since she thought she was "pretty near dead."

"Dr. Brett asked one of my boys if I was a cripple before. If I was lame before."

Dr. Fred Brett (Men Who are Making Green Bay 1897)

Jerome told Dr. Brett his mother had always been able-bodied, a hard worker. Right before the accident, she was employed at Huybrecht's gardens and earned seventy-five cents a day.

After the accident, Pauline testified, she had irreversible injuries. "I can't go afoot no more; I have got to go with a rig, with a horse and buggy. I [can walk] slow for a block, or a block and a half, maybe three blocks, if I take my time ... I can't even bend down to pick up anything. All my body is sore; I can't work nor do nothing."

Pauline's civil trial began on December 12, 1899, and Judge Samuel D. Hastings officiated. The jury deliberated on December 13 for two hours and awarded Pauline $700 in damages. The sum was far less than $5,000, yet Pauline was pleased. But not for long. Attorney Huntington appealed Pauline's case to the Wisconsin Supreme Court.

After three long years, while Pauline continued to suffer, that Court ordered the city of Green Bay to pay Pauline $827.61 (about $33,000 in current valuation). It was a good amount of money, and while it could not repair her physical health, the settlement helped Pauline and Henry purchase their own home at 528 Day Street.

Despite her injury, Pauline enjoyed her family as she aged. She was proud of the life she and Henry had built together. They had overcome so much. On May 21, 1915, Pauline died at a local hospital at the age of seventy. She had suffered another fall in January, breaking three ribs. Her doctor had believed Pauline's ribs had knitted together until she had taken ill. Only then did the physician discover that one of the rib bones had penetrated her lung.

Pauline had lived in Brown and Kewanee counties for sixty years, thirty-three years in Green Bay. Besides her husband, Henry, she was survived by four sons, Anton, Jerome, George, and Frank; two daughters, Mrs. Flora Geyer of Green Bay and Mrs. Delia Jakubovsky of Kewaunee; one brother Desire Coppersmith and two sisters, Mrs. Fannie Vandenbusch and Mrs. William Lancelle. In addition, there were Pauline's grandchildren including fourteen-year-old William Villiessse, the son of Jerome, and nephews like Vital Coppersmith, the twenty-six-year-old son of her brother Isadore.

Pauline's funeral service was held at the Church of the Blessed Sacrament, and she was buried at Fort Howard cemetery. Henry published a "Card of Thanks" in the *Green Bay Gazette*: "We hereby extend our heartfelt thanks to all our relatives, friends, and neighbors for the kindness and sympathy shown during the illness and death of our beloved mother ... Henry Villiesse and family."

William Villiesse (Grandson of Pauline) (Permission granted by Brian Schultz)

Henry died at the age of ninety-two, four years after Pauline.

They died not knowing what happened to Elvira. They died knowing J.P. Soquet was still on the loose. The trauma of it all had faded over time, but it was a weight they carried to their graves.

FINAL DISCOVERIES AND THE UNKNOWN

IN KEWAUNEE, WISCONSIN, in 1990, a man named John Mertens took an active interest in uncovering his ancestry. Mertens' great-grandmother was Julia Englebert, who had immigrated to the Green Bay township in 1855 with her parents Francois and Virginia Francart. Virginia was the only sister of August Minsart, who had died from arsenic poisoning in 1873.

Felix and Julia Englebert (August Minsart's niece) (Courtesy John Mertens)

John uncovered the newspaper articles connected to August Minsart's death and that discovery led to further research into August's wife, Elvira, and her second husband, Jean Philippe Soquet. John produced a twenty-nine-page booklet titled *Tale of a Portrait: Julia Francart Englebert, Her Untold Story* that primarily focused on the trials of Jean Philippe Soquet and his subsequent escape.

Six years after John produced his booklet, the genealogy platform Ancestry.com was launched. John reached out to possible family connections of Jean Philippe Soquet through Ancestry.com. Among those connections, information was pieced together from the descendants of the Beno-Soquet families passed down through their history.

In 1885, two years before J.P. Soquet's first trial, the Beno family lived about five doors down the road from the Soquet farm. One of their sons, Fred, married J.P. Soquet's daughter, Josephine. Descendants recalled information about J.P. Soquet's 1890 escape from the Wisconsin State Prison in Waupun, following his conviction at his second trial.

Fred and Josephine Soquet Beno Family
(Photo used with permission of Ancestry.com member)

Some Beno descendants believe J.P. Soquet was met outside the prison by "two of the boys" who had a buckboard. The two boys were believed to be J.P.'s twenty-four-year-old son, Jule, and J.P.'s thirty-two-year-old son-in-law, Fred Beno. After the second trial, the judge had allowed J.P. time to talk to his relatives including Jule and Fred. Maybe they had discussed a plan for J.P.'s escape, knowing he would likely be assigned work on the prison farm.

Some descendants believe J.P.'s escape was planned, others believe it was not. In any case, they agreed he made his way back to the Soquet farm. He stayed hidden in the attic of the Soquet home for almost two weeks before he and his son Jule left on a train in mid-October of 1890 and traveled to Idaho near the Ontario, Oregon, border. According to one descendant, J.P. and Jule possibly made a stop in Bessmer, Michigan, about 220 miles northwest of Green Bay where J.P.'s daughter, Jennie Soquet-Jesmer, lived. A few months earlier, Jennie had testified for her father at his second trial in Oshkosh.

Many descendants had heard that J.P.'s facial hair had been shaved off, and he had dressed in nun's clothing to escape on the train. Some say that one of the boys had rummaged through the laundry at the local convent and stole some clothing. Others believe the nun's clothing had come from his daughter, Jennie, who had left the convent to marry Nelson Adolfus Jesmer on March 29, 1890, two months before J.P.'s second trial.

In October of 1890, the Green Bay, Winona & St. Paul Railroad train departed from Green Bay heading west at 6:10 a.m. or 3:20 p.m. The train station was situated over the Mason Street Bridge in the city of Fort Howard. The distance from the farm would have been about ten miles. J.P. and Jule likely took the 6:10 a.m. train in October of 1890 when it still would have been dark.

When J.P. and his son arrived in Idaho, Jule found work for a man named Joe Ego. Since Jule Soquet could not read or write English, he purposely learned how to write his employer's simple and short name. Jule and J.P. left Idaho and arrived in Newberg, Oregon, in Yamhill County, where they both changed their names. Jule became Joseph Ego and J.P. Soquet became John Raino. Under Jule's new name, he purchased ten acres of farmland in 1896 for $350, twenty additional acres in 1898, twenty more in 1900, and a final 172 in 1904.

In 1894, at the age of twenty-eight, Jule Soquet, alias Joseph Ego, married eighteen-year-old Emma Reetz, also from Wisconsin, and the couple lived with J.P. Soquet, alias John Raino. Joseph and Emma Ego had six children who called their grandfather "gaga." One descendant said that J.P. had written to the Soquet-Beno family about once a year until he died.

Jule Soquet (Alias Joe Ego) (Photo used with permission of Ancestry.com member)

In J.P.'s later years, his son, Jule, sent "gaga" to the Washington County Asylum and Poor House. But J.P. escaped numerous times. On each occasion, he headed back to Jule's place, about a day's walk away, begging for food along the way. Jule's wife took "gaga" back to the asylum about two or three times. Jule's daughter Alvaretta remembered "gaga" as a "mean, ornery man." It appeared as if Jule had shared the information about his father's heinous past, and Alvaretta was afraid for her own children. She knew the Bible says that "The sins of the father will go into the third to fourth generations."

J.P. Soquet died in 1910 at age eighty-three under the name of John Raino. He was said to have been buried on Jule's property and an iron bed frame marked the grave. In that era, a bed frame symbolized the final resting place for the deceased and offered an affordable alternative to stone markers. J.P.'s Oregon Death Certificate states he died of "senile debility due to enlarged prostate."

Jule Soquet (Alias Joe Ego) and eldest daughter Alvaretta Ego (Ancestry.com)

On Alvaretta's deathbed, she told family members about her grandfather, whose real name was Jean Philippe Soquet. She revealed his crimes and the final locations of his last two murdered wives. That information was passed down to the current generation. The remains of J.P.'s second wife, Esperance, were "buried in a manure pile," and his third wife, Elvira, "was cooked in the oven." These outcomes for Esperance and Elvira can never be proven; they serve only to add to the story's mystery and legend.

J.P. Soquet lived out his life as a free man in Oregon. But the disappearance of his eldest son, Gregorie Frederick "Fred" Soquet, born in 1861, who allegedly found his mother's arm while plowing the fields, was still a mystery.

In recent years, a California woman named Ann M. Schoenfeld has investigated her great grandfather's past. His name was Frederick John Freeman. He lived in the small, isolated lumber town of Eureka, California. In 1893, he married a local girl, Caroline Clark, and together they raised five children. He said he was born in Minnesota in 1862, and his mother, Mary, had died when he was young. Because he had not gotten along with his new stepmother, he said he had left home with a band of gypsies who had taken him across the country and dropped him off at a California mill with two dollars and a knapsack of food.

When Fred Freeman suffered a stroke in his later years, rather than conversing in English, he began to speak in a French dialect. A Catholic nun, who nursed him back to health, spoke a French-Canadian dialect. But she noted that Fred's language was unrecognizable to her. Fred eventually reverted back to English when his health improved.

Through multiple Ancestry.com DNA matches, Ann positively identified that her great grandfather Fred Freeman was the missing eldest son of J.P. and Esperance Soquet. Ann determined this through her own DNA match and those of her cousins, which connected Ann's family to Genevieve "Jennie" Soquet-Jesmer, the eldest sister to Gregorie Frederick "Fred" Soquet. Ann documented this information in her book called *Hope For A Free Man* and stated she felt "a strange combination of shame and outrage" at learning she was related to a serial wife murderer and at least one of his victims.

Soquet Sisters (Josephine, Jennie and Elisabeth
(Photo used with permission of Ancestry.com member)

There is much that will never be known about what happened to J.P. Soquet and his family. There are speculations and theories and inferences to be made, but the truth of what he did and its impact on his family and their community will remain lost to history.

J.P. Soquet luckily never married again, sparing a fourth wife from being added to his tally.

AUTHOR'S NOTE

PEOPLE ASK ME WHY I was inspired to write *Disposable Wives.* In 1997, my husband and I sold our home at 644 S. Jackson Street in the Astor Historic District of Green Bay. We moved with our two boys to a home on the shore of Green Bay, just down the hill from Bay Settlement. The Bay Settlement area and its rich history intrigued me. I realized I had moved from one historic district to another. I knew this area of Brown County had been settled by Belgian immigrants. My own ancestors came from North Brabant, Netherlands, which borders Belgium's Antwerp province.

At the time of my family's move from the Astor neighborhood, I was an active marathon runner, and the steep Church Road climb was part of my training course. At the top was Holy Cross Church across from the Gregoire Denis Historic House. From there, I would run south on Bay Settlement Road and admire the views of the bay and the adjacent farmland. This stretch of my run was the same path Pauline Villiesse maneuvered in the first chapter of *Disposable Wives.*

Current Holy Cross Church (wikipedia)

In recent years, as a Brown County Historical Society board member, I have participated in one of our society's major events called "If Tombstones Could Talk," where former Brown County citizens are portrayed within three local cemeteries. One of the citizens previously portrayed was Frank Tilton, an 1880s *Green Bay Advocate* newspaper editor. Instead of focusing solely on Tilton's life, the portrayer and researcher, Dennis Jacobs, discussed, as Tilton, a story which had stood out during his newspaper career: the murders of Jean Philippe Soquet.

Dennis Jacobs, who grew up in the Bay Settlement area, shared his research with me, and the idea for *Disposable Wives* took hold. My prior historical true crime, *The Maid and the Socialite: The Brave Women Behind Green Bay's Scandalous Minahan Trials*, was released in 2023. During my research for *Disposable Wives*, I discovered some of the legal and medical characters, such as Attorney Charles E. Vroman, Judge Samuel D. Hastings Jr., Attorney Patrick H. Martin, and Dr. Benjamin C. Brett, had played roles in *The Maid and the Socialite* as well.

By writing *Disposable Wives*, I hope to have brought Brown County's early years to life while honoring the Belgian people who were instrumental in the county's growth. But the major reason I wrote this book was for the same reason I wrote *The Maid and the Socialite*: to give the forgotten and abused but brave women of those eras a voice. Too many women of the past suffered horrible fates that garnered little notice during their own times. My hope is to share their stories today and to do what little I can to bring them justice for what they suffered.

READING GROUP GUIDE

1. How do the Belgian immigrants navigate their dual identities as newcomers to America while maintaining their cultural heritage? What role does language play in their integration and success in Wisconsin?
2. What does Pauline's pursuit of justice reveal about the values and limitations of the Belgian community? How does their tight-knit culture both enable and hinder her efforts?
3. Xavier Martin finds himself caught between personal desires and community responsibilities. How do you view his choices throughout the story? What does his internal conflict suggest about the pressures facing community leaders?
4. The economic uncertainty of the Panic of 1873 creates desperation in the community. How does financial hardship drive the story's conflicts, and what does this reveal about survival in frontier farming communities?
5. How important is community reputation versus personal happiness in this story? What are the lasting impacts of scandal on families like the Villiesses and Soquets?
6. The trial scenes reveal tensions between the Belgian community and the broader legal system. How effective is the American justice system at serving this particular community, and what barriers exist?
7. Pauline must balance protecting her family's reputation with pursuing justice. Where do your sympathies lie in this conflict, and how would you have acted in her position?
8. What role does gossip and rumor play in revealing truth? When does community suspicion become valid evidence?
9. How much responsibility does the Belgian immigrant community

bear for J.P. Soquet's crimes? What role did silence and protecting community reputation play in allowing the violence to continue?

10. Pauline's family initially keeps J.P.'s admissions about Esperance's poisoning secret to protect Elvira. Do you think this was the right decision? How does Pauline's evolution from protective sister to key witness reflect changing attitudes about justice?
11. Elvira is both a victim of J.P.'s abuse and complicit in at least one crime, helping exhume Esperance's body, and perhaps poisoning August. How do you view her character? Can you sympathize with her choices given the constraints women faced in that era?
12. The legal system prevented J.P. from testifying against Elvira once they married and she against him. How did marriage laws of that era enable abusers? What parallels exist with modern protections for domestic violence victims?
13. The book's title suggests that certain women were considered disposable. How were Esperance, Elvira, Mary, and Clara viewed differently by society based on their gender, class, or family status?
14. We never learn definitively what happened to Elvira after her divorce. How does this unresolved ending affect your reading of the entire narrative? What does it say about women who disappeared without trace?
15. The author's goal is to give voice to forgotten, abused, but brave women of the past. What makes this 19th-century Wisconsin story relevant to contemporary conversations about domestic violence, justice, and gender?

Contact me at lyndadrews@gmail.com if you would like me to participate in a book club meeting in person or over Zoom or Facetime.

MAJOR RESEARCH SOURCES

THE SOUTHERN DOOR PENINSULA of Wisconsin still contains the largest rural settlement of people of Belgian origin in America. I was fortunate to have two amazing research repositories nearby: the Belgian Heritage Center in Brussels, Wisconsin, and the University of Wisconsin-Green Bay Belgian-American Research Collection. Each house critical information about the Walloon settlements in Brown, Door, and Kewaunee Counties. Those resources included books, photographs, oral histories, maps and manuscripts, highlighting the experiences of people of Belgian descent. The Area Research Center at the University of Wisconsin-Green Bay also housed the archival court records for the numerous court cases included in this book.

The court records for J.P. Soquet's first-degree murder trials in Green Bay and Oshkosh were lost. But the Wisconsin Supreme Court briefs still exist and are housed in the Lavinia Goodell Wisconsin State Law Library. Those records include the quoted testimony errors from Soquet's first trial. I used that information as well as newspaper articles to reconstruct the State vs. Soquet Green Bay trial. For Soquet's second first-degree murder trial in Oshkosh, I relied on newspaper articles.

Xavier Martin authored "The Belgians of Northeast Wisconsin" in 1895, which provided me with his first-hand insight into the resilient Belgian immigrants who managed to survive in their adopted country and his own part in their survival. J.P. Soquet's frequent arrests reported in the newspapers as well as the devastating Villiesse fires provided me a timeline to carry the story of Xavier and Pauline forward.

I regret that I could not locate photos of J.P. Soquet, Elvira Minsart-Soquet, and Pauline Villiesse. But the photos from their descendants can provide a glimpse into what these major characters might have looked like.

John Mertens, a descendant of August Minsart's sister, generously shared his research to write his unpublished work *Tale of a Portrait: Julia Francart Englebert, Her Untold Story*. Ancestry.com and Familysearch.com provided me with connections to Coppersmith, Villiesse, and Soquet descendants. Through communications with them, I could provide the surprising ending to this story.

BIBLIOGRAPHY

1883 Sanborn Fire Insurance Map Page 8. Elvira Soquet's house location on Main Street.

1883 Sanborn Fire Insurance Map 1883 Page 9. Pauline Villiesse home on Main Street.

Brown County Plat Map 1889 Southern Part of Green Bay.

1889 Brown County Plat Map North Half of Green Bay.

1887 Green Bay Sanborn Fire Insurance Map Page 8.

Ahnapee Record, Wisconsin. May 19, 1887.

Appleton Crescent, Wisconsin. May 24, 1890.

Ashcraft, Jenny. "Horse and Buggy: The Primary Means of Transportation in the 19th Century." 2019, blog.newspapers.com/horse-and-buggy-the-primary-means-of-transportation-in-the-19th-century/.

Atkinson v. Goodrich Transp. Co., 60 Wis. 141, 18 N.W. 764, 765 (1884). Case brief, Exhibit A.

Austin. "Winnebago County Courthouses-Part 2." The Weekend Historian, 14 Oct 2016, theweekendhistorian.com/2016/10/14/winnebago-county-courthouses-part-2/.

"Woman Poison her husband." *Baraboo Republic*, 26 Mar 1873.

Belgian-American Research Collection: University of Wisconsin-Green Bay. uwgb.edu/archives/collections/belgian/.

Belgian Heritage Center. belgianheritagecenter.org/en-us/default.aspx.

Belgian Laces, Volume #27-104, Official Quarterly Bulletin of the Belgian Researchers, Belgian American Heritage Association. July 2005.

Berlier, Moniquer. May 1999. "Picturing Ourselves: Photographs of Belgian Americans in Northeastern Wisconsin, 1888-1950." Unpublished Thesis. The University of Iowa.

Berryman, John R. *History of The Bench and Bar of Wisconsin, Vol. II.*, Chicago: H.C. Cooper, JR., & CO., 1898.

Blodgett, Fay Willis. Photos and letters provided from the Xavier Martin family (Xavier, Augusta, Amelia, Rudolph, Arthur). Willis died in 1996 and was married to Ruth Martin, the daughter of Pauline Martin, Xavier's daughter by Augusta.

Brown County Circuit Court Records of Indictments and Information. Brown Series 81. Volume 2, p 135. University of Wisconsin Green Bay. Green Bay, Wisconsin.

Brown County Circuit Court. Case Files. Beno, Ferdinand vs. Soquet, John P. et al. Brown Series 65. File Box 157, folder 1. University of Wisconsin-Green Bay. Green Bay, Wisconsin.

Brown County Circuit Court. Case Files. Martin, Mary Rebecca vs. Martin, Xavier. Brown Series 65. File Box 96, Folder 9. University of Wisconsin-Green Bay. Green Bay, Wisconsin.

Brown County Circuit Court. Case Files. Villiesse, Pauline vs. City of Green Bay. Brown Series 65. File Box 217, Folder 37. University of Wisconsin-Green Bay. Green Bay, Wisconsin.

Brown County Circuit Court. Case Files. Villiesse, Henry vs. Everard, Joseph. Brown Series 65. File Box 249. University of Wisconsin-Green Bay. Green Bay, Wisconsin.

Brown County Circuit Court. Minute Books. Brown Series 26. Volume 7, pages 409-415. University of Wisconsin-Green Bay. Green Bay, Wisconsin.

Brown County Circuit Court Records of Indictments and Information. Brown Series 81. Volume 2, p 179. University of Wisconsin-Green Bay. Green Bay, Wisconsin.

Brown Series 145, Brown County Probate Case Files, Box 3, Case File 123, Maria Soquet, 1885.

Brown Series 145, Brown County Probate Case Files, Box 3, Case File 119, Clara Soquet (Neglected Child), 1882 (2).

Brown Series 4 Tax Rolls Humboldt. 1871, 1872, 1873. Property owned by August Minsart.

Brown Series 65 - Case File 328, Beno vs. Jesmer et al. Box 561, Folder 28, February 2, 1921.

Burlington Hawkeye, Iowa. May 6, 1887.

"Catholic Traditions for Burial at Gravesite." Catholic Cemeteries Association of the Archdiocese of Hartford, Inc.

Chamberlain, P. Jr. Penn Carey Law: Legal Scholarship Repository Recent American Decision, 1888, Supreme Court of Wisconsin, *Soquet v. The State.*

"The Child Abuse Prevention and Treatment Act: 40 Years

of Safeguarding America's Children." Children's Bureau, An Office of the Administration for Children and Families, 2015, https://acf.gov/cb/training-technical-assistance/child-abuse-prevention-and-treatment-act-40-years-safeguarding.

Civil Records of Brown County: Death, Marriage, Probate and Real Estate including taxes, deeds, and mortgages.

Commemorative Biographical Record of the Counties of Brown, Kewaunee, and Door, Wisconsin. Chicago: J.H. Beers & Co., 1895.

Commemorative Biographical Record of the Fox River Valley Counties of Brown, Outagamie and Winnebago. Chicago: J.H. Beers & Co., 1895.

Commemorative Biographical Record of the West Shore of Green Bay, Brown, Oconto, Marinette, and Florence. Chicago: J.H. Beers & Co., 1896.

Connelly, Hon. Rebecca B., United States Bankruptcy Judge Western District of Virginia. "A Brief Look at (Some of) the History of Voluntary Bankruptcy in America: How Bankruptcy went from Punitive in the 19th Century to Rehabilitative in the 20th Century." https://www.mow.uscourts.gov/sites/mow/files/Connelly_history_doc.pdf (pages 6-10).

Cook, Jane Stewart. "Belgian Americans." everyculture.com/multi/A-Br/Belgian-Americans.html.

Courier, Waterloo, Iowa. 1890 (May 28, Oct 8); Jul 20, 1891.

Cruea, Susan M. "Changing Ideals of Womanhood During the Nineteenth-Century Woman Movement." General Studies Writing Faculty Publications, 2005.

Daily Northwestern, Oshkosh, Wisconsin. 1887 (Mar 23, Jul 16, Jul 22); 1890 (Feb 10, May 7, May 9, May 12-17, May 31, Sep 30, Oct 6).

Daily State Gazette, Green Bay. Oct 17, 1872; 1873 (May 24, Jun 30, Oct 14, Dec 7, Dec 13, Dec 20); 1874 (Feb 7, Mar 7, Jul 10, Jul 13, Oct 10); 1875 (Mar 1, Mar 18, Mar 20, Mar 22, Mar 23, Mar 25, Mar 27, Mar 30, Apr 2-3, Apr 7, Apr 15, May 22, Jun 26); Jul 26, 1877; 1879 (Feb 8, Feb 22, Dec 26); 1880 (Apr 29, May 6, Jun 11, Jun 12, Jun 17, Jun 27, Oct 14); 1881 (Apr 7, Jul 30, Sep 16); Mar 3, 1883; 1882 (Feb 1, Feb 25, Apr 29, Sep 16); 1883 (Feb 24, Mar 1, Jun 14); Sep 11, 1884; 1885 (Mar 21, May 9, May 19); Oct 2, 1886; 1887 (Jan 4, Jan 18, Feb 17, Feb 21, Feb 23, Mar 22, Mar 23, Mar 25-30, May 1-4, May 6, Jun 10, Jun 11); 1888 (Jun 16, Feb 24-25); 1889 (May 24, Sep 30); 1890 (Apr 7, May 5-May 20, Jun 9, Jul 12, Sep 30, Oct 4, Oct 7-8); 1891 (Jan 19, Jan 20, Jul 29); Feb 1, 1893; Dec 22, 1897; 1899 (May 10, Dec 13, Dec 15); Jan 18, 1900; 1902 (Jan 1, Jan 10); Nov 7, 1908.

Decatur Morning Review, Iowa. 1890 (May 24, Oct 3).

Defnet, Ducat, Eggericx, Poulain. *From Grez Doiceau to Wisconsin.* Brussels, Belgium, 1986.

Delvaux, Cletus. "The Sisters of the Holy Cross at Bay Settlement." *Voyageur Northeast Wisconsin's Historical Review*, Winter/Spring 2026, Volume 42, N. 2, p. 32-34.

Delvaux, Cletus. "Father Daems Bay Settlement's Extraordinary Missionary." *Voyageur Northeast Wisconsin's Historical Review*, Summer/Fall 2023, Volume 40, N. 1, p. 22-26.

Depere News, Wisconsin. Jan 10, 1874.

Dominica Sister M, OSF, The Chapel. Our Lady of Good Help, Green Bay, The Sisters of St Francis of Bay Settlement, 1955.

Door County Pulse, Sturgeon Bay, Wisconsin. doorcountypulse.com/.

Dull, J. Alfred. *Green Bay and Fort Howard directory 1874.* Reid and Miller, digital. library.wisc.edu/1711.dl/67QQWM3LTEWXC8M.

Eau Claire News, Wisconsin. August 13, 1887.

Ellis, William S. "Wisconsin's Door Peninsula." *National Geographic*, vol. 135, n3, Mar 1969, pp. 347-371.

Evon, Dan. "Reasons for Admission to Insane Asylums in the 19th Century." Snopes Inc, 08 Feb 2016, snopes.com/fact-check/reasons-admission-insane-asylum-1800s/.

Falk, Cynthia G. "The Evolving History of the Agricultural Silo: Hay Storage in the New World." 17 Mar 2015.

Family Search. J.P. Soquet (Alias John Raino) death certificate in Oregon. ancestors.familysearch.org/en/KCR5-B22/jean-philippe-soquet-1827-1910.

"Father Daems." Belgian Heritage Center, Facebook, 12 Feb 2019, trsSnodpoei12h 5ghc1013b1u69uu5Fgue0a92ct9ayi1 921rml,2rc27c.

Fond du Lac Commonwealth, Wisconsin. Nov 8, 1890.

Fort Howard Review, Wisconsin. 1887 (Mar 5, May 7).

Galveston Daily News, Texas. June 2, 1890.

Gaber, Brian. Email correspondence to provide Villiesse family information.

Glover, W. H. "Hiram Smith (1817-1890)." Agricultural History 31(1):60-61, 1957.

Goodell, Lavinia. "Was at the prison most of the day." Lavinia Goodell, *The*

Private Life and Public Trials of Wisconsin's First Woman Lawyer, 18 Mar 1879, laviniagoodell.com.

Green Bay Daily Advocate, Wisconsin. 1873 (Dec 18, Dec 25); Jan 1, 1874; 1884 (Mar 20, Jul 3); 1887 (Apr 5, Apr 28, May 4, May 6, Jul 12, Jul 19, Jul 28, Jul 29); Jan 17, 1889; 1890 (May 8, May 15, Oct 9).

Green Bay Press-Gazette, Wisconsin. May 21, 1915; Jul 2, 1918; 1919 (Jul 31, Oct 14); Jul 10, 1920; Aug 25, 1925.

Hall, Sylvia. *Farewell to the Homeland: European Immigration to N.E. Wisconsin*, 1840-1900, Brown County Historical Society, 1 Jan 1995.

Hartnett, Sean G. "Harvesting the New Land: A Geographical Appraisal of the Wheat Frontier in the Upper Midwest, 1835-1885." Unpublished Master's Thesis, Department of Geography, University of Wisconsin, Madison, 1981.

Heinrich, Dorothy L. & Lynn C. McAuley. *Belgian-American Research Materials*, University of Wisconsin-Green Bay Library Special Collections, 1976.

Heming, Harry H. *The Catholic Church in Wisconsin 1895 – 1896.* Catholic Historical Publishing Company, Milwaukee Wi., page 599.

Hill, Charles. "John V. Robbins, Pioneer Agriculturalist." *Wisconsin Magazine of History*, 1951.

Hofer, Ronald R. "The Best Interest of the Child Doctrine in Wisconsin Custody Cases." *Marquette Law Review* Vol 64, Issue 2, Article 4, Winter 1980.

Holand, Hjalmar Rued. *Wisconsin's Belgian Community.* Door County Historical Society, Sturgeon Bay, Wis, 1933.

Holubetz, Sylvia & Burridge, George Nau, et al. *The Astor Historic District—Its History and Houses.* Green Bay, WI: Astor Neighborhood Association, 1981.

"Holy Cross Church and Convent National Register of Historic Places Form 10-900." United States Department of Interior National Park Service, January 1992.

"In the Palm of His Hand." (A History of the Sisters of St. Francis of the Holy Cross, Bay Settlement, Wisconsin). Local History & Genealogy in Brown County Library, 2 Feb 1988.

Inter Ocean, Chicago. May 4, 1887

"Women on the Trail and Farms." Iowa Pathways, Iowa PBS, iowapbs.org/iowapathways/mypath/2463/women-trail-and-farm.

Jarstad, Anton, "The Melting Pot in Northeastern Wisconsin." *Wisconsin*

Magazine of History, vol. 26, 4, June 1943, pp. 426-432.

Juneau Telephone, Wisconsin. Apr 1, 1887

Kelling, George, L. "Early Detective work in 1870s in Wisconsin." *Britannica*, 2026, britannica.com/topic/police/Early-police-in-the-United-States.

Kenosha News, Wisconsin. Feb 19, 1925.

Kewaunee Enterprise, Wisconsin. Feb 1874.

Kaukauna Times, Wisconsin. 1890 (May 8, May 14, May 15).

Kinnard, Tim. "Why Farmers Often have Large Families." *Tim Kinnard Podcast*, The Kinnard Homestead.

Lampereur, Steve. "The Belgian Midas of Bay Settlement." Peninsula Belgian American Club, Facebook, 16 Sept 2024, belgianamericanclub/posts/10160886188003611/.

Laws of Wisconsin - CH. 118-119. docs.legis.wisconsin.gov/1882/related/acts/119.pdf.

Lempereur, Francoise and Xavier Istasse. *The Walloons in Wisconsin.* 2012.

Manitowoc Pilot, Wisconsin. Feb 5, 1874.

Martin, Morgan L. "Narrative of Morgan L. Martin." Library of Congress, Western Historical Co., 1881, loc.gov/resource/lhbum.7689a_0401_0433.

Martin, Odile. "Find a Grave." findagrave.com/memorial/146380758/mary-odile-swartz.

Martin, Xavier, "The Belgians of Northeast Wisconsin." *Wisconsin Historical Collections*, vol. XIII, Madison, Wisconsin State Historical Society, 1895, pp. 375-396.

Men Who are Making Green Bay. The Gazette Publishing Co, 1897.

Mertens, John Henry. *The Second Battle – A story of Our Belgian Ancestors in the American Civil War 1861-1865.* 1986.

Mertens, John Henry, *The Tale of a Portrait Julia Francart Englebert Her Untold Story.* Unpublished work. 1990.

Metzner, Lee W. "The Belgians in the North Country." *Wisconsin Magazine of History*, vol. 26, 3 Mar 1943, pp. 280-288

Milwaukee Daily Journal, Wisconsin. 1887 (Feb 25, Feb 26, Mar 23).

Milwaukee Journal, Wisconsin. 1887 (Feb 25, Feb 26, Mar 23).

Morrison, Robert G. Supreme Court of Wisconsin. Soquet v. The State. *The American Law Register* (1852-1891), Vol. 37, No. 8, New Series Volume 28 (Third Series, Vol. 2) (Aug., 1889), pp. 480-499 (20 pages).

National Library of Medicine. "The Attempt to Understand Puerperal Fever in the Eighteenth and Early Nineteenth Centuries: The Influence of Inflammation Theory." The University of Manchester, UK, pmc.ncbi.nlm.nih.gov/articles/PMC1088248/.

Neenah Daily Times, Wisconsin. 1890 (May 15, May 21).

Oregon State Board of Health, Bureau of Vital Statistics, Certificate of Death - John Raino. Oct 21, 1910.

Oshkosh Times, Wisconsin. 1887-1904, Oshkosh, Wis: Edgar W. Viall & Co. 1890 (May 8, May 9, May 14, May 15).

Oshkosh Northwestern, Wisconsin. Dec 2, 1889; 1890 (May 8, May 12-14, May 16, May 31, Jun 12); 1891 (Jul 11, Sep 28); Aug 6, 1892.

Peninsula Belgian American Club. "Historical Timeline." 2018, belgianamerican.org/history.html.

Portage Daily Democrat, Wisconsin. Oct 1, 1890.

Preston, Samuel H. and Haines, Michael R. "Fatal Years: Child Mortality in Late Nineteenth-Century America." Princeton University Press Volume. 1991, nber.org/books/pres91-1

Property Deed, Brown County, Wisconsin: Soquet, November 16, 1877, No. 103212), familysearch.org/en/united-states

Reiherzer, Lee. "An Illustrated History of the Oshkosh House Saloon and Hotel, Oshkosh Beer - A History of Beer, Breweries, and Saloons in Oshkosh, Wisconsin." 06 May 2019, oshkoshbeer.blogspot.com/2019/05/an-illustrated-history-of-oshkosh-house.html.

Rentmeesters, Jules. "Port of Antwerp Belgian Emigration." Printed in Belgium, 1989.

Richardson MD, B.L. *History of Medicine in Brown County, Wisconsin 1816-2000.* Quality Books.

Riney-Kehrberg, Pamela. "Childhood on the Farm: Work, Play, and Coming of Age in the Midwest". University Press of Kansas, 09 Jun 2005.

Rudolph, Jack. *A Pictorial History Green Bay.* Norfolk, Virginia: The Donning Company, 1893.

Rudolph, Jack. *Birthplace of a Commonwealth.* Green Bay, WI: Brown County Historical Society, 1976.

Rudolph, Jack. *The Green Bay Area in History and Legend.* Green Bay, WI: Brown County Historical Society, 2004.

Salina Daily Journal, Kansas. May 6, 1887.

Schafer, Joseph. 1922. "A History of Agriculture in Wisconsin." State Historical

Society of Wisconsin, Madison.

Schoenfeld, Ann M. *Hope for a Free Man: A Secret Family History of Murder, Escape and Discovery*. 2025.

Schroeder, Bertha (Mrs. Herb). "Feeding a Threshing Crew." Mennonite Heritage and Agricultural Museum.

Siegel, David. *Forces of Change: Events that led to the development of the Green Bay Fire Department, 1836-1895*. M&B Global Solutions, Green Bay, Wisconsin, 2016.

Simonar, Mrs. Carol J. (Gerald), "The Simonart Descendants History and Genealogy, Luxemburg, Wisconsin." 1980.

Sisters of St Francis of the Holy Cross Archival Records. harcsm.org/sisters-of-st-francis-of-the-holy-cross/.

Sisters of St. Francis of the Holy Cross website information on Father Daems gbfranciscans.org/content/about/community-founders.

Soquet Ancestry.com page, from the owner who prefers to remain anonymous, provided permissions to family photos and history. ancestry.com/family-tree/tree/15236274/family?cfpid=253578128).

Soquet v. State, 72 Wis. 659, 40 N.W. 391. (1888) (State of Wisconsin in Supreme Court John P. Soquet, Plaintiff in Error vs. The State of Wisconsin Defendant in Error - Dec. 1888.)

Soquet v. State, November 8, 1888, Supreme Court of Wisconsin. Jstor, American Law Register (1852-1891) vol. 37 No. 8, jstor.org/stable/3305285?seq=1.

Stiles, C.O. *Souvenir of Green Bay*. 1903.

Stout, Claude D. "The Legal Status of Women in Wisconsin." *Marquette Law Review* Volume 14 Issue 2 February 1930.

Times-Enterprise, Minnesota. Oct 9, 1890.

United States House of Representatives. "The Women's Rights Movement, 1848-1917." History Arts and Archives.

United States Census. Brown County. 1870 and 1880. ancestors.familysearch.org/en/LYLZ-Y4X/frederick-soquet-1861.

VandeCreek, Drew E. "Panic of 1873-1876." Northern Illinois University Libraries, Northern Illinois Digital Library digital.lib.niu.edu/illinois/gildedage.

Vernon County Censor - Viroqua, Wisconsin. Nov 18, 1891.

Warsh, Cheryl Krasnick. "The First Mrs. Rochester: Wrongful Confinement,

Social Redundancy, and Commitment to the Private Asylum, 1883-1923." *Historical Papers*, 1988.

Waterloo Daily Courier, Iowa. 1890 (May 28, Oct 8), Jul 20, 1891.

Waupun Times, Wisconsin. 1890 (Sep 30, Oct 7).

Webster, John C. "Memorabilia of the Class of '64 in Dartmouth College." All Biographies, Webster, Shepard & Johnston, Printers, 1884, Chicago, all-biographies.com/historical/john_tracy.htm.

Weekly Wisconsin, Milwaukee, Wisconsin. 1887 (Feb 26, Apr 2, May 14, Jul23, Nov 10, Dec 7); 1890 (Jan 11, Jun 7, Oct 4); 1892 (Feb 26, Feb 27).

Weissmann, G. "Puerperal Priority." The Lancet, 349, 122-125.

Wilson, Mary Ellen. "First case of child abuse and establishment of SPCC." en.wikipedia.org/wiki/Mary_Ellen_Wilson.

"Historic Building Materials and Methods." Wisconsin Historical Society, wisconsinhistory.org.

Wisconsin State Journal, Wisconsin. Apr 16, 1870; 1887 (Mar 24, Aug 2); Nov 8, 1889; 1890 (Jun 9, Oct 6).

Wisconsin State Prison. Inmate Conduct Records. Jean Soquet. Series 1379 Volume 8, Reel 8. Wisconsin State Historical Society. Madison, Wisconsin.

Wisconsin State Prison. Inmate Conduct Records. Jean Soquet. Series 1379 Volume 9, Reel 9. Wisconsin State Historical Society. Madison, Wisconsin.

Wisconsin State Prison (Waupun Correctional Institution). Historical Essay. Wisconsin Historical Society, 2002, wisconsinhistory.org.

Wright's Directory of Green Bay & Ft. Howard. Brown County Library.1893, 1894.

Wrights Directory of Green Bay and Fort Howard. 1894-95.

OTHER BOOKS BY LYNDA DREWS

Run at Destruction
Circle of Innocence
Desperate Parallels
The Maid and the Socialite

ACKNOWLEDGMENTS

DISPOSABLE WIVES took extensive research. To aid me in that effort I would like to thank the following individuals:

- John Mertens, a descendant of August Minsart's niece, who graciously shared his prior research into his unpublished booklet: *Tale of a Portrait: Julia Francart Englebert, Her Untold Story*. John is a wealth of knowledge related to the early Belgians in the 1800s including those who served in the Civil War and Xavier Martin. John shared photos and letters with me from Fay Willis Blodgett (1907–1996), a descendent of Xavier's daughter Pauline.
- Debra Anderson and her staff from the University of Wisconsin–Green Bay Archives and Area Research Center who helped me research court records, photos, and maps to provide the authentic details within my book.
- Dennis Jacobs, Brown County Library and Brown County Historical Society board member who provided me with the idea to write this book. It was wonderful to be able to bounce ideas off of him and use his skilled knowledge of Green Bay and the Bay Settlement in the 1800s to provide me accurate details to tell this story. He helped with securing some of the photos and also creating the map that is included in the front matter of my book.
- Julie Rheingans, Barb Chisholm, and Ann Jinkens – all connected to the Belgian Heritage Center—who have supported this effort through providing photos and directing me to the resources within the Belgian Heritage Center.
- Mary Jane Herber, Brown County historian and genealogist, who helped me research maps for proper locations within Green Bay and pointed me to numerous resources.

- Debra Lytie Riggs, a friend of my family since she was a little girl, who painted the beautiful cover for *Disposable Wives.* https://www.debrariggs.com/works
- My amazing editors and publisher: Melissa Wulske, Cassidy Sachs, and Kristin Mitchell who provided their expertise, empathy, and keen insight into my book.

Most importantly, I would like to thank my family and friends for all their support during my four-year journey to write *Disposable Wives.* Without their encouragement and valued opinions, I could never have completed this book.

ABOUT THE AUTHOR

WHEN LYNDA made the decision to retire from IBM after her thirty-year marketing career, she returned to an earlier passion. Her true-crime memoir, *Run at Destruction*, about her Green Bay running friend's mysterious death, was the outcome. *Publishers Weekly* said, "the author and victim's shared moments are remarkable." Best-selling true-crime author Anne Rule said Lynda's book was "wonderfully written ... a must for true crime readers," and Netflix and the I.D. Channel both adapted her book into true-crime segments.

Following Lynda's first book, she authored two novels before writing *The Maid and the Socialite*, a historical true crime set in Green Bay, Wisconsin, which has changed the city's history. *Disposable Wives* continues Lynda's passion of researching and writing stories about forgotten, abused, but brave Wisconsin women of past eras to give them a voice. Lynda is active in the Brown County Historical Society, the Brown County Community Women's Club, and Write On Door County. She and her husband Jim have lived in Brown County, Wisconsin, since 1974, the setting for each of her true crime books. (lyndadrews@gmail.com)